Gossip and Metaphysics

Tupelo Press Poetry in Translation

Abiding Places: Korea, South and North, by Ko Un
    Translated from Korean by Hillel Schwartz and Sunny Jung
Invitation to a Secret Feast: Selected Poems, by Joumana Haddad
    Translated from Arabic by Khaled Mattawa with Najib Awad,
    Issa Boullata, Marilyn Hacker, Joumana Haddad,
    Henry Matthews, and David Harsent
Night, Fish, and Charlie Parker, by Phan Nhien Hao
    Translated from Vietnamese by Linh Dinh
Stone Lyre: Poems of René Char
    Translated from French by Nancy Naomi Carlson
This Lamentable City: Poems of Polina Barskova
    Edited by Ilya Kaminsky and translated from Russian by the
    editor with Katie Farris, Rachel Galvin, and Matthew
    Zapruder
New Cathay: Contemporary Chinese Poetry
    Edited by Ming Di and translated from Chinese by the editor
    with Neil Aitken, Katie Farris, Christopher Lupke, Tony
    Barnstone, Nick Admussen, Jonathan Stalling, Afaa M.
    Weaver, Eleanor Goodman, Ao Wang, Dian Li, Kerry Shawn
    Keys, Jennifer Kronovet, Elizabeth Reitzell, and Cody Reese
Ex-Voto, by Adélia Prado
    Translated from Brazilian Portuguese by Ellen Doré Watson
Gossip and Metaphysics: Russian Modernist Poems and Prose
    Edited by Katie Farris, Ilya Kaminsky, and Valzhyna Mort,
    with translations by the editors and others

Edited by Katie Farris,
Ilya Kaminsky, and
Valzhyna Mort

Gossip and Metaphysics

Russian Modernist Poems and Prose

T|P

TUPELO PRESS
North Adams, Massachusetts

GOSSIP AND METAPHYSICS: RUSSIAN MODERNIST POEMS AND PROSE

Compilation copyright © 2014 Tupelo Press. Translations and individual elements are copyrighted by the authors, translators, and/or previous publishers, as cited on pages 300–306, which represent an extension of this copyright page.

Library of Congress Cataloging-in-Publication Data

Gossip and metaphysics : Russian modernist poems and prose / edited by Katie Farris, Ilya Kaminsky, and Valzhyna Mort.
     pages ; cm. – (Tupelo Press poetry in translation)
  Summary: A selection of poems and seminal prose texts about poetics from major Russian writers of the Modernist era.
  ISBN 978-1-936797-47-9 (pbk. : alk. paper)
  1. Russian poetry--20th century–Translations into English. 2. Modernism (Literature)--Soviet Union. I. Farris, Katie, editor. II. Kaminsky, Ilya, 1977- editor. III. Mort, Valzhyna, 1981- editor. IV. Series: Tupelo Press poetry in translation.
  PG3237.E5G67 2014
  891.71'408--dc23   2014025763

First edition: September 2014.

Cover and text designed by Ann Aspell.

Cover and title page art: Wassily Kandinsky (1866–1944), "Free Curve to the Point — Accompanying Sound of Geometric Curves," 1925, Ink on paper. 15-3/4 x 11-7/8 inches. Image copyright © The Metropolitan Museum of Art. Image Source: Art Resource, NY.

Tupelo Press
P.O. Box 1767, North Adams, Massachusetts 01247
Telephone: (413) 664–9611 / Email: editor@tupelopress.org
www.tupelopress.org

 transcript   ART WORKS.

The publication of this book was effected under the auspices of the Mikhail Prokhorov Foundation TRANSCRIPT Programme to Support Translations of Russian Literature, with additional support from the Antonia and Vladimer Kulaev Cultural Heritage Fund and the National Endowment for the Arts.

Elena Karina Canavier, *Botticelli* (1979).
Porcelain clay, 13 x 12 inches.

*Tupelo Press is grateful to
the Antonia and Vladimer Kulaev Cultural Heritage Fund
for a generous grant in support of this book's creation
and publication, in honor of artist
Elena Karina Canavier*

Wassily Kandinsky (1866–1944), "Free Curve to the Point—Accompanying Sound of Geometric Curves," 1925, Ink on paper. 15-3/4 x 11-7/8 inches. Image copyright © The Metropolitan Museum of Art. Image Source: Art Resource, NY.

Contents

Introduction

by Katie Farris

Writing poetry is rewriting it.

—MARINA TSVETAEVA

If you were to sit down and read this volume in one sitting, you might be overwhelmed by the clatter of voices—Kharms bellowing into the darkness, Akhmatova grinding her syllables out against the walls of the Soviet prison that held her son, Tsvetaeva gasping and stuttering her way toward a self-contradictory, paradoxical truth—all speaking to and for and about history, truth, logos, and one another. It's a little like sitting down late to a poets' dinner in the kitchen of a Russian restaurant, with conversation and vodka-drinking well under way. Some conversations have begun long ago and there's no one there to help catch you up; some end abruptly when one party or another leaves to smoke a cigarette or salt the soup. What keeps you there is the heady and unmistakable knowledge that you are in the proximity of genius.

Or, if you will permit another metaphor, this book's structure more resembles textile than codex. Many common threads run through it—intertwining, doubling back, sometimes unraveling—creating a matrix of poetic conversation: Mayakovsky on Khlebnikov, Pasternak on Mayakovsky, Tsvetaeva on Pasternak, Brodsky on Tsvetaeva, Akhmatova on Mandelstam. Shared themes range from the expected (the word) to the serendipitous

(Tsvetaeva and Mandelstam on the ocean). These poets are obsessed with proximity—proximity to God, to history, to nature, to their poetic predecessors, to language (their own and others), to place, and always, ever, to the inexpressible. And the prose in this collection evinces a common action: *the reaching out.*

First and perhaps foremost, poets reach out to other poets. Brodsky's playful and occasionally crude "Letter to Horace" muses on how he might communicate with the Latin poet, given the fact that his own Latin "stinks," and the modern poet settles on the notion that meter could be their common tongue: "...meters are always meters, in the underworld especially. Iambs and dactyls are forever...More exactly: whenever. Not to mention, wherever." In contrast, Mandelstam's essay "Conversation about Dante" is an attempt to communicate *through* Dante; this is a Menelauan attempt to grapple with metaphor in the *Commedia* as it metamorphoses from granite to crystal and from orchestral composition to scientific experiment, becoming an ode to its very mutability: "Dante is the greatest, the unrivaled master of transmutable and convertible poetic material, the earliest and simultaneously the most powerful chemical conductor of the poetic composition existing only in the swells and waves of the ocean..."

Many poets are invoked in these pages, but a reader would be hard pressed not to notice the pervasiveness of Pushkin. Mandelstam, who struggled all his life to negotiate the appropriate place for a poet in a rapidly (and violently) changing world, speaks about "a purely Pushkinian, *Kammerjunker* struggle for social dignity and a recognized social position for the poet." In her essay "Art in the Light of Conscience," Tsvetaeva invokes Pushkin as a great poet: "Whenever you mention art's holiness call to mind this confession of Pushkin's..." As he strolls under the Pushkin monument in Moscow, Pasternak muses on what happens to a poet after death: "But who will understand or believe that it was suddenly given to the Pushkin of 1836 to recognize himself as the Pushkin of any year, as the Pushkin, say, of 1936?" The Russian literary landscape of the Modernists was an echo-chamber, declaiming and amplifying Pushkin's influence.

Of course, not all writers are so respectful of their elders; for revolutionaries, Pushkin functioned as a useful symbol of the establishment. Kharms's examination of Pushkin retains his slapstick, somewhat brutal prose style, turning his meditation on literature into literature, a sort of literary cartoon: "In fact, compared to Pushkin, all people are little kids, except Gogol. Compared to him, Pushkin is a little kid. And so, instead of writing about Pushkin, I would rather write about Gogol." The humor is there, and the rough, raw truth that Kharms evokes in his poetry. In his Beckettian (though really it was Beckett who was Kharmsian) short play "Pushkin and Gogol," Pushkin and Gogol trip over one another endlessly, a humorous loop that evokes our modern gif, the short-format video loops found online.

While many of the poets in this volume are in conversation with the past, other poets seem to be reaching into the future. Mandelstam notices this tendency in Dante: "It is inconceivable to read Dante's cantos without directing them toward contemporaneity. They were created for that purpose. They are missiles for capturing the future. They demand commentary in the *futurum*." Another break with the past comes, unsurprisingly, from the Futurist manifesto, "A Slap in the Face of Public Taste" by Mayakovsky and Khlebnikov, et alia, in which they call for a revolution: "The past is too tight. The Academy and Pushkin are less intelligible than hieroglyphics. Throw Pushkin, Dostoyevsky, Tolstoy, etc., etc., overboard from the Ship of Modernity." If nothing else, Kharms, Mayakovsky, and Khlebnikov remind us that in order to stand on the shoulders of giants, we must first climb them like tree trunks.

In "Art in the Light of Conscience," Tsvetaeva's reflexively argumentative meditation on morality, poetry, and nature, she develops what could be read as an early foray into ecopoetic theory. In the essay, she explores the three-way intersection she sees between art as "an offshoot of nature (a species of its creation)"; the need for artistic amorality as a consequence of art's natural origins; and the paradoxical necessity of spiritual greatness in the great poet. In order to resolve this gridlock she has presented — that art is essentially natural, yet artists must transcend the earthly in order to achieve necessary perspective — Tsvetaeva produces a lovely atmospheric metaphor and applies it both to the necessary placement of art and to the necessary placement of the great artist's soul: "...starting from the earth [art] is the first millimeter of sky over it...the soul, that first, lowest sky of the spirit." This hovering just barely above the earth, this limited levitation, allows for the poet to act as a kind of translator, or incarnator:

"...a poet's whole labor amounts to a fulfillment, the physical fulfillment of a spiritual task...the will to embody physically what already exists spiritually (the eternal) and to embody spiritually (to inspirit) what doesn't yet exist spiritually and desires to ...to embody the spirit that desires a body (ideas) and to inspirit the bodies that desire a soul (the elements). The word is body to ideas, soul to the elements."

Whether the poets in this volume are speaking backward or forward in time, in Russian or Latin, to their neighbors, or over enormous, impossible distances, even speaking to death itself, they speak with the urgency of creators in the *process* of creating, engaging in a lively argument with writers long dead and those yet to come.

This book came about because there is no other anthology in English dedicated to Russian modernist poetics. For a group of poets so widely admired, relatively little seems to be known about their philosophy of poetry and their poetic influences, and although there is tremendous aesthetic diversity in this group, they have more in common than many Anglophone readers assume. For example, it is not unusual to hear an American poet say that Mayakovsky, the most preeminent Soviet poet, and Pasternak, the author of *Doctor Zhivago*, had nothing in common literarily. We hope the moving excerpt from Pasternak's autobiography *Safe Conduct* puts that misconception to rest—he as much as admits that his entire poetics came about in reaction to Mayakovsky, precisely because he had been such a profound influence. It's also been widely assumed that Mandelstam and Khlebnikov were divided by their Acmeist/Futurist poetics; however, reading Mandelstam's essay on Dante alongside Khlebnikov's thoughts on the importance of *sound* in poetry indicates just how influential Khlebnikov was on Mandelstam's poetry during the 1930s. American readers who already love Kharms's "Symphonies" may want to read Andrei Bely's "Symphonies," written several decades earlier. Russian poetry was a small world, made even smaller by the arrests, pogroms, famine, assassinations, disappearances, and political conflagration of the modernist period, and aesthetic disagreements were not as divisive as they have been made to seem.

There are two major difficulties associated with putting together an anthology of poetry in translation: the first is the selection process, and the second is the choice of translations. Russian literature has had its struggles with translation; think of Constance Garnett's renderings of nearly every nineteenth-century Russian author of note. While she did Anglophone readers a tremendous service by making these works available, her translations have been denigrated by those familiar with the Russian language, because she translated them all with the same tone, modulation, prose style—Tolstoy and Dostoyevsky became a sort of homogenous Tolstoyevsky. The difficulty with Russian to English translation was perhaps even more pronounced when it came to Russian poetry. Vladimir Nabokov's translation of *Eugene Onegin* comes in two volumes—the translation, and a hefty volume of notes and commentary on the untranslatable. Brodsky would go into a "flying rage" if you asked him about translations of Mandelstam or Akhmatova into English. The editors of this volume empathize with native speakers, but we're much more interested in how these translations might re-sound and reshape the Anglophone literary tradition. We believe, along with Ezra Pound, that every new great age of English poetry is a great age of translation.

In this volume, therefore, you will find many non-native Russian speakers as translators; we believe that the final poem's incarnation in its new language is the most important qualification. Many readers, and especially native Russian speakers, encountering Christian Wiman's translations of Mandelstam, will recognize how Wiman finally managed to capture, in English, something essential about Mandelstam's poetry—the intricate wordplay and elision of sound/meaning that are only possible when one knows a language intimately. Mandelstam himself understood that the first mandate of translation is immediacy, not literal accuracy; his biographer, Clarence Brown, describes reading Mandelstam's translations of Petrarch into Russian:

"I had received the texts alone, with no indication of where the originals might be among Petrarch's hundreds of sonnets, so my first concern was naturally to seek these out. It was an awful headache. No sooner would I have identified this or that image in an opening line or two than some wild divergence would convince me that Mandelstam must have been working from another original. The 'other original' stubbornly refusing to turn up, I was driven back to my starting point, and had to conclude what is the point of this little narrative: that Mandelstam had translated Petrarch not into Russian, but into Mandelstam."

Scandalized scholars need not detain us, then, for we must understand that in the end any translation lives or dies on the strength of its own readability in its new language. Ergo, our sole criteria for the selection of poetry in this book: readability.

This book is not meant to be an exhaustive or definitive compilation. Unfortunately, for reasons of space and copyright, numerous important poets, such as Blok, Gumiliov, Essenin, Vvedensky, Zabolotsky, Shvarts, and Prigov, among others, have not been included. The book is also not intended to function as a scholarly compendium, complete with critical apparatus, but was put together by practicing poets attempting to better understand how writers read other writers, learn from them, and use that knowledge to make art.

Therefore, this book is intended primarily for writers and avid readers—for those who long to glimpse what happened before the final drafts of the poems, who wish to peek into one window on the raucous, continuing conversation about poetics that has been taking place for millennia. For this reason, we've chosen not to place the poets in chronological order, but rather in conversation with one another.

Anna Akhmatova once claimed she was interested in only two things: gossip and metaphysics. We hope this book provides you with some of both.

1 Boris Pasternak

(1890–1960)

*To read the poems of Pasternak is to get one's throat clear,
to fortify one's breathing... I see Pasternak's My Sister—Life as a
collection of magnificent exercises in breathing...
a cure for tuberculosis.*

—Osip Mandelstam

*My Sister—Life! The first thing I did, when I'd borne it all, from
the first blow to the last, was spread my arms out wide, so that the
joints all cracked. I was caught in it,
as in a downpour... a downpour of light.*

—Marina Tsvetaeva

*Pasternak did not pluck fruits from the tree of reason, the tree of
life was enough for him. Confronted by argument, he replied with
his sacred dance... Pasternak's poetry is antispeculative, anti-
intellectual... His worship of life meant a fascination with what
can be called nature's moods—air, rain, clouds,
snow in the streets, a detail changing thanks to
the time of the day or night, to the season.*

—Czeslaw Milosz

WILD VINES

Beneath a willow entwined with ivy,
we look for shelter from the bad weather;
one raincoat covers both our shoulders—
my fingers rustle like the wild vine around your breasts.

I am wrong. The rain's stopped.
Not ivy, but the hair of Dionysus
hangs from these willows. What am I to do?
Throw the raincoat under us!

— a version by Robert Lowell

For Anna Akhmatova

It seems I am choosing words that will stand,
and you are in them,
but if I blunder, it doesn't matter —
I must persist in my errors.

I hear the soiled, dripping small talk of the roofs;
the students' black boots drum eclogues on the boardwalks,
the undefined city takes on personality,
is alive in each sound.

Although it's spring, there's no leaving the city.
The sharp customers overlook nothing.
Day bends to its sewing until it weeps;
sunrise and sunset redden the same red eye.

You ache for the calm reaches of Ladoga,
then hurry off to the lake for a change
of fatigue. You gain nothing,
the shallows smell like closets full of last summer's clothes.

The dry wind dances like a dried-out walnut
across the waves, across your stung eyelids —
stars, branches, milestones, lamps. A white
seamstress on the bridge is always washing clothes.

I know that objects and eyesight vary greatly
in singleness and sharpness, but the iron
heart's vodka is the sky
under the northern lights.

BORIS PASTERNAK   3

That's how I see your face and expression.
This, not the pillar of salt, the "Lot's Wife" you pinned down
in rhyme five years ago to show up our fear,
limping forward in blinders, afraid of looking back.

How early your first dogged, unremitting idiom
hardened — no unassembled crumbs!
In all our affairs, your lines throb
with the high charge of the world. Each wire is a conductor.

— a version by Robert Lowell

PART THREE, *from* Safe Conduct

I

In the winters the chain of boulevards cut through Moscow behind a double veil of blackened trees. Lights gleamed yellow in the houses, like small star-shaped circles of lemons cut through the centres. Blizzardy sky hung down low on the trees, and, all around, everything white was blue.

On the boulevards poorly dressed young people were hurrying along, bending as if they were going to butt. Some of them I was acquainted with, most of them I didn't know, but all of them were my coevals, that is — the countless faces of my childhood.

They had just begun to be addressed by their patronymics, endowed with rights and initiated into the secret of the words "possess," "profit," "acquire." They displayed a haste that is worthy of closer analysis.

There is death and foreknowledge in the world. The unknown is dear to us, the known in advance is terrifying, and every passion is a blind jump aside from inevitability which rolls towards us. Living species would have nowhere to exist and repeat themselves if passion had nowhere to leap to off the common path, along which rolls the common time, the time of the gradual demolition of the universe.

But life does have somewhere to live and passion somewhere to leap, because alongside the common time there exists an unceasing infinity of roadside arrangements, which are reproduced immortality, and every new generation is one of these.

Young people, bending as they ran, hurried through the blizzard, and, although each one had his reasons for haste, yet they were spurred along by something they had in common more than by all their personal promptings, and this was their historical wholeness — their surrender to the passion with which mankind, escaping from the common path and avoiding its end for yet one more innumerable time, had just sped into them. And so as to screen from them the duality of their run through inevitability, and so that they should not go mad, abandon what they had begun and hang themselves, the whole earth's globe of them, a power kept watch behind the trees on all the boulevards, a much tested and terribly experienced power which accompanied them with its intelligent eyes. Art stood behind the trees, art which makes us out so splendidly that you always wonder from what non-historical worlds it has brought its ability to see history in silhouette. It stood behind the trees, terribly similar to life, and was endured in life, because of this likeness, as portraits of wives and mothers are endured in the laboratories of scholars dedicated to natural science, that is to the gradual solution of death.

What kind of art, then, was it? It was the youthful art of Scriabin, Blok, Kommissarzhevskaya, Bely — advanced, gripping, original. And so astounding that not only did it not call up thoughts of replacing it but, just the contrary, one wanted to repeat it all from the foundation up, in order to make it more stable, only to repeat it more strongly, more hotly, more wholly. One wanted to re-say it all in a single breath, but this was unthinkable without passion, and passion kept leaping aside all the time, and so in this way the new came into being. But the new didn't come to take the place of the old, as is usually supposed — on the contrary, it arose in an enraptured reproduction of the model. That is the kind of art it was. And what kind of generation was it?

The boys close to me in age were thirteen years old in 1905, and twenty-one just before the war. Their two critical periods coincided with two red-letter dates in our country's history.

Their boyish maturity and their coming of call-up age both went straightaway as clamps to strengthen a transitional epoch. Our age is stitched through and through with their nerves and has been obligingly put by them at the disposal of old men and children. To characterize them fully, however, one must bear in mind the system whose air they breathed.

Nobody knew it was a Charles IV or a Louis XVI on the throne. Why is it that last monarchs seem to be monarchs in the fullest sense of the word? There is evidently something tragic in the very essence of hereditary power.

A political autocrat takes up politics only in those rare cases where he is a Peter the Great. Such examples are exceptional and are remembered for thousands of years afterwards. More often, nature limits the sovereign all the more firmly in that she is not parliament and the limits she sets are absolute. In the form of a centuries-hallowed rule, the name "hereditary monarch" is given to a person who is obliged to live through, ceremonially, one of the chapters of a dynasty's biography — that's all. Sacrificial custom survives in this, more stark than in a bee-hive.

What happens then to people of this terrible vocation if they're not Caesars, if their experience does not boil over as politics, if they lack genius — the one thing that could free them from the fate of "life" in favour of a posthumous fate?

Instead of gliding they slip, instead of diving they sink, instead of living they accommodate themselves to trivialities which reduce life to a mere decorative vegetating. At first these trivialities are hourly, then minute-by-minute; first they are genuine, then imaginary; first the accommodating takes place without external help, then with the help of table-turning.

When they see a cauldron, they fear its gurgling. Ministers assure them it is all in the order of things, and the more perfect the cauldron, the more fearful. The technique of state reforms is expounded, which consists in the conversion of heat energy into motor energy and which declares that states flourish only when they threaten explosion yet do not explode. Then, screwing up their eyes from fear, they take the handle of a whistle and, with all their innate gentleness, organize a Khodynka, a Kishinyov pogrom and a Ninth of January, and walk away shyly to their family and briefly interrupted diary.

Ministers clasp their hands to their heads. It becomes finally clear that vast territories are being governed by small minds. Explanations are in vain. Counsels don't attain their goal. The latitude of abstract truth is not once experienced by them. They are slaves of what is nearest at hand and most obvious, they conclude from like to like. It is too late to re-educate them, the denouement approaches. Everyone submits to the notice of dismissal and leaves them to the mercy of what is coming.

They see it approach. They rush from its threats and demands away to whatever is most alarming and demanding in their home. The Henriettas, Marie-Antoinettes and Alexandras are given more and more of a voice in the terrible choir. They estrange the advanced aristocracy from themselves, as if the market-place were interested in the life of the palace and were demanding that it reduce its comfort. They turn to gardeners from Versailles, lance-corporals from Tsarskoe Selo, autodidacts from the common people, and then the Rasputins surface and quickly rise: the monarchy's never-acknowledged capitulations to the people — which it thinks of as the "folk" — its concessions to the spirit of the time, wildly contrary to everything required of true concessions, for they are made to one's own detriment alone without benefiting the other person; and usually it is this particular absurdity that, laying bare the doomed nature of the terrible vocation, decides its fate and — by the tokens of its weakness — itself gives the provoking signal for an uprising.

When I came back from abroad it was the centenary of the year of the Fatherland. The Brest line had been renamed the "Alexandrovsky." Stations were whitewashed, the guards who rang the bell were dressed in clean shirts. The Kubinka station building had flags stuck all over it, extra guards stood at the doors. An imperial inspection was taking place nearby and on account of this the platform shone with a vivid profusion of loose sand not yet trodden down in all places.

In the travelers' minds this did not arouse recollection of the events being celebrated. One sensed in the jubilee decorations the reign's chief characteristic: indifference to its own history. And if anything was affected by the festivities, it wasn't the movement of people's thoughts but the movement of the train which was stopped at stations for longer than the timetable required and was held up in the countryside by signals oftener than usual.

I could not help calling to mind Serov, who had died the previous winter, and his stories of the time when he was painting the Tsar's family; caricatures made by artists at the Yusupovs' sketching evenings; odd incidents that had accompanied the Kutepov edition of *The Tsar's Hunt*; and many trifles relevant to this moment and connected with the school of painting which was under the control of a Ministry of the Imperial Court and in whose building we had lived for some twenty years. I might have recalled the year 1905 as well, the drama in the Kasatkin family and my own half-baked revolutionism, which went no further than braving a Cossack whip and its lash on the back of a quilted overcoat. And finally, as for the guards, stations and flags, of course they too heralded a very serious drama and were not at all the innocent vaudeville act my shallow apoliticism saw in them.

The generation was apolitical, I might have said, were I not aware that the tiny part of it I came in contact with is not even enough to judge the whole intelligentsia by. This was the side of itself, I shall say, that it turned towards me, but it was also the side that it turned towards the age when it came forth with its first declarations of a science, a philosophy and an art of its own.

II

However, culture does not fall into the arms of the first comer. All the things listed had to be won by battle. The notion of love as a duel applies here too. Art could cross over to the adolescent only as the result of a militant attraction experienced as a personal event in all its excitement. The literature of the beginners abounded in symptoms of this condition. The novices formed groups. The groups divided into the epigonic and the innovatory. These were parts — inconceivable in isolation — of that upsurge which had been left to chance with such insistence that it already permeated everything with the atmosphere of a romance no longer merely expected but actually happening. The epigones represented an impetus without fire or gift, the innovators — a militancy moved solely by an emasculated hatred. These were the words and gestures of a serious disagreement, overheard by an ape and spread around in bits, disjointed and verbatim, in all directions, with no idea of the meaning that inspired the storm.

Meanwhile the fate of the conjectural poet-elect already hung in the air. It was almost possible to say what kind of person he would be, though not yet possible to say who would be it. To judge by appearance, dozens of young people had the same restlessness, thought the same thoughts, made the same claims to originality. As a movement the innovators were distinguished by an apparent unanimity. But, as in the movements of every age, this was the unanimity of lottery tickets whirling and swarming in the mixing drum. The movement's fate was to remain forever a movement — a curious case of the mechanical shifting of chances — from the moment of one of the tickets, coming away from the lottery wheel, blazed up with the fire of winning, of conquest and of having a face and the significance of a name. The movement was called Futurism.

The conqueror and the justification of the draw was Mayakovsky.

III

We became acquainted in the constrained atmosphere of group prejudice. Long before this, Yulian Anisimov had shown me his poems in A *Trap for Judges*, the way one poet displays another. But that was in the epigonic circle, Lirika, for the epigones were not ashamed of their sympathies and in their circle Mayakovsky had been discovered as a phenomenon of great promise and imminence, like some huge bulk.

But in the innovators' group, Centrifuga, of which I became a member shortly after, I learned (this was in 1914, in the spring) that Shershenevich, Bolshakov and Mayakovsky were our enemies and that we were due to have a far from jocular confrontation with them. The prospect of a quarrel with someone who had already made an impression on me and was attracting me more and more from the distance did not surprise me at all. Here lay the innovators' whole originality. The birth of Centrifuga had been accompanied all winter by interminable brawls. All winter I did nothing but play at group discipline, sacrificing to it conscience and taste. Now once again I got ready to betray whatever was required when the moment came. But this time I overestimated my strength.

It was a hot day at the end of May, and we were already sitting in the tea-room on the Arbat when the three I have mentioned came noisily and youthfully in from the street, handed their hats to the porter, and, not moderating the sonorousness of their talk, which had been drowned out by trams and carts till then, made their way towards us with unforced dignity. They had beautiful voices. Here, the later declamatory style in poetry had its beginning. Their clothes were elegant, ours were slovenly. In all respects the enemy's position was superior.

While Bobrov was wrangling with Shershenevich—the essence of which was that they had taunted us on one occasion and we had replied still more coarsely and an end had got to be put to all this—I was watching Mayakovsky, not taking my eyes off him once. I think this was the first time I had seen him so closely.

The way he said "e" instead of "a," setting his diction rocking like a piece of sheet-iron, was the trait of an actor. One could easily imagine his deliberate abruptness as the distinguishing characteristic of other professions and statuses. He was not the only striking one. Beside him sat his comrades. One of them acted the dandy like him, the other, like him, was a genuine poet. But these similarities didn't diminish Mayakovsky's exceptionalness, rather they underlined it. As distinct from playing at one single thing, he played everything at once; and in contrast to the playing of roles, he played—with life. This could be sensed at the first glance, without the least thought of what his end would be. This was what was riveting about him and frightening.

Although everyone, when they walk or stand, can be seen at their full height, yet when Mayakovsky made his appearance this fact seemed a miracle and made everyone turn to look at him. In his case the natural seemed supernatural. The cause was not his height but another, more general, more elusive quality. More than others are, he was wholly contained in his manifestation. There was as much of the expressed and the definitive in him as there is little of it in the majority of people, who rarely, only under some special shock, emerge from the murk of half-fermented intentions and unrealised suppositions. He existed as if on the day after some enormous spiritual life that had been lived on a large scale and stored up ready for all eventualities, and now everyone met him sheafed in its irreversible consequences. He would sit in a chair as though it were the saddle of a motorcycle, bend forward, cut and rapidly swallow a Wiener schnitzel, play cards with sidelong glances, not turning his head, majestically stroll along the Kuznetsky, drone out, like bits of the liturgy, dully and nasally, specially profound lines of his own and others' verse: he scowled, grew, travelled, appeared in public, and in a depth behind all this, as behind the upright stance of a skater going at full speed, one perpetually glimpsed the one day preceding all his days when the amazing initial run had been taken which had straightened him up so largely and uninhibitedly. Behind his way of holding himself one sensed something like a decision once it has been acted on and its results can no longer be revoked. Such a decision was his own genius, for the encounter with it had once so astonished him that it became to him a thematic prescription for all time and he gave himself up wholly to its embodiment without pity or hesitation.

But he was still young and the forms this theme was to take still lay ahead. While the theme was insatiable, it endured no putting off. And so, at the beginning, in order to please it, he was obliged to anticipate his future, and anticipation realised in the first person is posing.

From these poses, which are natural in the world of the highest self-expression, as the rules of propriety are in everyday life, he selected the pose of an outward integrity, the hardest for an artist and the noblest in relation to friends and intimates. He kept up this pose with such perfection that it is now practically impossible to say what lay beneath it.

And yet the mainspring of his lack of shyness was wild shyness, and under his pretended willpower lay hidden a phenomenally suspicious lack of will and an inclination to causeless gloom. The mechanism of his yellow blouse was just as deceptive. By its means he was fighting not the jackets of the bourgeoisie but the black velvet of the talent inside himself, whose cloying black-browed forms had begun to disturb him earlier than happens in the lives of the less gifted. For no one knew as he did the whole vulgarity of the natural fire before it has been gradually roused to a fury by cold water, and no one knew as he did that the passion which suffices for the continuation of the race does not suffice for creation, and that this needs a passion sufficient for the continuation of the race's image, that is, one which inwardly resembles the Passion and whose newness inwardly resembles the Divine Promise.

The parley ended abruptly. The enemies we were supposed to annihilate went away untrampled. Rather, the peace terms arrived at were humiliating to us.

It had grown darker outside in the streets meanwhile. It had started to drizzle. In our enemies' absence the tea-room seemed drearily empty. Flies became noticeable along with the half-eaten cakes and the glasses blinded with hot milk. But the thunderstorm didn't take place. Lushly the sun struck at the pavement netted with little mauve spots. It was May of the year 1914. The vicissitudes of history were so near! But who thought of them? The crass town glowed with enamel and tinfoil, as in "The Golden Cockerel." The poplars' lacquered green was glittering. For the last time, colours had that poisonous grassiness they were shortly to part with forever. I was crazy about Mayakovsky and missing him already. Do I need to add that the ones I betrayed were *not* the ones I'd meant to?

IV

Chance brought us together the following day under the awning of the Greek café. The large yellow boulevard lay flat, spreading between the Pushkin monument and Nikitsky Square. Lean dogs with long tongues lay yawning, stretching and laying their muzzles more comfortably on their front paws. Gossipy pairs of nannies were chattering away, continually bewailing something or other. Butterflies would fold their wings for a moment and melt away in the heat, then suddenly open out again, lured sideways by irregular waves of sultry heat. A small girl in white, who must have been wet through, hung in mid-air as she whipped her whole body by the heels with a skipping-rope's whistling circles.

I caught sight of Mayakovsky from a distance and pointed him out to Loks. He was playing heads or tails with Khodasevich. At that moment Khodasevich got up, paid what he had lost, and, leaving the awning, went off in the direction of Strastnoi Boulevard. Mayakovsky remained at the table alone. We went in, greeted him, and got into conversation. After a while he offered to recite something.

The poplars were green, the lime trees a dryish gray. Driven out of all patience by fleas, the drowsy dogs kept jumping up on all four paws, calling Heaven to witness their moral impotence against brute force and dropping to the sand again in a state of indignant sleepiness. Throaty whistles were uttered by engines on the Brest railway, now renamed the Alexandrovsky line. And around us hair was being cut and whisker shaved, baking and roasting were going on, people were selling things and moving about—and were wholly unaware.

It was the tragedy *Vladimir Mayakovsky*, which had just come out. I listened with overwhelmed heart and held breath, oblivious. I'd never heard anything like it before. Everything was in it. Boulevard, dogs, poplars and butterflies. Hair-dressers, bakers, tailors and steam engines. What's the use of quoting? We all remember this sultry, mysterious, summery text, now available to everyone in its tenth edition.

Far off, locomotives roared like great whales. And the same unconditional distance as there was upon the earth was there in the throaty territory of his creation. This was that unfathomable spirituality without which there is no originality, that infinity which opens out in life from any point and in any direction and without which poetry is just a misunderstanding not yet cleared up.

And how simple it all was! Art was called a tragedy. Which is what it should be called. The tragedy was called *Vladimir Mayakovsky*. The title concealed a discovery which had the simplicity of genius: that the poet is not the author but the subject of poetry that addresses the world in the first person. The title was not the name of the author but the surname of the content.

V

Actually I carried the whole of him with me that day from the boulevard into my life. But he was enormous; there was no holding onto him when apart from him. And I kept losing him. Then he would remind me of himself. With *A Cloud in Trousers*, *Backbone Flute*, *War and the Universe*, *Man*. What was weathered away in the intervals was so huge that the reminders too had to be extraordinary. And such they were. Each of the stages I've mentioned found me unprepared. At each one, he was grown out of all recognition and wholly reborn like the first time. It was impossible to get accustomed to him. So what was so unusual about him?

He possessed relatively permanent qualities. My admiration too was comparatively stable. It was always ready for him. It would seem that under such conditions I could have grown used to him without having to make any leaps. Nonetheless, this was how matters stood.

While he existed creatively, I spent four years trying to get used to him but could not do it. Then I got used to him in two and a quarter hours, the time taken by the recital and discussion of his uncreative "150,000,000." Then for more than ten years I carried the burden of being used to him. Then suddenly, all at once, in tears, I lost it, when he gave a reminder of himself "at the top of his voice," as he had used to do, but now from beyond the grave.

What one could not get accustomed to was not so much him as the world which he held in his hands and which he would now set in motion, now bring to a halt, just as the whim took him. I shall never understand what he gained from demagnetizing the magnet when the horseshoe that before had made every imagination rear up on end and drawn to itself all possible weights "with the [oaken] feet of its lines," now without any apparent change, ceased to shift as much as a grain of sand. There can scarcely be another instance in history of someone going so far in a new experience and then — at the hour he himself had predicted, just when that experience, even if at a cost of discomforts, had become so vitally needed — rejecting it so completely. His place in the Revolution, outwardly so logical, inwardly so forced and empty, will always be a mystery to me.

What one could not get accustomed to was the Vladimir

Mayakovsky of the tragedy, *the surname of its content*, the poet contained in the poetry from time immemorial, the potentiality that only the strongest realize — and not the so-called "interesting person."

I had gone home from the boulevard charged with this unaccustomedness. I was renting a room with a window looking out at the Kremlin. From over the river, Nikolai Aseev was likely to turn up at any moment. He would come from the S— sisters, a profoundly and diversely gifted family. When he entered I would recognize a vivid, disheveled imagination in him, an ability to transform triviality into music, the sensitivity and the guile of a genuine artistic nature. I loved him. He was enthusiastic about Khlebnikov. I can't understand what he found in me. From both art and life, we were trying to obtain different things.

VI

The poplars were green, and reflections of gold and of white stone were running like lizards over the water of the river when I drove by way of the Kremlin to the Pokrovka on my way to the station and from there with the Baltrushaitises to the Oka in the province of Tula. There, right next to us, lived Vyacheslav Ivanov. The other dachas too were occupied by people from the artistic world.

Lilac was still in bloom. It had run far out onto the road to arrange a lively welcome on the broad drive leading into the estate, lacking only the music and the bread-and-salt. Beyond it an empty yard, trodden in by cattle and overgrown with patchy grass, sloped a long way down towards the houses.

It promised to be a hot, rich summer. I was translating Kleist's comedy *The Broken Jug* for the Chamber Theatre, then just coming into existence. There were a lot of snakes in the park. People talked about them every day. They talked about snakes while eating fish soup and while bathing. And whenever I was asked to say something about myself, I would start talking about Mayakovsky. This was no mistake. I had made a god of him, personified in him my own spiritual horizon. Vyacheslav Ivanov was the first, as I remember, to compare him to the hyperbolism of Hugo.

VII

When war was declared, the weather changed for the worse, it began to rain a good deal, the women's first tears began falling. The war was still new and quakingly terrible in its newness. People didn't know what to do with it; they entered it like very cold water.

The passenger trains by which the local men travelled from the *volos* to the assembly centres departed by the old timetable. The train would set off and a surge of lamentation would roll in pursuit of it, banging its head against the rails and not like weeping at all, but unnaturally tender and bitter like the rowanberry. Someone's arm would gather up an elderly woman warmly wrapped in unsummery clothes. And the relatives of the recruit would take her away, uttering short sounds of exhortation, under the arches of station.

This keening, which was kept up only in the first months, was wider than the grief of the mothers and young wives that streamed forth in it. It was introduced all along the line like an emergency measure; stationmasters touched their caps as it travelled past; telegraph poles made way for it. It transformed the region and was visible from every side in a pewter icon-setting of foul weather, because it was a thing of burning vividness which people had got unused to and hadn't touched since previous wars but had taken out of storage just the night before, brought on horseback to the train in the morning, and would lead out by the arms from the station arches and drive home again through the bitter mud of a country road. But the soldiers who went in ready-formed marching units straight to the very heart of the terror were met and seen off without any wailing. In their close-fitting clothes they jumped down onto the sand from the high goods trucks, not at all in the manner of peasants, ringing their spurs and trailing their crookedly flung-on greatcoats in the air. Others stood by the planks fixed across the truck doors and gave a few slaps to the horses stamping the filthy wood of the rotting floor with haughty hoof-blows. The platform was giving away no apples, had plenty of cheeky answers and grinned into the corners of tightly pinned kerchiefs, blushing crimson.

September was ending. Garbage-golden and burning in the hollows like the mud of a fire put out with water, a grove of hazels, all bent and broken by the winds and by climbers after nuts, made a chaotic image of ruin, twisted from all its joints by a stubborn resistance to disaster.

One noon in August the knives and plates on the terrace had turned green, dusk had fallen on the flowerbeds and the birds had gone quiet. The sky began trying to tear from itself the bright net of night deceitfully thrown on it like a cloak of invisibility. The park had died out and was looking sinisterly, obliquely upward at the humiliating enigma through which the earth, whose loud glory it had been drinking so proudly with all its roots, was being rendered unimportant. A hedgehog rolled out onto the path. A dead viper lay there in the shape of a knot, like an Egyptian hieroglyph. It shifted it, then suddenly stopped and froze. And again it broke and shed its dry bunch of needles, and first poked out, then hid, its pig-like muzzle. All the while that the eclipse lasted, that ball of prickly suspicion kept gathering itself, first in the shape of a small boot, then in that of a pine-cone, till a presage of renascent certainty drove it back into its lair.

VIII

In the winter one of the S — sisters, Z.M.M., came to live on Tverskoi Boulevard. People visited her. I. Dobrovein, a remarkable musician with whom I was friends, used to drop in. Mayakovsky sometimes came to her house. By then I was accustomed to seeing in him the leading poet of the generation. Time showed I was not mistaken.

It is true there was Khlebnikov with his subtle genuineness. But part of his merit remains inaccessible to me even now, for poetry as I understand it proceeds, after all, in history and in collaboration with actual life.

There was Severyanin too, a lyric poet who poured himself forth in spontaneous stanzas, in ready forms like Lermontov's, and who, with all his untidiness and vulgarity, was impressive just because of this rare structure of his open, unfettered talent.

But the peak of poetic destiny was Mayakovsky, and this was later confirmed. After this, every time the generation expressed itself dramatically, lending its voice to a poet, whether it was Esenin or Selvinsky or Tsvetaeva, an echo was heard of Mayakovsky's kindred note; it was heard in the very way they were bound to their generation—in the way they addressed the world from out of their own time. I am saying nothing about such masters as Tikhonov and Aseev because, both here and in the rest of what I shall say, I am confining myself to this dramatic line which is closer to me, while they chose a different one.

Mayakovsky rarely turned up alone. Usually his retinue consisted of Futurists, men of the movement. In M—'s household around this time, I saw the first primus stove of my life. This invention didn't yet give off a stink, and who thought it would bring so much filth into our lives and come into such wide use? Its clean roaring body threw out a high-pressure flame. Chops were fried on it one by one; the elbows of our hostess and her helpers got covered with chocolate-coloured Caucasian suntan. The cold little kitchen was transformed into a settlement in the Tierra del Fuego whenever we dropped in on the ladies from the dining-room and, as innocent of technology as wild Patagonians, we bent over the copper disk that embodied something bright and Archimedean. And—kept dashing out for beer and vodka.

A tall Christmas tree in the sitting room held out its paws towards the grand piano, secretly in league with the trees on the boulevard. It was solemnly dark as yet. The whole divan was piled with glittering tinsel, like heaps of sweets, some of it still inside cardboard boxes. Special invitations were issued for the decorating of the tree, in the morning if possible, which meant three in the afternoon.

Mayakovsky recited, made everyone laugh and ate his supper in haste, almost unable to wait for the game of cards. He was bitingly polite and with great skill hid his incessant agitation. Something was going on in him, some sort of crisis was taking place. His destiny had become clear to him. He was openly posing, but with such hidden anxiety and fever that on his posing there stood drops of cold sweat.

IX

But he was not always attended by the innovators. Often he would come in the company of a poet who had emerged with honour from the test that Mayakovsky's vicinity usually set. Of the many people I had seen at his side Bolshakov was the only one I could see next to him without strain. It didn't matter which of them spoke first, they could both be listened to without violence to one's hearing. Like his later and even stronger union with his lifelong friend, Lilya Brik, this friendship was understandable, it was a natural one. One's heart didn't ache for Mayakovsky in Bolshakov's company, he was on his own level, wasn't lowering himself.

But usually his sympathies aroused bewilderment. This poet with his overwhelmingly large self-awareness, who had gone further than anyone else in laying bare the essence of the lyrical and had with medieval boldness brought it close to a theme in whose vast design poetry almost began to speak with the tongue of sectarian identification — this poet took up just as hugely and broadly another, more local, tradition.

He saw beneath him a city which had gradually risen up to him from the depths of *The Bronze Horseman, Crime and Punishment,* and *Petersburg,* a city in a haze which people called, with unnecessary vagueness, the problem of the Russian intelligentsia, but essentially a city in the haze of eternal divinations about the future, a precarious Russian city of the nineteenth and twentieth centuries.

He could embrace such views, yet, alongside these immense contemplations, he was faithful, almost as if duty-bound, to all the dwarf undertakings of his random, hastily assembled clique which was invariably mediocre to the point of indecency. This man with an almost animal craving for truth surrounded himself with petty, finicky people of fictitious reputations and false, unjustified pretensions. Or, to come to the main point: to the very end he went on finding something in the veterans of a movement which he himself had long ago permanently discarded.

These were probably the consequences of a fatal loneliness which, once established, is later deliberately intensified, with that pedantry with which the will sometimes moves in a direction it has recognized to be inevitable.

X

All this was to show itself later, however. At the time there were only faint signs of the strange things to come. Mayakovsky recited Akhmatova, Severyanin and his own and Bolshakov's works about the war and the city, and the city we emerged into at night from the homes of friends was a city deep in the rear of the war.

Already we were failing in the matters always difficult for immense, inspirational Russia — transport and supplies. Already the new words — "detail," "medical kit," "licensing," "refrigeration" — were hatching the first larvae of profiteering. While the profiteers were thinking in truck-loads, those same trucks were exporting large consignments of fresh indigenous population, night and day, in haste, with songs, in exchange for damaged batches coming back in the hospital trains. And the best of the girls and women had gone as nurses.

The place for authentic positions was the front, and the rear would have fallen into a false one in any case, even if, on top of this, it hadn't grown skilled in voluntary falsehood. The city hid behind phrase-making like a cornered thief, although no one at the time was attempting to trap it. Like all hypocrites, Moscow lived an intensified external life and was vivid with the unnatural vividness of a flower-shop window in winter.

By night it seemed the very image of Mayakovsky's voice. What was happening in this city, and what was being heaped up and hurled to pieces by this voice, were as alike as two drops of water. But this was not the similarity dreamt of by naturalism, rather it was the link that combines anode and cathode, artist and life, the poet and his time.

Opposite M—'s house stood the house of the Moscow chief of police. There, in the course of several days that autumn I ran into Mayakovsky, and Bolshakov, too, I think, at one of the formalities required for the registration of volunteers. We had been concealing this procedure from one another. I didn't carry it through to the end, despite my father's sympathy. But, unless I am mistaken, nothing came of it in the case of my friends either.

Shestov's son, a handsome lieutenant, drew from me a solemn promise to give the idea up. Soberly and positively he told me what it was like at the front, warning me I would find there exactly the opposite of what I expected. Soon after this he perished, in the first battle after his return to the front from that leave.

Bolshakov entered the Tver Cavalry School, Mayakovsky was later called up when his turn came, but, following my release that summer just before the war, I was released again at all subsequent medical examinations.

A year later I went away to the Urals. Before that I spent a few days in Petersburg. The war was less noticeable there than in Moscow. Mayakovsky, who was called up by then, had been there for some time.

As always, the animated movement of the capital was tempered by the generosity of its dreamy spaces, which the needs of life could never exhaust. The very streets were the colour of winter and dusk, and their impetuous silveriness did not need much lamplight and snow to send them dashing and sparkling into the distance.

I walked down Liteinyi Avenue with Mayakovsky; he trampled miles of street with sweeping strides, and I was amazed, as always, by the way he was able to be a kind of frame or edge to any landscape. In this he suited gray, sparkling Petrograd even better than Moscow.

This was the time of the *Backbone Flute* and the first drafts of *War and the Universe*. A *Cloud in Trousers* had come out as a little book with an orange cover. He told me about the new friends he was taking me to, about his acquaintance with Gorky, about how the social theme was taking a bigger and bigger place in his plans and enabling him to work in a new way, at definite times, in measured portions. And that was the first time I visited the Briks.

Still more naturally than in the capital cities, my thoughts about him spread out into the semi-Asiatic wintry landscape of *The Captain's Daughter* in the Urals and in the Kama region of Pugachov.

I returned to Moscow soon after the February Revolution. Mayakovsky had come from Petrograd and was staying in Stoleshnikov Lane. In the morning I called on him at his hotel. He was getting up and, while dressing, he recited his new *War and the Universe* to me. I did not expatiate on the impression it made on me. He read it in my eyes. In any case, he knew the extent of his effect upon me. I talked about Futurism and said how marvelous it would be if he could now openly send all that to the devil. He laughed and almost agreed.

XI

Hitherto I have shown how I perceived Mayakovsky. But there is no love without scars and sacrifices. I have told what sort of person Mayakovsky was as he entered my life. It remains to tell how it was changed by this. I shall now fill this gap.

When I came back from the boulevard that day, completely overwhelmed, I couldn't think what to do. I felt I was utterly untalented. This would not have mattered terribly. But I was aware of a kind of guilt towards him which I couldn't quite make sense of. Had I been younger, I would have given up literature. But my age prevented this. After all my metamorphoses, I couldn't decide to re-define myself a fourth time.

What happened was something else. The time and common influences made me akin to Mayakovsky. Some things in us coincided. I noticed them. I realised that if I didn't do something to myself, they would occur more often in the future. I had to protect him from their banality.

Although I could not have given it a name, I resolved to renounce what led to them. I renounced the Romantic manner. This was how the unromantic style of *Over the Barriers* came into being.

But the Romantic manner which I forbade myself from then on contained a whole conception of life. This was the conception of life as the life of the poet. It had come to us from the Symbolists, and the Symbolists had adopted it from the Romantics, principally the Germans.

Blok had been possessed by this idea for a certain period only. In the form in which it was natural to him it was not able to satisfy him. He had either to heighten it or to abandon it altogether. He abandoned the idea. Mayakovsky and Esenin heightened it.

In the poet who lays himself down as the measure of life and pays for this with his life, the Romantic conception is irresistibly vivid and is irrefutable in its symbols, that is, in everything that figuratively touches upon Orphism and Christianity. In this sense something intransient is incarnate in the life of Mayakovsky and in the fate of Esenin too, a fate that defies all epithets in the self-exterminatory way that it begs to become myth and recedes into myth.

But outside the legend the Romantic scheme is false. The poet who is its foundation is inconceivable without the non-poets to bring him into relief, for this poet is not a living personality absorbed in moral cognition but a visual biographical emblem which demands a background to make its contours visible. Unlike the passion plays, which needed a Heaven in order to be heard, this drama needs the evil of mediocrity in order to be seen, as Romanticism always needs philistinism and loses half its content with the disappearance of the petty-bourgeois outlook.

The conception of biography as spectacle was inherent in my time. I share this conception with everyone else. I parted from it while it was still mild and non-compulsory among the Symbolists, before it began to presuppose heroism and before it smelt of blood. And, in the first place, I freed myself from it unconsciously, by rejecting the Romantic devices for which it served as basis. In the second place, I avoided it consciously as well, as a brilliance unsuited to me because, having confined myself to my craft, I feared any kind of poetizing that would place me in a false and unsuitable position.

But when My Sister — Life appeared, a book in which wholly uncontemporary aspects of poetry were expressed, that had been revealed to me in the revolutionary summer, I became utterly indifferent as to the name of the force that had given me the book, because it was immensely bigger than me and the poetic conceptions surrounding me.

XII

From Sivtsev Vrazhek, into a dining-room not cleared up for months, peered winter twilight and the roofs and trees of the quarter round the Arbat. The apartment's owner, a bearded newspaperman of extreme absentmindedness and kindliness, gave the impression of being a bachelor, although he had a family in the province of Orenburg. Whenever he had any spare time he would rake up from the table a whole month's newspapers of every possible persuasion and carry them in armfuls into the kitchen, together with the petrified remains of breakfasts that used to accumulate between his morning readings in regular deposits of bacon rinds and loaf ends. Till my conscience pricked me, there would be a bright, loud, odorous flame in the stove on the thirtieth of every month, as in Dickens's Christmas tales of roast geese and counting-house clerks. With the approach of darkness, sentries on point duty would open enthusiastic fire from their revolvers. Sometimes whole bursts were fired and sometimes sparse separate shots like inquiries into the night, full of a piteous unanswered fatality, and as it was impossible for them to fall into rhythm and many were killed by stray bullets, one wanted, for safety's sake, to set metronomes from pianos along the side-streets instead of militiamen.

Sometimes their cracking changed to a barbarous wail. And, as often happened in those days, you couldn't tell at first whether it was in the street or the house. But this was the sole inhabitant of the study, a portable one with a plug, calling for someone to go to it — like moments of lucidity in a continuous delirium. It was from here that I was invited by telephone to a private house in Trubnikovsky Lane for a gathering of all the poetic forces that could possibly be found at that moment in Moscow. On this same telephone, though a good deal earlier, before the Kornilov revolt, I'd had a disagreement with Mayakovsky.

Mayakovsky informed me that he had put me on his poster, alongside Bolshakov and Lipskerov, but also along with the most faithful of the faithful, including, it seemed, one who could break thick planks with his forehead. I was almost pleased to have the opportunity to talk to my idol for the first time as if he were a stranger, and, getting more and more irritated, I parried his self-justifying arguments one by one. It was not so much his lack of ceremony that surprised me as the poverty of imagination it displayed, for, as I pointed out, this incident consisted not in his unbidden use of my name but in his annoying conviction that my two-year absence had altered neither my life nor my interests. He ought first to have inquired whether I was still alive and whether I had not given up literature for something better. To this he replied quite reasonably that we had already met since the Urals, one day in the spring. But in a most surprising way this piece of reasoning failed to get through to me. And with misplaced stubbornness I demanded that he publish a correction of the poster in the press, which was impracticable as the evening was so near, and, since I was quite unknown at that time, it was affected nonsense as well.

But though I was still hiding *My Sister — Life* and concealing what was going on in me, I could not endure it when those around me assumed that everything was the same as before. Besides which, precisely that spring conversation Mayakovsky alluded to so unsuccessfully was doubtless dimly alive in me, and I was irritated by the inconsistency of this invitation after all that had been said then.

XIII

He reminded me of this telephone skirmish some months later, in the house of the amateur verse-writer A—. Present were Balmont, Khodasevich, Baltrushaitis, Erenburg, Vera Inber, Antokolsky, Kamensky, Burliuk, Mayakovsky, Andrei Bely and Tsvetaeva. I could not know, of course, what an incomparable poet Tsvetaeva was to develop into. But even without knowing her remarkable *Mileposts*, written at that time, I instinctively set her apart from the others in the room because of her striking simplicity. I sensed something akin to me in her: a readiness to part at any moment with all privileges and habits if something lofty were to kindle her and set her admiration aflame. On this occasion, we exchanged a few sincere, friendly words. At that evening gathering, she was a living palladium for me against the people of two movements, the Symbolists and the Futurists, who thronged the room.

The reading began. People read by seniority, with no perceptible success. When Mayakovsky's turn came, he stood up, put one arm round the edge of the empty shelf in which the back of the divan ended, and started reading *Man*. Like a bas-relief, as I have always seen him against the background of the age, he towered among the others who were sitting or standing, and, supporting his fine head with one hand or pressing his knee into the bolster of the divan, he recited a work of extraordinary depth, elation and inspiration.

Opposite him, with Margarita Sabashnikova, sat Andrei Bely. He had spent the war in Switzerland. The Revolution had brought him back to his own country. This was possibly the first time he had seen and heard Mayakovsky. He listened as if spellbound, and though he did nothing to betray his rapture his face was all the more eloquent. Astonished and grateful, it flew to meet the reader. Part of the audience was out of sight to me, including Tsvetaeva and Erenburg. I watched the others. Most kept within the boundaries of an enviable self-esteem. All felt themselves to be names, thought of themselves as poets. Bely alone was listening with complete self-abandon, carried far, far away by the joy that regrets nothing because on the heights where it is at home there is nothing other than sacrifice and the eternal readiness for it.

Chance was bringing together before my eyes the two geniuses who justified two literary movements which had become exhausted, one after the other. In Bely's vicinity, which I experienced with pride and delight, I felt Mayakovsky's presence with double force. His essence was revealed to me in all the freshness of a first encounter. I knew it that evening for the last time.

After this many years passed. One year passed and when I read the poems of *My Sister* to Mayakovsky before anyone else, I heard ten times more from him than I ever expected to hear from anyone. Another year passed. In a small group of friends he read his "150,000,000." And for the first time I had nothing to say to him. Many years passed, during which we met at home and abroad, tried to be friends, tried to work together, and all the time I was understanding him less and less. Others will tell about this period, for in those years I came up against my understanding's limits and it seemed they were not to be overcome. My memories of that time would be pale and would add nothing to what has been said already. And so I shall go straight on to what I still have to tell.

XIV

I shall tell of the strangeness that is repeated from age to age and that may be called the last year of a poet.

All of a sudden, an end is put to projects that have been resisting completion. Often nothing is added to their unfinished state except for a new — hitherto unpermitted — certainty that they are complete. And this certainty is conveyed to posterity.

They change their habits, cherish new plans, boast endlessly of being in high spirits. And all of a sudden — the end, sometimes violent, more often natural, but very like suicide even then because of the lack of desire for self-defence. And then one is suddenly brought up short and one notes similarities. They were cherishing plans, editing *The Contemporary*, making preparations to establish a peasant journal. They were opening an exhibition of twenty years' work, taking steps to obtain a foreign passport.

But it turns out that others had seen them during those very same days depressed, complaining, weeping. Men who had spent whole decades in voluntary solitude were suddenly afraid of it like children frightened of a dark room and would seize the hands of chance visitors, clutching at their presence, only not to be left along. The witnesses of these states of mind could not believe their ears. Men who had received far more corroborations from life than it ever grants to others were now reasoning as if they had not yet begun to live and had had no experience or support in the past.

But who will understand or believe that it was suddenly given to the Pushkin of 1836 to recognize himself as the Pushkin of any year, as the Pushkin, say, of 1936? That a time comes when the responses coming long since from other hearts in answer to the beats of the main one, which is still alive and still pulsing, thinking and wanting to live, are suddenly fused into one heart, expanded and transmuted? That the irregular, constantly accelerating beats are coming at last so thick and fast that all at once they even out and, coinciding with the main heart's tremors, start to live one life with it, beating in unison with it from now on? That this is no allegory. That this is experienced. That this is a kind of age of life, impulsive, felt in the blood and real — only as yet unnamed. That this is a kind of non-human youth, but a youth that rends the continuity of one's preceding life with such abrupt joy that, because there exists no name for it and because comparisons are inevitable, its abruptness makes it, more than anything else, resemble death. That it resembles death but — is *not* death, not death at all, and if only, if only people did not want complete resemblance...

And together with the heart, a displacement occurs between memories and work, works and hopes, the created world and the world yet to be created. What kind of personal life did he have? — people sometimes ask. You shall now be enlightened about his personal life. A huge region of utter contradiction contracts, concentrates, smoothes itself out and, suddenly, shuddering with simultaneity in every part of its structure, begins to exist physically. It opens its eyes, takes a deep breath and flings off the last remnants of the pose that was given it as a temporary support.

And if one recalls that all this sleeps by night and wakes by day, walks on two feet and is called a human being — it is natural to expect corresponding phenomena in its behavior.

A large, real, really existing city. It is winter there. Darkness comes early there, there the working day goes by in an evening light.

Once, long, long ago it was terrible. It had to be conquered, its refusal to give recognition had to be broken. Much water has flowed by since then. Recognition has been wrung from it; its submission has become a habit. A great effort of memory is needed to imagine how it could once have inspired such agitation. Lamps twinkle in it, people cough into handkerchiefs and click their abacuses. It gets covered with snow.

Its uneasy immensity would have swept past unnoticed were it not for this new, wild impressionability. What is the shyness of adolescence beside the vulnerability of this new birth? And again, as in childhood, everything is noticed. Lamps, typists, door pulleys, galoshes, storm clouds, the crescent moon and the snow. Terrible world!

It bristles with backs of fur-coats and sleighs. Like a penny rolling across the floor, it rolls on its edge along the rails, rolls away into the distance and tenderly falls off its rim into the mist, where a signal-woman in a sheepskin coat bends to pick it up. It rolls about and grows tiny and teems with fortuities. It is so easy to stumble, there, against a slight want of attention. These are deliberately imagined annoyances. They are blown up consciously from nothing. But even when blown up, they are still utterly trivial next to the wrongs one strode over so majestically only a short while ago. But that's just the point, that there can be no comparison, because that was in the previous life it was such a joy to tear up. Oh, if only this joy were more equable and more credible.

But it is incredible and incomparable, and yet nothing in life ever flung one so much from extreme to extreme as does this joy.

What lapses into despondency are here. What repetition of the whole of Hans Christian Andersen and his unhappy duckling. What elephants are here made out of flies.

But perhaps the inner voice is lying? Perhaps the terrible world is right? "No smoking." "Please state your business briefly"? Are these not truths?

"Him? — What, hang himself? Don't you worry." "Love? — What, him? — Ha-ha-ha! He only loves himself."

A large, real, really existing city. It is winter there, it is freezing there. Squeaking and willow-woven, the air, in its twenty degrees of frost, stands across the road as if on stilts hammered into the ground. Everything in it is misting over, rolling away and becoming lost. But can things be as sad as this when they are so joyful? So isn't this a second birth? So is this death?

— translated by Angela Livingstone

from A LETTER TO MARINA TSVETAEVA
(March 25, 1926)

At last I am with you. Since all is clear to me and I believe in fate, there is no need for me to speak. I could leave everything to fate, who serves me with an undeserved loyalty that makes me dizzy with joy. Yet this is joined to so much feeling for you — if not all of my feeling — that I can scarcely cope with it.

You are filled with such beauty, you are a sister to me, you are my life, sent directly from heaven, and at the time of my soul's greatest ordeal. You are mine and have always been mine; all of my life is — you.

Four evenings in a row I have thrust into my coat pocket a fragment of a haze-moist, smoke-dim Prague night, now with a bridge in the distance, now with you there, before my very eyes; I lurch into someone seen standing in line or fished out of my memory, and in a trembling voice recite to him that endless sequence of poignant lyrics of Michelangelesque breadth and Tolstoyan quietude which is called "Poem of the End." I came upon the poem by chance, a typed copy, without punctuation.

What else is there to say but to describe the table on which it lay?

You made me think again of our God, of my own self, of my childhood, of that part of me which always inclined me to look upon a novel as a textbook (of you know what), and upon a lyrical poem as the *etymology* of feelings (in case you missed the point about the textbook).

Truly, truly. Precisely that, precisely that thread which is spun by reality; precisely that which a person always *does* and never *sees*. As when a genius, that half-crazed creature, moves his lips. Just as you do in the first part of your poem. With what excitement one reads it! As if playing a part in a tragedy. Every sigh, the slightest nuance, is explicit in the verse.

"Excessively, excessively, that is,"
"But when the train had drawn up, the hander-in,"
"With business secrets and talcum for ballroom floors,"
"That means one needn't, it means there's no need," -
"Love is of flesh and blood,"
"We're pawns, you see, and someone plays with us,"
"Separating, coming apart?"

(By these phrases, you realize, I express whole pages at a time, so that:

"All I am is a beast with someone's charge in the belly."
"Aforesaid by the chess game.")

Probably I have left something out, the poem lies at my right hand, I could pick it up and verify it but I don't wish to, it is better this way, from memory, more alive, with the exclamations I keep uttering wherever I go: "A gift from heaven!" "Beloved!" "Astonishing!" "Marina!" or anything else you can pull out of my depths just by rolling up your sleeves and reaching for it.

This is how it affects people. After reading it aloud to them (and *how* I read it!) there is silence, surrender, an atmosphere in which they begin to feel "the assault of the tempest." How is it achieved? Sometimes by the mere lifting of an eyebrow. I sit bent, bowed, aged. I sit reading as if you were watching me, and I love you and want you to love me. Then, when my listeners are reborn through your greatness, your wisdom, your unqualified profundity, all I have to do is murmur, without changing my pose, merely lifting an eyebrow, "Well? What do you say? Isn't she colossal?" to cause my soul (open to everyone when I chatter, but, despite occasional slips, preserved in secrecy by its own nature) to plunge into the vast spaces you open up.

What a great, what a devilishly great, artist you are, Marina! But not another word about the poem or I will be constrained to drop you, my work, my family, and, turning my back on everybody, sit down and write about art, about genius, about the revelations of objectivity (a subject that has not yet been worthily treated), and about the joyful gift of feeling a oneness with the world, because you, like any true artist, have fixed your sights upon the bull's-eyes of these lofty targets.

I have but one small criticism to make, of an expression you use. I fear we are not always at one in our choice of words, that even though we both withdrew from the world at an early age you and I have not fought off prevailing clichés in the same way. You perhaps left the words "artist" and "objectivity" to the circles you ran away from. If this is so, you naturally hear in them only Sivtsev-Vrazhek overtones, enveloped in cigarette smoke and stained with wine; you parted company with them forever by dropping them in some familiar vestibule.

I picked them up. I will say nothing about artistry — if that theme does not constitute my entire theology, at least it makes a volume too big and heavy to lift. As for objectivity, this is what I would like to say. It is a term I apply to that magical, elusive, and rare feeling you know in the highest degree. There, I have put it in a nutshell. As you read this, see if it doesn't fit you, consider your poems, meet me halfway.

When Pushkin said (you can quote this more exactly; forgive my ignorance and approximation) "Can you believe it? My Tatiana is getting married!" he was probably giving fresh and novel expression to a feeling unacknowledged in those days.

— *translated by Margaret Wettlin and Walter Arndt*

‖ MARINA TSVETAEVA

(1892–1941)

I instinctively set her apart from the others in the room because of her striking simplicity. I sensed something akin to me in her: a readiness to part at any moment with all privileges and habits if something lofty were to kindle her and set her admiration aflame.

—BORIS PASTERNAK

Of all Russian poets, Tsvetaeva is the sincerest. Her sincerity, however, is the sincerity of sound—when one screams out in pain. Pain is biographical, while a scream is impersonal. Her "I refuse" encompasses the refusal of everything and anything...

—JOSEPH BRODSKY

[A KISS ON THE FOREHEAD...]

A kiss on the forehead—erases misery.
I kiss your forehead.

A kiss on the eyes—lifts sleeplessness.
I kiss your eyes.

A kiss on the lips—is a drink of water.
I kiss your lips.

A kiss on the forehead—erases memory.

—*a version by Ilya Kaminsky and Jean Valentine*

[I KNOW THE TRUTH ...]

I know the truth! Give up all the other truths.
No time on earth for people to kill each other.
Look — it's evening; look, it's nearly night. No more
of your talk, poets, lovers, generals.

Now no wind, and the earth is sprinkled with drizzle,
and soon the blizzard of stars will go quiet.
And soon, soon, to sleep, under the earth, all of us,
us who alive on earth don't let us sleep.

— a version by Ilya Kaminsky and Jean Valentine

[I WOULD HAVE LOVED TO LIVE WITH YOU...]

I would have loved to live with you
in a town
of eternal twilight
and eternal bells.
In a small provincial hotel
a thin chime
of an antic clock—like the droplets of time.
And at times at night from some
attic—
a flute
and a flutist himself in the window.
And large tulips on windowsills.
And you might not have even loved me.

In the middle of the room we'd have had a huge tile stove
and on each tile—an image:
a rose—a heart—a ship.
And in the only window—
Snow, snow, snow.

You would have lain there stretched—how I love you: lazy,
indifferent, volatile.

Now and then a sharp crack
of a match.

A cigarette lights and burns out,
and for a long time a short stump of ash
trembles on its tip.
You are too lazy to take it out —
and the whole cigarette flies into the fire.

— translated by by Valzhyna Mort

from ART IN THE LIGHT OF CONSCIENCE

"Art is holy," "holy art": however much a commonplace, this does have a certain meaning, and one in a thousand does think what he is saying and say what he is thinking.

That one in a thousand who consciously affirms the holiness of art is the person I am addressing.

What is holiness? Holiness is a condition the reverse of sin. Our contemporary age does not know sin, it replaces the concept "sin" with the concept "harm." It follows that for an atheist there can be no question of the holiness of art: he will speak either of art's usefulness or of art's beauty. Therefore, I insist, what I say is addressed exclusively to those for whom God — sin — holiness — *are*.

If an atheist starts speaking of the loftiness of art, then what I say will partly concern him too.

What is art?

Art is the same as nature. Don't seek in it other laws than its own (don't look for the self-will of the artist, which isn't there — only look for the laws of art). Perhaps art is just an offshoot of nature (a species of its creation). What is certain: a work of art is a work of nature, just as much born and not made. (And all the labour towards its realisation? But the earth labours too — in French, "la terre en travail." And isn't birth itself labour? Female gestation and the artist's gestation of his work have been talked of so often they don't need insisting on: all know — and all know correctly.)

So what is the difference between a work of art and a work of nature, between a poem and a tree? There's none. Whatever the paths of labour and miracle, yet it *is*. I am!

That means the artist is the earth, which gives birth, and gives birth to everything. For the glory of God? And spiders? (There are some in works of art too.) I don't know for the glory of whom, and I think the question here is not of glory but of power.

Is nature holy? No. Sinful? No. But if a work of art is the same as a work of nature, why do we ask something of a poem but not of a tree? At most we'll regret that it grows crooked.

Because earth, the birth-giving, is irresponsible, while man, the creating, is responsible. Because the sprouting earth has but one will—to sprout—whereas man has got to will the sprouting of the good which he knows. (It is telling that the only thing that can be called "wicked" is the notorious "individual" quality, the unipersonal; there is no "wicked epic" or "wicked nature.")

The earth didn't eat the apple in Paradise, Adam ate it. It didn't eat and doesn't know, he did eat and does know, he knows and is answerable. And insofar as the artist is a human being and not a monster, an animated bone-structure and not a coral bush, he has to answer for the work of his hands.

So, a work of art is the same as a work of nature, but one that is supposed to be illumined by the light of reason and conscience. Then it serves the good, as a stream turning a mill-wheel serves the good. But to call every work of art "a good" is like calling every stream "useful." It is sometimes useful and sometimes harmful, and how much oftener harmful!

It is good when you take it (take yourself) in hand.

The moral law can be introduced into art, but can a mercenary corrupted by so many changes of master ever make a soldier of the regular army?

Poet and elements

Poetry is God in the holy dreams of the earth

There is an ecstasy in battle
and on the sombre chasm's edge.

Ecstasy, that is to say, intoxication, is a feeling that is not good
in itself, it is outside goodness, and anyway—intoxication with
what?

Whatever threatens us with doom
hides in itself, for mortal hearts,
unspeakable pleasures...

Whenever you mention art's holiness call to mind this confes-
sion of Pushkin's.
—Yes, but further on it says...
—All right. Let's dwell on that line, then, the one trump card
for goodness: "...guarantee/perhaps of immortality!"
What kind of immortality? In God? In such vicinity the very
sound of the word is wild. A guarantee of the immortality of
nature itself, of the elements themselves—and of us insofar as
we are they, are it. A line, if not blasphemous, at least manifestly
pagan.
And further on, in black and white:

And so, all praise to thee, O Plague!
We're not afraid of murky tombs,
we're not confounded by your call!
As one we lift our frothing cups

and drink the rose maiden's breath
although that breath be — breath of Plague!

Not Pushkin, the elements. Nowhere and never have the elements spoken out so strongly. Visitation of the elemental — upon whom, doesn't matter, this time upon Pushkin. It is written in tongues of flame, in ocean waves, in desert sands — in anything you like, only not in words.

And this capital letter for Plague: plague no longer as a blind elemental force, but as a goddess, the proper name and face of *evil*.

The most remarkable thing is that we all love these lines, none of us judges them. If one of us said this in real life or, better, did it (set fire to a house, for instance, blew up a bridge), we'd all come to and shout "Crime!" Yes, come to — from a spell, wake up — from a sleep, that dead sleep of conscience, with nature's powers, our own, awake within it, that sleep into which we were cast by these few measured lines.

Genius

Visitation of the elemental, upon whom? Doesn't matter. Today upon Pushkin. Pushkin, in the little song of the Wilson tragedy, is a genius primarily because it *came upon* him.

Genius: the highest degree of subjection to the visitation — one; control of the visitation — two. The highest degree of being mentally pulled to pieces, and the highest of being — collected. The highest of passivity, and the highest of activity.

To let oneself be annihilated right down to some last atom, form the survival (resistance) of which will grow — a world.

For in this, this, this atom of resistance (resistivity) is the whole of mankind's chance of genius. Without it there is no genius—there is the crushed man who (it's still the same man!) bursts the walls not only of the Bedlams and Charentons but of the most well-ordered households too.

There is no genius without will, but still more is there none, still less is there any, without the visitation. Will is that unit to the countless milliards of the elemental visitation thanks to which alone they *are* milliards (realize their milliardness) and without which they are noughts—bubbles above a drowning man. While will without the visitation is—in creativity—simply a post. Made of oak. Such a poet would do better to go for a soldier.

Pushkin and Walsingham

Walsingham was not the only one visited by the plague. To write his *Feast in Time of Plague* Pushkin had to *be* Walsingham— and cease to be him. Repentant? No.

To write the song of the *Feast*, Pushkin had to fight down in himself both Walsingham and the priest, and pass through into some third thing as through a door. Had he dissolved himself in the plague, he could not have written this song. Had he warded off the plague with signs of the Cross, he could not have written this song (the link would have snapped). From the plague (the element) Pushkin escaped, not into the feast (the plague's, that is, Walsingham's triumphal feast over him) and not into prayer (the priest's), but into song.

Pushkin, like Goethe in *Werther*, escaped from the plague (Goethe from love) by giving his hero the death he himself longed to die. And by putting into his mouth a song that Walsingham could not have composed.

Had Walsingham been *capable* of that song, he would have

been saved, if not for life everlasting, at least for life. But Walsingham, as we all know, is long since upon the black cart.

Walsingham is Pushkin with no way out into song.
Pushkin is Walsingham with the gift of song and the will to sing.

—

Why do I arbitrarily identify Pushkin with Walsingham and not with the priest, whose creator he also is?

This is why: in the *Feast*, the priest doesn't sing. (—Priests never do sing. —Yes, they do: prayers.) Had Pushkin been the priest as much (as powerfully) as he was Walsingham, he could not have helped making him sing; he'd have put into his mouth a counter-hymn—a prayer to the plague—just as he put the delightful little song (of love) into the mouth of Mary, who is in the *Feast* (while Walsingham is what Pushkin *is*) what Pushkin loves.

The lyric poet betrays himself by song, and always will, for he cannot help making his favourite (his double) speak in his own, poet's, language. A song, in a dramatic work, is always love's give-away, an unwitting sign of preference. The author tires of speaking for others and gives himself away—in song.

What remains to us of the *Feast* (in our ears and souls)? Two songs. Mary's and Walsingham's. A love-song and a plague-song.

Pushkin's genius lies in his not giving a counterweight to Walsingham's "Hymn," an antidote to plague, a prayer. Had he done so, the work would have been stabilized, and we satisfied, from which no increase of good would have come; for by slaking our thirst for a counter-hymn Pushkin would have extinguished it. And so, with only the "Hymn to the Plague," God, the good and prayer remain—outside, as the place we not only aspire to but are thrown back to; the place to which the plague throws us back. The prayer Pushkin doesn't give is there, unavoidable. (The priest in the *Feast* speaks in the performance of his duty and we not only feel nothing, we don't even listen, knowing in advance what he will say.)

Pushkin could hardly have thought of all that. One can only plan a work backwards from the last step taken to the first, retracing with one's eyes open the path one had walked blindly. Think the work *through*.

A poet is the reverse of a chess-player. He not only doesn't see the pieces and the board, he doesn't see his own hand — which indeed may not be there.

In what lies the blasphemy of Walsingham's song? There is no reviling of God in it, only praise of the plague. Yet is there any blasphemy stronger than this song?

Blasphemy, not because from fear and despair we feast in a time of plague (thus children laugh from fear!), but because in the song — the apogee of the feast — we have lost our fear; because we turn punishment into a feast, turn punishment into a gift; because we dissolve not in the fear of God, but in the bliss of annihilation. If (as everyone believed, in those days, we do too while reading Pushkin) the plague is God's will to punish and vanquish us; if it really is God's scourge.

We throw ourselves under the scourge, as foliage under sunbeams, as foliage under the rain. Not joy in the teaching, but joy in the beating. Pure joy in the blow as such.

Joy? More than that! Bliss, with no equal in all the world's poetry. Bliss of complete surrender to the elemental — be it Love, or Plague, or whatever else we may call it.

For after the "Hymn to the Plague" there was no longer any God. And having come in ("enter Priest"), what else is there for the priest to do, but to go out.

The priest went away to pray, Pushkin—to sing. Pushkin goes away after the priest, he goes away last, tearing himself with effort (as if by the roots) from his double, Walsingham; or rather, at this moment Pushkin divides: into himself as Walsingham and himself as poet, himself doomed and himself saved.

But Walsingham sits at the table eternally. But Walsingham rides on the black cart eternally. But Walsingham is dug in with a spade eternally.

For that song by which Pushkin was saved.

⌁

A terrible name—Walsingham. It's no wonder Pushkin named him only three times in the whole play (named as if invoking him, and, like an invocation, thrice). The anonymous "President," which lends the work a sinister modern relevance, is still closer to us.

⌁

Walsinghams aren't needed by the elements. They defeat them in their stride. To conquer God in Walsingham is, alas, easier than to conquer song in Pushkin.

The plague, in *Feast in Time of Plague*, coveted not Walsingham but Pushkin.

And—*wonder of wonders!*—Walsingham, who is to the plague only an occasion for getting hold of Pushkin, Walsingham, who is for Pushkin only an occasion for his own elemental (his plaguey)

self, that very Walsingham rescues Pushkin from the plague—
into song, without which Pushkin cannot be his elemental self.
By giving him the song and taking upon himself the end.
The last atom of resistance to the elemental, to the glory of
the elemental, is what art is. Nature conquering herself to her
own glory.

—

So long as you are a poet, you shall not perish in the elemental,
for everything returns you to the element of elements: the word.
So long as you are a poet, you shall not perish in the elemen-
tal; for that is not to perish but to return to the lap of nature.
The poet perishes when he renounces the elemental. He
might as well cut his wrists without ado.

—

The whole of Walsingham is an exteriorisation (a carrying out-
side his limits) of the elemental Pushkin. You cannot live with
a Walsingham inside you: either a crime or a poem. Even if
Walsingham *existed*,—Pushkin would still have *created* him.

—

Thank the Lord the poet has the hero, the third person—*him*—
as a way out. Otherwise, what a shameful (and uninterrupted)
confession.
Thus, at least the appearance is saved.

—

The "Apollonian principle," the "golden mean": don't you see that this is nothing more than bits of Latin stuck in a schoolboy's head?

Pushkin, who created Walsingham, Pugachov, Mazeppa, Peter, who created them from inside himself, who didn't create them but disgorged them...

The Pushkin of the sea "of the free element."

—There was also another Pushkin.

—Yes, the Pushkin of *Walsingham's deep thought.*

(Exit Priest. The President remains, sunk in *deep thought.*)

November 1830. Boldino. A hundred and one years ago. A hundred and one years later.

Art's lessons

What does art teach? Goodness? No. Commonsense? No. It cannot teach even itself, for it is—given.

There is no thing which is not taught by art; there is no thing the reverse of that, which is not taught by art; and there is no thing which is the only thing taught by art.

All the lessons we derive from art, *we* put into it.

A series of answers to which there are no questions.

All art is the sole givenness of the answer.

Thus, in *Feast in Time of Plague*, it answered before I asked, plied me with answers.

All *our* art is in managing (in time) to put, to each answer before it evaporates, *our* question. This being outgalloped by answers is what inspiration is. And how often—a blank page.

—

One reads *Werther* and shoots himself, another reads *Werther* and, because Werther shoots himself, decides to live. One behaves like Werther, the other like Goethe. A lesson in self-extermination? A lesson in self-defense? Both. Goethe, by some law of the particular moment in his life, *needed* to shoot Werther; the suicidal demon of the generation needed to be incarnated precisely through Goethe's hand. A twice fateful necessity, and as such—without responsibility. And *very* fraught with consequences.

Is Goethe guilty of all the subsequent deaths?

He himself, in his profound and splendid old age, replied: no. Otherwise we wouldn't dare say a single word, for who can calculate the effect of any one word? (I'm putting it my own way, this is the substance of it.)

I too shall reply for Goethe: no.

He had no evil will, he had no will at all except the creative one. Writing his *Werther*, he not only forgot all others (that is, their possible troubles), but forgot himself too (his own trouble!).

All-forgetfulness, forgetfulness of everything which is not the work: the very basis of creation.

Would Goethe have written *Werther* a second time, after everything that had happened, if (improbably) he had again had just as urgent a need to? And would he then have been indictable? Would Goethe have written—knowingly?

He'd have written it a thousand times if he had needed to, just as he would not have written even the first line of the first one if the pressure had been the tiniest bit lighter. (Werther, like Walsingham, is a pressure from within.)

—And would he then have been indictable?

As a man, yes. As an artist, no.

Moreover, as an artist Goethe would have been both indictable and condemned if he had immolated Werther in himself with the aim of preserving human lives (fulfilment of the commandment: Thou shalt not kill). Here the law of art is exactly the reverse of the moral law. An artist is guilty in two cases only: in that refusal I have mentioned to create the work (for whoever's benefit), and in the creation of an inartistic work. Here his lesser responsibility ends, and his boundless responsibility as a human being begins.

Artistic creation is in some cases a sort of atrophy of conscience—more than that: a necessary atrophy of conscience, the moral flaw without which art cannot exist. In order to be good (not lead into temptation the little ones of this world), art would have to renounce a fair half of its whole self. The only way for art to be wittingly good is—not to be. It will end with the life of the planet.

Tolstoy's crusade

"An exception in favour of genius." Our whole relation to art is an exception in favour of genius. Art is itself that genius in whose favour we are excepted (excluded) from the moral law.

What is our whole relation to art if not this: conquerors are not judged; and who else *is* it—this Art—but a notorious conqueror (seducer) of, above all, our conscience.

The reason why, despite all our love for art, we respond so warmly to Tolstoy's clumsy, extra-aesthetic challenge to art (for he went, and he led, against his own grain) is that this challenge comes from the lips of an artist, seduced and seducing lips.

In Tolstoy's call for the annihilation of art, what is important are the lips that do the calling; if it did not sound from such a dizzying artistic height—if it were one of *us* calling us—we would not even turn our head.

In Tolstoy's crusade against art, what is important is Tolstoy: the artist. We *forgive* the artist the shoemaker. *War and Peace* cannot be eradicated from our relation to him. Ineradicable. Irreparable.

Through the artist we *consecrate* the shoemaker.

In Tolstoy's crusade against art, we are seduced once again— *by* art.

All this is no reproach to Tolstoy, but a reproach to us, the slaves of art. Tolstoy would have given his soul to make us listen—not to Tolstoy, but to *the truth*.

An objection.

Whose preaching of poverty is more convincing (that is to say, more deadly to wealth): the poor man's, poor from birth, or the rich man's who has renounced his riches?

The latter, of course.

The same applies to Tolstoy. Whose condemnation of pure art is more convincing (more deadly to art): that of the Tolstoyan who has been nothing in art, or that of Tolstoy himself who has been everything?

So we start by placing our eternal credit with Tolstoy the

artist, and end by recognizing the complete discrediting—by Tolstoy the artist—of art itself.

—

When I think of the moral essence of that human individual, the poet, I always recall the definition of the Tolstoy father in *Childhood and Boyhood*: "He belonged to that dangerous breed of people who can narrate one and the same action as the greatest baseness and as the most innocent joke."

The sleeper

Let us return to Goethe. Goethe, in his *Werther*, is just as innocent of the bad (the destruction of lives) as (example of the second reader who because of *Werther* decides to live) innocent of the good. Both—death and desire to live—are consequence, not purpose.

Whenever Goethe had a *purpose*, he realised it in his life: he built a theatre, proposed a series of reforms to Karl-August, studied the customs and soul of the ghetto, worked at mineralogy. In short, when Goethe had some purpose or other, he realised it directly, without this great round-about way of art.

The sole purpose of a work of art during its making is that it should be completed, and not even that the whole work should be completed, but each individual particle of it, each molecule. The very work itself, as a whole work, steps back before the realization of this molecule; or rather, each molecule *is* this whole, whose purpose is everywhere in its entire length and breadth, ubiquitous, omnipresent—and it itself, as a whole, is an end-in-itself.

At its completion it may turn out that the artist had made

something bigger than he planned (was able to do more than he thought he could!), something other than he'd planned. Or others will say so, as they did to Blok. And Blok was astonished every time, he always agreed with everyone, agreed almost with the first comer, so new to him was all this (that is, the presence of any purpose whatsoever).

Blok's *The Twelve* arose under a spell. The demon of that hour of the Revolution (who is Blok's "music of Revolution") inhabited Blok and compelled him.

Then the naive moralizer, Z. G., spent a long time wondering whether or not to shake hands with Blok, while Blok patiently waited.

Blok wrote *The Twelve* in one night and got up in complete exhaustion, like one who has been ridden.

Blok did not know *The Twelve*, never read it from a stage. ("I don't know *The Twelve*. I don't remember *The Twelve*." Truly, *he did not know*.)

And one can understand his terror when in 1920 on the Vozdvizhenka he seized his companion's hand: "Look!" And only five paces later: "Katka!"

In the Middle Ages (yet what *extreme* ones!), whole villages were possessed by a demon and suddenly started talking Latin.

A poet? A sleeper.

Art in the light of conscience

One woke up. A man sharp-nosed and waxen-faced who, in the hearth of the Sheremetev house, burned a manuscript. The second part of *Dead Souls*.

Lead not into temptation. A more than medieval — *propriomanual* — casting of one's creation into the flames. Self-judgment, which I say is the only judgment.

(The shame and failure of the Inquisition lies in the fact that it itself did the burning, instead of leading people to do their own burning; burned manuscripts, when it should have burned out the soul.)

— But Gogol was mad by that time.

A madman is one who burns down a temple (not built by him) to achieve fame. Gogol, burning the work of his hands, burned his fame as well.

And I recall the words of a shoemaker (Moscow 1920), a case where the shoemaker really is higher than the artist: "You and me, Marina Ivanovna, are not out of our minds, but them — they're short of mind."

—

That half-hour of Gogol's at the fireplace did more for good, and against art, than all Tolstoy's many years of preaching.

For here is a deed, a visible deed of the hands, that movement of the hand which we all thirst for, and which is not to be out-weighed by any "movement of the spirit."

—

Maybe we would not have been tempted by the second part of *Dead Souls*. Certainly we'd have been glad to have it. But that gladness of ours would have been nothing in comparison with our actual gladness in Gogol, who, out of love for our living souls, burned his *Dead* ones. On the fire of his own conscience.

The first were written with ink.

The second — in us — with fire.

Art without artifice

Yet in the very heart of art, and at the same time on its heights, there are works that make you say: "This is not art any more. It's more than art." Everyone has known works of this sort.

Their sign is their effectiveness despite their inadequacy of means, an inadequacy which nothing in the world would make us exchange for any adequacies and abundances, and which we only call to mind when we try to establish: how was it done? An essentially futile approach, for in every born work the ends are hidden.

Not yet art, but already more than art.

Such works often come from the pens of women, children, self-taught people—the little ones of this world. Such works often come from no pen at all, being unwritten but kept (or lost) orally. Often they are the sole works of a lifetime. Often—the very first. Often—the very last.

Art without artifice.

Here is a verse by a four-year-old boy who did not live long.

> Over there, lives a white bird.
> Over there, walks a pale boy
> Surely! Surely! Surely!
> There *is*—far away.

(*Vedno* ["surely"]—a childish and folk form of *vedomo* ["known"] which here sounds like both *verno* ["right"] and *zavedomo* ["wittingly"]: wittingly right. While *tam-ot* ["far away"] is a nanny's word for distance.)

Here is the last line of a poem by a little girl of seven who has never walked, and who prays to be able to stand up. I heard the poem only once, twenty years ago, and have kept only the last line: "So that I may *stand up* to pray!"

[...]

Attempt at a hierarchy

Major poet. Great poet. Lofty poet.

A major poet is what anyone—any major poet—can be. To be a major poet, it is enough to have a major poetic gift. To be a great poet, even the most major gift is too small: he needs an equivalent gift of personality—of mind, soul, will—and the aspiration of this whole towards a definite aim; that is, its organization. But a lofty poet is something that even a quite minor poet, bearer of the most modest gift, can be—such as Alfred de Vigny, who wins our recognition as a poet by the power of his inner worth alone. In his case, the gift just reached to the brim. A little less and he'd have been merely a hero (that is to say, immeasurably more).

The great poet includes—and counterbalances—the lofty poet. The lofty poet does *not* include the great one, otherwise we'd call him "great." Loftiness as the sole sign of existence. So, there is no poet bigger than Goethe, but there are poets who are loftier—his younger contemporary Hölderlin, for instance, an incomparably poorer poet, yet a *dweller* upon those highlands where Goethe is but a guest. And the lofty is after all less than the great, even if they are of equal height. Thus: the oak is great, the cypress lofty.

The early foundation of genius is too vast and stable to let it disappear into loftiness. Shakespeare, Goethe, Pushkin. If

Shakespeare, Goethe, Pushkin, had been loftier they would have left many a thing unheard, unanswered, would simply not have condescended to many things.

Genius: a resultant of counteractions, that is, ultimately, equilibrium, that is, harmony; while the giraffe is a freak, creature of a single dimension, his own neck; the giraffe is neck. (Every freak is a part of itself.)

"The poet soars among the clouds" — true, but true of only one breed of poet: the only-lofty, the purely-spiritual. And he doesn't even soar, he sojourns. The humpback pays for his hump, the angel too pays for his wings while on earth. Fleshlessness, so close to fruitlessness, rarefied air, thought instead of passion, utterances instead of words — these are the earthly signs of heavenly guests.

A single exception: Rilke. A poet not only equally lofty and great (this can be said of Goethe too), but one who has that same exclusive loftiness which here excludes nothing. As if God, who, when giving other poets of the spirit their one gift, took everything else away from them, left to Rilke that everything else. Into the bargain.

⸻

Loftiness does not exist as parity. Only as primacy.

⸻

For the merely major poet, art is always an aim in itself — that is, a mere function without which he cannot live and for which he is not responsible. For the great and for the lofty, it is always a means. He himself is a means in someone's hands — as is, indeed, the merely major poet, in other hands. The whole difference, apart from the basic difference of which hands, is in the degree of consciousness the poet has of being held. The spiritually greater the poet—that is, the loftier the hands that hold him—the more powerfully conscious he is of this being-held (being in service). Had Goethe not known a higher force above himself and his work, he would never have written the last lines of the last *Faust*. Only to the innocent is it *given*—or to the one who knows *everything*.

In essence, a poet's whole labour amounts to a fulfillment, the physical fulfillment of a spiritual task (not assigned by himself). And a poet's whole will—to the laboring will to realisation. (No such thing as individual creative will.)

The will to embody physically what already exists spiritually (the eternal) and to embody spiritually (to inspirit) what doesn't yet exist spiritually and desires to, regardless of the qualities of this desirer. To embody the spirit that desires a body (ideas), and to inspirit the bodies that desire a soul (the elements). The word is body to ideas, soul to the elements.

Every poet is, in one way or another, the servant of ideas or of elements: sometimes, (as already mentioned) of ideas alone; sometimes, of both ideas and elements. Sometimes, of the elements alone. But even in this last case, he is still the first low sky of something: of those same elements and passions. Through the element of the word, which alone among all elements, is—from its very beginning—made sense of, that is to say, made spirit of. *The low close sky of the earth.*

In this ethical approach (the demand for idea-content, for loftiness, in a writer) may lie the whole solution to something at first glance incomprehensible: the nineties' preferring Nadson to Pushkin, who, if not obviously idea-less is certainly less clearly idea-full than Nadson, and the previous generation's preferring Nekrasov-the-citizen to just Nekrasov. All that fierce utilitarianism, all the Bazarovism, is only the affirmation of and demand for loftiness as the basic principle of life—it is *only the Russian form of loftiness.* Our "usefulness" is only conscience. Russia, to her honour—or rather, to the honour of her conscience, not the honour of her artistry (two things that don't need each other)— always approached writers—rather, always *went* to writers—the way the peasant went to the Tsar—for the truth. And it was excellent when that Tsar turned out to be Lev Tolstoy and not Artsybashev. For Russia also learned to live from Artsybashev's *Sanin!*

Prayer

What can we say about God? Nothing. What can we say *to* God? Everything. Poems to God are prayer. And if there are no prayers nowadays (except Rilke's and those little ones', I know of none), it is not because we don't have anything to say to God, nor because we have no one to say this anything to—there is something and there is someone—but because we haven't the conscience to praise and pray God in the same language we've used for centuries to praise and pray absolutely everything. In our age, to have the courage for direct speech to God (for prayer) we must either not know what poems are, or forget.

Loss of trust.

———

The cruel thing Blok said about the early Akhmatova: Akhmatova writes poems as if a man were watching her, but you should write them as if God were watching you—adapting the first, denunciatory half of the sentence to fit every one of us—holily, in the end. As if before God, *standing in the divine presence.* But what in us shall then withstand, and who among us?

Point of view

In relation to the spiritual world: art is a kind of physical world of the spiritual.

In relation to the physical world: art is a kind of spiritual world of the physical.

Starting from the earth, it is the first millimetre of air over it (of sky, that is, for the sky begins right from the earth, or else there is no sky at all. Check this by distances, which clarify phenomena).

Starting from the top of the sky, it is that same first millimetre above the earth, but the last when seen from the top; that is, it is almost earth from there, and from the very top it is entirely earth. *Where you look from.*

⟶

In the same way, the soul, which the common man supposes to be the peak of spirituality, is for the spiritual man—almost flesh. The analogy with art is not accidental, for poetry—which I never take my eyes off when I say "art," the whole *event* of poetry, from the poet's visitation to the reader's reception—takes place entirely within the soul, that first, lowest sky of the spirit. Which is in no way contradictory to art as nature. There is no soul-less nature; there is only uninspired—spirit-less—nature.

Poet, poet! The most soul-animated—and how often (perhaps just *because* of that) the most uninspired object!

"*Fier quand je me compare*"— no! Because whatever is below the poet does not even count: there is still enough pride not to level oneself down. For I look up—from below,—and my point of support is not in my own lowness, but in that height.

"*Humble quand je me compare, inconnu quand je me considère,*" for in order to contemplate something one must rise above the contemplated thing; place between oneself and the thing all the vertical, the refusal, of height. For I look down—from above! The highest in me—at the lowest in me. And what remains to me of this confrontation—but amazement... or recognition.

> She took the faded pages
> And gazed upon them strangely
> As souls look from on high
> At bodies they've cast off.

This is how I too shall one day (indeed, I already do) look at my poems...

Poet's heaven

—A priest serves God in his way, you in yours.

—Blasphemy. When I write my poem *The Swain*—about a vampire's love for a girl and hers for him—I don't serve any God: I know what God I serve. When I describe Tatars in open spaces, I again don't serve any God except the wind (or a wizard: a forefather). All my Russian works are elemental, that is, sinful. One has to distinguish what forces are *im Spiel*. And when shall we finally stop taking power for truth, and magic for holiness?

Art is a temptation, perhaps the last, subtlest, most insuperable of the earth's seductions, that last cloud in the last sky, at which gazed the dying *brother of a brother*, Jules Goncourt—no longer looking at anything, yet attempting to get its colouring into words—having by then forgotten all words.

A third kingdom with its own laws, from which we so seldom escape into the higher one (and how often into the lower!). A third kingdom, the first sky from the earth, a second earth. Between the heaven of the spirit and the hell of the species, art is purgatory which no one wishes to leave for paradise.

When, at the sight of a priest, a monk, even a nurse, I—invariably, irresistibly!—lower my eyes, I know why I lower them. My shame at the sight of a priest, a monk, even a nurse—this shame is visionary.

—You are doing God's work.

—If my works release, enlighten, purify—yes; if they seduce—no, and it would be better to hang a stone round my neck.

But how often in one and the same work, on one and the same page, in one and the same line, they both release *and* seduce. Like the dubious swill in a witch's cauldron — what *hasn't* been heaped into it and boiled?

How many it has ruined; how few, saved!

And the immediate riposte of the accused:

Dark power!
Craft of *Mra*!
How many — ruined!
How few — saved!

I fear that even when dying... *Mra*, by the way, I take here as
a feminine noun, a feminine ending, the sound of death. *Mor*
(masculine), *Mra* (feminine). Death could have had this name;
perhaps at some time, somewhere, it did have this name: *Mra*.
Word-creation, like any creation, only means following the track
of the hearing ear of nation and nature. A journey by ear. *"Et
tout le reste n'est que littérature."*

—

Polytheism of the poet. I'd say our Christian God is at best *one*
among the host of his gods.
　　Never an atheist. Always a polytheist, with the sole difference
that the higher knows the older (knows what there was in pagan
times too). But the majority don't know even this, and blindly
alternate Christ with Dionysus, not realising that the very juxta-
position of these names is blasphemy and sacrilege.
　　Art would be holy if we lived then, or those gods now. The
poet's heaven is just on a level with the pedestal of Zeus: the
summit of Olympus.

Kernel of the kernel

　　　...and you send reply.
　　　But to you there is no response...
　　　Such, poet, are you as well!

Not-poet, above-poet, more than poet, not only poet: but where and what is the *poet* in all this? *Der Kern des Kernes*, the kernel of the kernel.

A poet is an answer.

From the lowest level of the simple reflex to the highest level of Goethe's great answer, the poet is a definite and invariable mental-artistic reflex. To what? may be simply a question of brain capacity. Pushkin said: to everything. A genius's answer.

This mental-artistic reflex is the kernel of the kernel which unites the anonymous author of a chastushka with the author *Faust* Part Two. Without it there is no poet, or rather, it *is* the poet. Miracle of the poet, not explicable by any convolutions of the brain.

A reflex before thought, even before feeling, the deepest and fastest—as by electric current—spearing of the whole being by a given phenomenon, and the simultaneous, almost preceding, answer to it.

An answer not to the blow, but to a quivering of the air—of a thing that has not yet moved. Answer to the pre-blow. Not an answer, but a pre-answer. Always to a phenomenon, never to a question. The phenomenon itself is the question. The thing self-strikes the poet—with itself; self-questions him—with itself. The command for an answer, coming from the phenomenon itself—which is not yet manifest and is manifested only through the answer. Command? Yes, if "SOS" is a command (the most unrepulsable of all).

Before it existed (well, it always existed, only hadn't yet reached time; thus the opposite shore has not yet reached the ferry). Why the poet's hand so often hangs in mid-air is that its support—in time—does not yet exist (*nicht vorhanden*). The poet's hand—even if hanging in mid-air!—creates the phenomenon (completes its creation). This hand hanging in the air is, in fact, the poet's imperfect, despairing, yet nonetheless creative, "*be.*" (Who called me?—Silence.—I must create, that is, name, the one who called me. Such is the poet's "responding.") One more thing. "Mental-artistic reflex." Artistic-vulneral, for the soul is our capacity for pain—pure and simple. (For pain which is not headache, not toothache, not throatache, not...not...not, etc.—pain pure and simple.)

This is the kernel of the kernel of the poet, leaving aside the *indispensable* artistry: the *strength of anguish.*

Truth of poets

Such then is the truth of poets, the most elusive, most invincible, most convincing and most unproven truth; truth that lives in us only for some primary *glimmer* of perception (what was that?) and remains in us only as a trace of light or loss (*was* it something?). Truth irresponsible and inconsequential, which—for God's sake—one should not even attempt to pursue, because it is irretrievable even for the poet. (A poet's truth is a path where all traces are straightway overgrown. Untraceable even for the poet, were he to follow in his own wake.) He didn't know he was about to *pronounce*, often didn't know what it was he was pronouncing. Didn't know it before the pronouncing, and forgot it immediately after. Not one of innumerable truths, but one of the innumerable faces of the truth, which destroy each other only when set side by side. Once-only aspects of the truth. Simply—a thrust in the heart of Eternity. The means: juxtaposition of two most ordinary words, which stand side by side just so. (Sometimes—separation by a single hyphen!)

There is a lock which opens only through a certain combination of figures: if you know this, opening it is nothing; if you don't, it's a miracle or chance. A miracle-chance which happened to my six-year-old son who, in one go, twisted and unfastened a fine chain of this sort that had been locked around his neck, to the horror of the chain's owner. Does the poet know, or not know, the combination of figures? (In the poet's case—since all the world is locked up and everything is waiting to be unlocked—it is different every time, to each thing its own lock; and behind the lock is a particular truth, different every time, once-only—like the lock itself.) Does the poet know *all* the combinations of figures?

My mother had a peculiarity: she would set the clock during the night, whenever it stopped. In response to not its ticking but its not-ticking—doubtless what woke her up—she would set it in the dark without looking. In the morning the clock showed *it*—the absolute time, I assume—which was never found by that unhappy crowned contemplator of so many contradictory clock-faces and listener to so many uncoinciding chimes.

The clock showed *it*.

Chance? Chance that is repeated every time is, in the life of a man, fate; in the world of phenomena, law. This was the law of her hand. The law of her hand's *knowledge*.

Not: "my mother had a peculiarity," but: her *hand* had the peculiarity—of truth.

Not playing like my son, not self-assured like the owner of the lock, and not visionary like the supposed mathematician—but both blind and visionary, obeying only his hand (which, itself, obeys what?): thus the poet opens the lock.

He lacks only one gesture: the self-assured, sure of self and of lock alike, gesture of the owner of the lock. A poet does not possess a single lock as his own. That is why he unlocks them all. And that is why, unlocking each at the first try, he won't open any of them a second time. For he is not the owner of the secret, only its passer-by.

Condition of creation

The condition of creation is a condition of entrancement. Till you begin—*obsession*; till you finish—*possession*. Something, someone, lodges in you; your hand is the fulfiller not of you but of *it*. Who is this *it*? That which through you wants to be.

Things always chose me by the mark of my power, and often I wrote them almost against my will. All my Russian work are of this sort. Certain things of Russia wanted to be expressed, they chose me. And how did they persuade, seduce me? By my own power: only you! Yes, only I. And having given in—sometimes seeingly, sometimes blindly—I would obey, seek out with my ear some assigned aural lesson. And it was not I who, out of a hundred words (not rhymes! but in the middle of a line), would choose the hundred and first, but *it* (the thing), resisting all the hundred epithets: that isn't *my* name.

The condition of creating is a condition of dreaming, when suddenly, obeying an unknown necessity, you set fire to a house or push your friend off a mountain-top. Is it your act? Clearly it *is* yours (after all, it is you sleeping, *dreaming*!). Yours—in complete freedom. An act of yourself without conscience, yourself as nature.

A series of doors, behind one of which someone, something

(usually terrible), is waiting. The doors are identical. Not this one—not this one—not this one—*that* one. Who told me? Nobody. I recognize the one I need by all the unrecognised ones (the right one by all the wrong ones). It's the same with words. Not this one—not this one—not this one—*that* one. By the obviously *not-this* I recognise *that*. Native to every sleeper and writer is the *blow of recognition*. Oh, the sleeper cannot be deceived! He knows friend and he knows enemy, knows the door and knows the chasm behind the door, and to all this—both friend and enemy, and door and pit—he is doomed. The sleeper cannot be deceived, even by the sleeper himself. Vainly I say to myself: I won't go in (through the door), I won't look (through the window)—I know that I shall go in, and even while I am saying I won't look, I am looking.

Oh, the sleeper is not to be saved!

There is a loop-hole, though, even in sleep: when it gets too terrible, I'll wake up. In sleep, I'll wake up; in poetry, I shall resist.

Someone said to me about Pasternak's poems: "Splendid poems when you explain them all like that, but they need a key supplied with them."

No, not supply a key to the poems (dreams), but the poems themselves are a key to understanding everything. But from understanding to accepting there isn't just a step, there is no step at all; to understand is to accept, there is no other understanding, any other understanding is non-understanding. Not in vain does the French *comprendre* mean both "understand" and "encompass"—that is, "accept" and "include."

There is no poet who would reject any elemental force, consequently any rebellion. Pushkin feared Nicholas, deified Peter, but loved Pugachov. It wasn't by chance that all the pupils of one remarkable and wrongly forgotten poetess, who was also a teacher of history, answered the question put by the district administrator: "Well, children, and who is your favourite tsar?"—(the whole class together:) "Grishka Otrepyev!"

Find me a poet without a Pugachov! without an Impostor! without a *Corsican!*—*within.* A poet might lack the power (the means) for a Pugachov, that's all. *Mais l'intention y est toujours.* What doesn't accept (rejects, even ejects) is the human being: will, reason, conscience.

In this realm the poet can have only one prayer: not to understand the unacceptable—let me not understand, so that I may not be seduced. The sole prayer of the poet is not to hear the voices: let me not hear, so that I may not answer. For to hear, for the poet, is already to answer, and to answer is already to affirm, if only by the passionateness of his denial. The poet's only prayer is a prayer for deafness. Otherwise there is the most difficult task of choosing what to hear according to its quality; that is, of choosing the forcible stopping of his own ears to a number of calls, which are invariably the stronger. Choice from birth, that is, to hear only what is important, is a blessing bestowed on almost no one.

(On Odysseus's ship there was neither hero nor poet. A hero is one who will stand firm even when not tied down, stand firm even without wax stuck in his ears; a poet is one who will fling himself forward even when tied down, who will hear even with wax in his ears, that is—once again—fling himself forward. The only things non-understood by the poet from birth are the half-measures of the rope and the wax.)

Thus Mayakovsky failed to vanquish the poet in himself, and the result was a monument to the Volunteer leader raised by the most revolutionary of poets. (The poem "Crimea," twelve immortal lines.) One can't help remarking the devilish cunning of whatever those forces are that pick themselves a herald from among their very enemies. The end of the Crimea just *had* to be depicted by Mayakovsky!

When, at the age of thirteen, I asked an old revolutionary: "Is it possible to be a poet and also be in the Party?," he replied, without a moment's thought: "No."

So I too shall reply: no.

—

What element was it then, what demon, that lodged in Mayakovsky at that hour and made him describe Wrangel? For the Volunteer movement, as everyone now recognises, was not elemental. (Unless—the steppe they went over, the songs they sang...)

Not the White movement, but the Black Sea; into which, kissing the Russian earth three times, stepped the Commander-in-chief.

The Black Sea of that hour.

—

I don't want to be a springboard for others' ideas, a loudspeaker for other people's passions.

Other people's? But is anything "other" to a poet? In *The Covetous Knight* Pushkin made even miserliness his own, in *Salieri* even untalentedness. And it was not through being other, but precisely through being *related*, that Pugachov knocked at me.

So I'll say: I don't want anything that isn't wholly mine, wittingly mine, most mine.

And what if the most mine (revelation of dream) is indeed Pugachov?

I don't want anything that I won't answer for at seven o'clock in the morning and won't die for (won't die without) at any hour of day or night.

I won't die for Pugachov—that means he is *not mine*.

—

The reverse extreme of nature is Christ.

The other end of the road is Christ.

Everything in between is—halfway along the road.

And it is not for the poet, from birth a man of many roads, to give up his many roads—the native cross of his crossroads!—for the halfway roads of social issues or whatever else.

To lay down one's soul for one's friends.

Only this can overpower the elemental in a poet.

—translated by Angela Livingstone

from POETS WITH HISTORY
AND POETS WITHOUT HISTORY

[…]

What is the "I" of a poet? It is—to all appearances—the human "I" expressed in poetic speech. But only to appearances, for often poems give us sómething that had been hidden, obscured, even quite stifled, something the person hadn't known was in him, and would never have recognised had it not been for poetry, the poetic gift. Action of forces which are unknown to the one who acts, and which he only becomes conscious of in the instant of action. An almost complete analogy to dreaming. If it were possible to direct one's own dreams—and for some it is, especially children—the analogy would be complete. That which is hidden and buried in you is revealed and exposed in your poems: this is the poetic "I," your dream-self.

The "I" of the poet, in other words, is his soul's devotion to certain dreams, his being visited by certain dreams, the secret source—not of his will, but of his whole nature.

The poet's self is a dream-self and a language-self; it is the "I" of a dreamer awakened by inspired speech and realised only in that speech.

This is the sum of the poet's personality. This is the law of his idiosyncrasy. This is why poets are all so alike and so unalike. Like, because all without exception have dreams. Unlike, in what dreams they have. Like—in their ability to dream; unlike—in the dreams.

All poets can be divided into poets with development and poets without development. Into poets with history and poets without history. The first could be depicted graphically as an arrow shot into infinity; the second—as a circle. Above the first (the image of the arrow) stands the law of gradual self-discovery. These poets discover themselves through all the phenomena they meet along their way, at every step and in every new object. Mine or others', the vital or the superfluous, the accidental and the eternal: everything is for them a touchstone. Of their power, which increases with each new obstacle. Their self-discovery is their coming to self-knowledge through the world, self-knowledge of the soul through the visible world. Their path is the path of experience. As they walk, we physically sense a wind, the air they cleave with their brows. A wind blows from them.

They walk without turning round. Their experience accumulates as if by itself, and piles up somewhere behind, like a load on the back which never makes the back hunch. One doesn't look round at the sack on one's back. The walker knows nothing of his rucksack until the moment he needs it: at the stopping-place. The Goethe of *Götz von Berlichingen* and the Goethe of the *Metamorphosis of Plants* are not acquainted with each other. Goethe put in his sack everything he needed from *himself of that time*, left himself in the wondrous forests of young Germany and of his own youth, and went—onward. Had the mature Goethe met the young Goethe at a crossroads, he might actually have failed to recognise him and might have sought to make his acquaintance. I'm not talking of Goethe the person, but of Goethe the creator, and I take this great example as an especially evident one.

Poets with history (like people with history in general and like history itself) do not even renounce themselves: they simply don't turn round to themselves—no time for it, only onward! Such is the law of movement and of pressing forward.

The Goethe of *Götz*, the Goethe of *Werther*, the Goethe of the *Roman Elegies*, the Goethe of the *Theory of Colours*, and so on—where is he? Everywhere. Nowhere. How many are there? As many as there are strides. Each step was taken by a different person. One set out, another arrived. *He* was no more than the tirelessness of the creative will, the muscle that lifted the walker's foot. The same is true of Pushkin. Maybe this is what genius is?

The loneliness of such walkers! People look for a person you yourself would no longer recognise. They fall in love with the one of you whom you have already disavowed. They give their trust to one you have outgrown. From Goethe, until he was eighty-three (the year of his death), people went on demanding *Götz* (Goethe at twenty!). And—a smaller but nearer example— from the Blok of *The Twelve* they still demand "The Unknown Woman."

This is what our Russian Goethean, the poet and philosopher Vyacheslav Ivanov, now living in Padua, meant when he wrote his fine lines:

> The one whose name you trumpet
> has taken another name,
> the one you love today
> has already ceased being loved.

It isn't a question of age; we all change. The point is that the mature Goethe didn't understand his own youth. Some poets grow young in their old age: Goethe's *Trilogy of Passion* was written by a seventy-year-old! It's a question of one thing replacing another, of opening horizons, of previously concealed spaces. It's a question of the quantity of minutes, of the infinity of tasks, of the immensity of his Columbus-like strengths. And the rucksack on the back (Goethe really did walk about with a bag for collecting stones and minerals) gets heavier and heavier. And the road keeps stretching ahead. And the shadows grow. And you can neither exhaust your strength nor reach the end of the road! Poets with history are, above all, poets of a theme. We always know what they are writing about. And, if we don't learn where they were going to, we do at least realize, when their journey is completed, that they had always been going somewhere (the existence of a goal). Rarely are they pure lyricists. Too large in size and scope, their own "I" is too small for them—even the biggest is too small—or they spread it out till nothing is left and it merges with the rim of the horizon (Goethe, Pushkin). The human "I" becomes the "I" of a country—a people—a given continent—a century—a millennium—the heavenly vault (Goethe's geological "I": "I live in the millennia"). For such a poet a theme is the occasion for a new self, and not necessarily a human one. Their whole earthly path is a sequence of reincarnations, not necessarily into a human being. From a human to a stone, a flower, a constellation. They seem to incarnate in themselves all the days of creation.

Poets with history are, above all, poets of will. I don't mean the will to fulfill, which is taken for granted: no one will doubt that a physically huge bulk like *Faust,* or indeed any poem of a thousand lines, cannot come into being by itself. Eight, sixteen, or, rarely, twenty lines may come about by themselves—the lyric tide most often lays fragments at our feet, albeit the most precious ones. I mean the will to choose, the will to have choice. To decide not merely to become another, but—this particular other. To decide to part with oneself. To decide—like the hero in the fairy tale—between right, left, and straight on (but, like that same hero, never backward!). Waking up one morning, Pushkin makes a decision: "Today I shall write Mozart!" This Mozart is his refusal to a multitude of other visions and subjects;

it is total choice—that is, a sacrifice. To use contemporary vocabulary, I'd say that the poet with history rejects everything that lies outside his general line—the line of his personality, his gift, his history. The choice is made by his infallible instinct for the most important. And yet, at the end of Pushkin's path, we have the sense that Pushkin could not have done otherwise than create what he did create, could not have written anything he did not write...And no one regrets that in Gogol's favor he refused the *Dead Souls* project, something that lay on Gogol's general line. (The poet with history also has a clear view of others—Pushkin had, especially.) The main feature of poets of this sort is the striving toward a goal. A poet without history cannot have a striving toward a goal. He himself doesn't know what the lyric flood will bring him.

Pure lyric poetry has no project. You can't make yourself have a particular dream or feel a particular feeling. Pure lyricism is the sheer condition of going though something, suffering something through, and in the intervals (when the poet is not being summoned by Apollo to holy sacrifice), in the ebbs of inspiration, it is a condition of infinite poverty. The sea has departed, carried everything away, and won't return *before its own time.* A continual, awful hanging in the air, on the word of honor of perfidious inspiration. And suppose one day it lets you go?

Pure lyric poetry is solely the record of our dreams and feelings, along with the entreaty that these dreams and feelings should never run dry...To demand more from lyricism...But what *more* could be demanded from it?

The lyric poet has nothing to grasp hold of: he has neither the skeleton of a theme nor obligatory hours of work at a desk; no material he can dip into, which he's preoccupied with or even immersed in, at the ebb times: he is wholly suspended on a thread of trust.

Don't expect sacrifices: the pure lyricist sacrifices nothing—he is glad when anything comes at all. Don't expect moral choice from him either—whatever comes, "bad" or "good," he is so happy it has come at all that to you (society, morality, God) he won't yield a thing.

The lyric poet is given only the will to fulfill his task, just enough for sorting out the tide's offerings.

Pure lyricism is nothing but the recording of our dreams and sensations. The greater the poet, the purer the record.

A walker and a stylite. For the poet without history is a stylite or—same thing—a sleeper. Whatever may happen around his pillar, whatever the waves of history may create (or destroy), he sees, hears, and knows only what is his. (Whatever may be going on around him, he sees only his own dreams.) Sometimes he seems to be really great, like Boris Pasternak, but the small and the great draw us equally irresistibly into the enchanted circle of dream. We too turn into stone.

To exactly the extent that other people's dreams, when they tell us them, are inexpressive and uninfectious, these lyric dreams are irresistible, affecting us more than our own!

Now beyond the slumbering mountain
the evening ray has faded.
In a resounding stream the hot
spring faintly sparkles...

These lines by the young Lermontov are more powerful than all my childhood dreams—and not only childhood, and not only mine.

It could be said of poets without history that their soul and their personality are formed in their mother's womb. They don't need to learn or acquire or fathom anything at all—they know everything from the start. They don't ask about anything—they make manifest. Evidence, experience are nothing to them. Sometimes the range of their knowledge is very narrow. They don't go beyond it. Sometimes the range of their knowledge is very wide. They never narrow it to oblige experience. They came into the world not to learn, but to say. To say what they already know: everything they know (if it is a lot) or the only thing they know (if it is just one thing).

They came into the world to make themselves known. Pure lyricists, only-lyricists, don't allow anything alien into themselves, and they have an instinct for this just as poets with history have an instinct for their own general line. The whole empirical world is to them a foreign body. In this sense they have the power to choose, or more exactly, the power to select, or more exactly still, the power to reject. But the rejection is done by the whole of their nature, not by their will alone. And is usually unconscious. In this, as in much, maybe in everything, they are children. Here is how the world is for them: "That's the wrong way."—"No, it's the right way! I know! I know better!" What does he know? That any other way is impossible. They are the absolute opposite: I am the world (meaning the human world—society, family, morality, ruling church, science, commonsense, any form of power—human organization in general, including our much-famed "progress"). Enter into the poems and the biography too, which are always a single whole.

For poets with history there are no foreign bodies, they are conscious participants in the world. Their "I" is equal to the world. From the human to the cosmic.

Here lies the distinction between the genius and the lyric genius. There do exist purely lyric geniuses. But we never call them "geniuses." The way this kind of genius is closed upon himself, and doomed to himself, is expressed in the adjective "lyrical." Just as the boundlessness of the genius, his impersonality even, is expressed by the absence, even impossibility, of any adjective whatever. (Every adjective, since it gives an exact meaning, is limiting.)

The "I" cannot be a genius. A genius may call itself "I," dress itself in a certain name, make use of certain earthly tokens. We must not forget that among ancient peoples "genius" signified quite factually a good higher being, a divinity from *above*, not the person himself. Goethe was a genius because above him there hovered a genius. This genius distracted and sustained him up to the end of his eighty-third year, up to the last page of *Faust* Part Two. That same genius is shown in his immortal face.

A last, and perhaps the simplest, explanation. Pure lyric poetry lives on feelings. Feelings are always the same. Feelings are not regular or consistent. They are all given to us at once, all the feelings we are ever to experience; like the flames of a torch, they are squeezed into our breast from birth. Feeling (the childhood of a person, a nation, the planet) always starts at a maximum, and in strong people and in poets it remains at that maximum. Feeling doesn't need a cause, it itself is the cause of everything. Feeling doesn't need experience, it knows everything earlier and better. (Every sentiment is also a presentiment.) Someone in whom there is love, loves; someone in whom there is anger, gets angry; and someone in whom there is a sense of hurt, is hurt, from the day he is born. Sensitivity to hurt gives rise to hurt. Feeling doesn't need experience, it knows in advance that it is doomed. There's nothing for feeling to do on the periphery of the visible, it is in the center, is itself the center. There's nothing for feeling to seek along any roads, it knows that it will come — will lead — into itself.

An enchanted circle. A dream circle. A magic circle.

Thus once again:

Thought is an arrow,
Feeling is a circle.

This is the essence of the purely lyrical sort of poet, the nature of pure lyricism. And if they sometimes seem to develop and change—it is not *they* that develop and change, but only their vocabulary, their linguistic equipment.

Few lyricists are given the right words, their own words, from the start! From helplessness, they often begin with others' words—not their own, but universal ones (and often it's precisely at that stage that they please the majority, which sees in them its own nothingness). Then, when they start talking their own language, sometimes very soon, we think they have changed and grown up. Yet it's not they who have grown, but their language-self, which has reached them in its growth. Not even the greatest musician can express himself on a child's keyboard.

Some children are born with a ready-made soul. No child is born with ready-made speech. (Or just one was—Mozart.) Pure lyricists, too, learn to talk, for the language of poets is the physics of their creativity, their soul's body, and each body has got to develop. The hardest thing of all for a lyric poet is to find his own language, not his own feeling, as he has that from his birth. But there is no pure lyricist who hasn't already conveyed himself in his childhood—his definitive and fated self—announced his whole self in some fairly complete and exhaustive stanza of four or eight lines, one that he will never offer again and that could stand as an epigraph to the whole of his work, a formula for his whole fate. A first stanza, which could also be the last: a pre-life stanza which could also be a pre-death one (inscription on a tombstone).

Such is Lermontov's "The Sail." Pure lyric poets, the majority of them, are children of very early development (and of very short life, both as persons and as writers)—or rather of very early insight, with a presentiment of their being doomed to poetry—*Wunderkinder* in the literal sense, having a wide-awake sense of fate, that is to say of themselves.

The poet with history never knows what is going to happen to him. It is his genius that knows this, guiding him and revealing to him only as much as he needs for free movement: a proximate goal, a sense of direction, constantly keeping the main thing hidden round a turning. The pure lyricist always knows that nothing is going to happen to him, that he will have nothing but himself: his own tragic lyric experience.

Take Pushkin who began with his *lycée* verses, and Lermontov who began with "The Sail." In Pushkin's first poems we discern nothing of Pushkin whatsoever—only the genius Derzhavin was able to glimpse the future genius in the living face, voice, and gesture of the youth. But in the eighteen-year-old Lermontov's "The Sail" all Lermontov is present, the Lermontov of turbulence, offence, duel, death. The young Pushkin could not have had such a poem as "The Sail"—but not because his talent was undeveloped: he was no less gifted than Lermontov. Simply, Pushkin, like every poet with history, and like history itself, began at the beginning—like Goethe too—and then spent all his life *im Werden* ("in becoming") while Lermontov—immediately—"was." To find himself, Pushkin had to live not one life, but a hundred. While Lermontov, to find himself, had only to be born.

Of our contemporaries I will name three exceptional cases of perfection in the innate lyrical quality: Anna Akhmatova, Osip Mandelstam, and Boris Pasternak, poets born already equipped with their own vocabulary and with maximum expressiveness.

When in the first poem of her first book, the young Akhmatova conveys the confusion of love in the lines:

I drew my left-hand glove
Onto my right hand —

she conveys at one blow all feminine and all lyric confusion (all the confusion of the empirical!), immortalizing with one flourish of the pen that ancient nervous gesture of woman and of poet who at life's great moments forget right and left—not only of glove, but of hand, and of country of the world, suddenly losing all their certainty. Through a patent and even penetrating precision of detail, something bigger than an emotional state is affirmed and symbolized—a whole structure of the mind. (A poet lets go the pen, a woman lets go her lover's hand, and immediately they can't tell the left hand from the right.) In brief, from these two lines of Akhmatova's, a broad, abundant flow of associations comes into being, associations which spread like circles from a flung pebble. The whole woman, the whole poet is in these two lines; the whole Akhmatova, unique, unrepeatable, inimitable. Before Akhmatova none of us portrayed a gesture like this. And no one did after her. (Of course, Akhmatova is not only this gesture; I'm giving just one of her main characteristics.) "Again or still?" was what I asked in 1916, about Akhmatova who in 1912 had begun by dipping the same jug into the same sea. Now, seventeen years later, I can see that then, without suspecting it, she had provided the formula for a lyric constant. Listen to the image: it has a depth. Look at its movement: it conveys roundness. The roundness of the dipping gesture, essentially deep. A jug. A sea. Together they constitute volume. Thinking about today, seventeen years later, I might say: "the same bucket into the same well," preferring an accurate image to a beautiful one. But the essence of the image would be the same. I offer this as yet another instance of lyric constancy.

I've never heard anyone say, about Akhmatova or Pasternak: "Same thing over and over again—boring!" Just as you cannot say "Same thing over and over again—boring!" about the sea, of which Pasternak wrote the following:

> All becomes dull, only you never grow familiar—
> days pass, years pass, thousands and thousands of
>   years...

For, both Akhmatova and Pasternak scoop not from the surface of the sea (the heart), but from its depth (the fathomless). They can't become boring, just as sleep can't be boring—which is always the same, but with always different dreams. Just as dreaming can't be boring.

When you approach something, you need to know what you may expect from it. And you must expect from it its own self, that which constitutes its being. When you approach the sea— and the lyric poet—you are not going for something new, but for the same again; for a repetition, not a continuation. Lyric poetry, like the sea, even when you're discovering it for the first time, is something you invariably re-read; while with a river, which flows past, as with Pushkin, who walks past—if it's on their banks you've been born—you always read on. It is the difference between the crossways, lulling, lyrical motion of the sea, and the linear, never-returning movement of a river. The difference between being somewhere and passing by. You love the river because it is always different, and you love the sea because it is always the same. If you desire novelty, settle by a river.

Lyric poetry, like the sea, rouses and calms itself, happens within itself. Not in vain did Heraclitus say: "Nobody steps twice into the same river," taking, as his symbol of flowing, not the sea which he saw before him every day and knew well, but—a river. When you go to the sea and to the lyricist, you are not going for the never-returning flow of the current, you're going for the ever-returning flow of the waves; not for the unrepeatable moment, not for the intransient, but precisely for the repeatability of the unforeseen in sea and in lyric, for the invariability of changes and exchanges, for the inevitability of your amazement at them.

Renewal! This is where their power over us lies, the might which sustains all worship of the divine, all sorcery, all magic, all invoking, all cursing, all human and non-human unions. Even the dead are summoned three times.

Who will say to the great and the genuine: "Be different!"

Be!—is our silent prayer.

To the poet with history we say: "Look further!" To the poet without history: "Dive deeper!" To the first: "Further!" To the second: "More!"

And if some poets seem dull because of their monotony, then this comes from the shallowness and smallness (the drying up) of the image, not from the fact that the image remains the same. (A dried-up sea is no longer a sea.) If a poet bores us with monotony, I'll undertake to prove that he is not a great poet, his imagery is not great. If we take a saucer for a sea, that is not its fault.

Lyricism, for all that it is doomed to itself, is itself inexhaustible. (Perhaps the best formula for the lyrical and for the lyric essence is this: being doomed to inexhaustibility!) The more you draw out, the more there remains. This is why it never disappears. This is why we fling ourselves with such avidity on every new lyric poet: maybe he'll succeed in drawing out all that essence which is the soul, thereby slaking our own? It's as if they were all trying to get us drunk on bitter, salty, green sea-water and each time we believe it is drinking-water. And once again it turns out bitter! (We must not forget that the structure of the sea, of the blood, and of lyricism—is one and the same.)

What's true of dull people is true of dull poets: what's dull is not the monotony, but the fact that the thing repeated—though it may be very varied—is insignificant. How murderously identical are the newspapers on the table, with all their various dissonances; how murderously identical are the Parisian women in the streets with all their variety! As if these things—advertisements, newspapers, Parisian women—were not varied, but were all the same. At all the crossroads, in all the shops and trams, at all auctions, in all concert-halls—innumerable, and yet, however many, they all amount to one thing! And this one thing is: everyone!

It is boring when, instead of a human face, you see something worse than a mask: a mold for the mass production of facelessness: paper money with no security in gold! When, instead of a person's own words, no matter how clumsy, you hear someone else's, no matter how brilliant (which, by the way, straightaway lose their brilliance—like the fur on a dead animal). It is boring when you hear from the person you're talking to not his own words, but somebody else's. Moreover, if a repetition has bored you, you can be pretty sure it's a case of someone else's words—words not created, but repeated. For one cannot repeat oneself in words: even the slightest change in the speech means it is not a repetition but a transformation with another essence behind it. Even if one tries to repeat a thought of one's own, already expressed, one will involuntarily do it differently every time; the slightest change and something new is said. Unless one learns it by heart. When a poet is obviously "repeating himself," it means he has abandoned his creative self and is robbing himself just as if he were robbing someone else.

In calling renewal the pivot of lyricism, I don't mean the renewal of my own or others' dreams and images, I only mean the return of the lyric wave in which the composition of the lyrical is constant.

The wave always returns, and always returns as a different wave.

The same water — a different wave.

What matters is that it is a *wave*.

What matters is that the wave *will return*.

What matters is that it will *always* return *different*.

What matters most of all: however different the returning wave, it will always return as a wave of the *sea*.

What is a wave? Composition and muscle. The same goes for lyric poetry.

Similarity, variation on the same, is not repetition. Similarity is in the nature of things, at the basis of nature itself. In the renewing (the constant developing) of the given forms of trees, not one oak repeats its neighbor, and on one and the same oak not one leaf repeats a preceding one. Similarity in nature: creation of the similar, not of the same; the like, not the identical; new, not old; creation, not repetition.

Each new leaf is the next variation on the eternal theme of

the oak. Renewal in nature: infinite variation on a single theme. Repetition does not happen in nature, it is outside nature, thus outside creativity too. That is the way it is. Only machines repeat. In "poets who repeat," the machine of memory, separated from the springs of creativity, has become a mere mechanism. Repetition is the purely mechanical reproduction of something which inevitably turns into someone else's, even when it is one's own. For, if I've learnt my own thought by heart, I repeat it as though it were someone else's, without the participation of anything creative. It may be that only the intonation is creative, is mine, the feeling, that is, with which I utter it and change its form, the linguistic and semantic vicinity in which I place it. But when, for example, I write on a blank page the bare formula I once found: "*Etre vaut mieux qu'avoir* (it's better to be than to have)," I repeat a formula which doesn't belong to me any more than an algebraic one does. A thing can only be created once.

Self-repetition, that is self-imitation, is a purely external act. Nature, creating its next leaf, does not look at the already-created leaves, doesn't look because it has in itself the whole form of the future leaf: it creates out of itself by an inner image and without a model. God created man in his own image and likeness without repeating himself.

In poetry, every self-repetition and self-imitation is, above all, imitation of form. One steals from oneself or from one's neighbor a certain verse-form, certain phrases, certain public figures or even a theme (thus everyone steals rain from Pasternak, for example, but no one loves it except him and no one serves it except him). No one has the power to steal the essence (their own or another's). Essence cannot be imitated. Therefore, all imitative poems are dead. If they're not dead but stir us with live agitation, then they're not an imitation but a transformation. To imitate means to annihilate in every case — it means destroying the thing to see how it is made; stealing from it the secret of its life, and then reinstating everything except the life.

———

Some poets start with a minimum and end with the maximum, some start with a maximum and end with the minimum (drying up of the creative vein). And some start with a maximum and stay with this maximum right up to their last line—among our contemporaries, Pasternak and Akhmatova, mentioned already. These never gave either more or less, but always stayed at a maximum of self-expression. If for some there is a path of self-discovery, for these there is no path at all. From their birth, they are here. Their childish babble is a sum, not a source.

> The soft careful break
> of a fruit off a tree
> amidst ceaseless music
> of deep forest quietness.

This quatrain by the seventeen-year-old Osip Mandelstam has in it the whole vocabulary and meter of the mature Mandelstam. A formula for himself. What was the first thing to touch the ear of this lyricist? The sound of a falling apple, the acoustic vision of roundness. What signs are there here of a seventeen-year-old? None. What is there here of Mandelstam? Everything. To be precise: this ripeness of the falling fruit. The stanza is that very falling fruit which he depicts. And, just as from the two lines by Akhmatova, there are unusually wide circles of associations. Of round and warm, of round and cold, of August, Augustus (the emperor), the Hesperides, Paris, Eden, Adam (the throat): Mandelstam gives the reader's imagination all this in a single stanza. (Evocative power of lyricists!) Characteristic of the lyrical: in conveying this apple, the poet did not explicitly name it. And, in a sense, he never departed from this apple.

Who can talk of the poetic path of (to take the greatest, most indisputable lyricists) Heine, Byron, Shelley, Verlaine, Lermontov? They have covered the world with their feelings, laments, sighs, and visions, drenched it with their tears, set fire to it on all sides with their indignation.

Do we learn from them? No. We suffer for them and because of them.

It is the French proverb, tailored in my Russian style: *"Les heureux n'ont pas d'histoire."*

One exception, a pure lyricist who did have development and history and a path: Alexander Blok. But, having said "development," I see that I've not only taken the wrong direction but used a word that contradicts Blok's essence and fate. Development presupposes harmony. Can there be a development that is—catastrophic? And can there be harmony when what we see is a soul being torn completely apart? Here, without playing with words, but making a severe demand on them and answering for them, I assert: Blok, for the duration of his poetic path, was not developing, but was tearing himself apart.

One could say of Blok that he was trying to escape from one himself to another. From one which tormented him. To another which tormented him even more. The peculiarity is this hope of getting away from himself. Thus a mortally wounded man will run wildly from the wound, thus a sick man tosses from land to land, then from room to room, and finally from side to side.

If we see Blok as a poet with history, then it is solely the history of Blok the lyric poet, of lyricism itself, of suffering. If we see Blok as a poet with a path, then the path consists of running in circles away from himself.

94

Stopping to draw breath.

And entering the house, to meet oneself there once again!

The sole difference is that Blok started running at birth, while others stayed in one place.

Only once did Blok succeed in running away from himself— when he ran onto the cruel road of the Revolution. That was the leap of a dying man from his bed, of a man fleeing from death into the street, which won't notice him, into the crowd, which will trample him. Into Blok's physically collapsing and spiritually undermined personality rushed the elemental force of the Revolution, with its songs and demons—and it crushed that body. Let us not forget that the last word of *The Twelve* is "Christ," which was one of the first words Blok spoke.

Such were this pure lyric poet's history, development, and path.

—*translated by Angela Livingstone*

from A LETTER TO BORIS PASTERNAK
(May 23, 1926)

[…]

But there's one thing, Boris: I don't like the sea. Can't bear it.
A vast expanse and nothing to walk on – that's one thing. In
constant motion and I can only watch it—that's another. Why,
Boris, it's the same thing all over again, i.e., it's my notorious,
involuntary immobility. My inertness. My beastly tolerance,
whether I want to be tolerant or not. And the sea at night?—cold,
terrifying, invisible, unloving, filled with itself—like Rilke (itself
or divinity, no matter). I pity the earth: it feels cold. The sea
never *feels* cold, it *is* cold — it is all its horrible features. They are
its essence. An enormous refrigerator (at night). An enormous
boiler (in the daytime). And perfectly round. A monstrous *sau-
cer. Flat*, Boris. An enormous flat-bottomed cradle tossing out
a baby (a ship) every minute. It cannot be caressed (too wet). It
cannot be worshiped (too terrible). As I would have hated Jeho-
vah, for instance, as I hate any great power. The sea is a dictator-
ship, Boris. A mountain is a divinity. A mountain has many sides
to it. A mountain stoops to the level of Mur (touched by him!)
and rises to Goethe's brow; then, not to embarrass him, rises
even higher. A mountain has streams, nests, games. A mountain
is first and foremost *what I stand on*, Boris. My exact worth. A
mountain is a great dash on the printed page, Boris, to be filled
in with a deep sigh.

—*translated by Margaret Wettlin and Walter Arndt*

from A LETTER TO RAINER MARIA RILKE
(July 6, 1926)

ST.-GILLES-SUR-VIE
Dear Rainer,

Goethe says somewhere that one cannot achieve anything of significance in a foreign language — and that has always rung false to me. (Goethe always sound right in the aggregate, valid only in the summation, which is why I am now doing him an injustice.)

Writing poetry is in itself translating, from the mother tongue into another, whether French or German should make no difference. No language is the mother tongue. Writing poetry is rewriting it. That's why I am puzzled when people talk of French or Russian, etc., poets. A poet may write in French; he cannot be a French poet. That's ludicrous.

I am not a Russian poet and am always astonished to be taken for one and looked upon in this light. The reason one becomes a poet (if it were even possible to *become* one, if one *were* not one before all else!) is to avoid being French, Russian, etc., in order to be everything. Or: one is a poet because one is not French. Nationality — segregation and enclosure. Orpheus bursts nationality, or he extends it to such breadth and width that everyone (bygone and being) is included. Beautiful German — there! And beautiful Russian!

[...]

— translated by Margaret Wettlin and Walter Arndt

III OSIP MANDELSTAM

(1891–1938)

What was the first thing to touch the ear of this lyricist?
The sound of a falling apple, the acoustic vision of roundness...
What is there here of Mandelstam? Everything.
To be precise: this ripeness of the falling fruit.
And...there are unusually wide circles of associations.
Of round and warm, of August, Augustus (the emperor),
the Hesperides, Paris, Eden, Adam (the throat): Mandelstam gives
the reader's imagination all this...

— MARINA TSVETAEVA

Mandelstam was a tragic figure. Even while in exile
in Voronezh, he wrote works of untold beauty and power.
And he had no poetic forerunners...In all of world poetry,
I know of no other such case. We know the sources of Pushkin
and Blok, but who will tell us where that new, divine harmony,
Mandelstam's poetry, came from?

— ANNA AKHMATOVA

TRISTIA

There is, I know, a science of separation
In night's disheveled elegies, stifled laments,
The clockwork oxen jaws, the tense anticipation
As the city's vigil nears its sun and end.
I honor the natural ritual of the rooster's cry,
The moment when, red-eyed from weeping, sleepless
Once again, someone hoists the journey's burden,
And to weep and to sing become the same quicksilver verb.

But who can prophesy in the word *good-bye*
The abyss of loss into which we fall;
Or what, when the dawn fires burn in the Acropolis,
The rooster's rusty clamor means for us;
Or why, when some new life floods the cut sky,
And the barn-warm oxen slowly eat each instant,
The rooster, harbinger of the one true life,
Beats his blazing wings on the city wall?

I love the calm and custom of quick fingers weaving,
The shuttle's buzz and hum, the spindle's bees.
And look — arriving or leaving, spun from down,
Some barefoot Delia barely touching the ground...
What rot has reached the very root of us
That we should have no language for our praise?
What is, was; what was, will be again; and our whole lives'
Sweetness lies in these meetings that we recognize.

Soothsayer, truth-sayer, morning's mortal girl,
Lose your gaze again in the melting wax
That whitens and tightens like the stretched pelt of a squirrel
And find the fates that will in time find us.
In clashes of bronze, flashes of consciousness,
Men live, called and pulled by a world of shades.
But women — all fluent spirit; piercing, pliable eye —
Wax toward one existence, and divining they die.

—translated by Christian Wiman

THE NECKLACE

Take, from my palms, for joy, for ease,
A little honey, a little sun,
That we may obey Persephone's bees.

You can't untie a boat unmoored.
Fur-shod shadows can't be heard.
Nor terror, in this life, mastered.

Love, what's left for us, and of us, is this
Living remnant, loving revenant, brief kiss
Like a bee flying completed dying hiveless

To find in the forest's heart a home,
Night's never-ending hum,
Thriving on meadowsweet, mint, and time.

Take, for all that is good, for all that is gone,
That it may lie rough and real against your collarbone,
This string of bees, that once turned honey into sun.

—translated by Christian Wiman

Leningrad

I've come back to my city. These are my own old tears,
my own little veins, the swollen glands of my childhood.

So you're back. Open wide. Swallow
the fish-oil from the river lamps of Leningrad.

Open your eyes. Do you know this December day,
the egg-yolk with the deadly tar beaten into it?

Petersburg! I don't want to die yet!
You know my telephone numbers.

Petersburg! I've still got the addresses:
I can look up dead voices.

I live on back stairs, and the bell,
torn out nerves and all, jangles in my temples.

And I wait till morning for guests that I love,
and rattle the door in its chains.

—*translated by Clarence Brown and W. S. Merwin*

"YOUR THIN SHOULDERS"

Your thin shoulders are for turning red under whips,
turning red under whips, and flaming in the raw cold.

Your child's fingers are for lifting flatirons,
for lifting flatirons, and for knotting cords.

Your tender soles are for walking on broken glass,
walking on broken glass, across bloody sand.

And I'm for burning like a black candle lit for you,
for burning like a blank candle that dare not pray.

—translated by Clarence Brown and W. S. Merwin

from CONVERSATION ABOUT DANTE

I

[…]

The quality of poetry is determined by the speed and decisiveness with which it embodies its schemes and commands in diction, the instrumentless, lexical, purely quantitative verbal matter. One must traverse the full width of a river crammed with Chinese junks moving simultaneously in various directions — this is how the meaning of poetic discourse is created. The meaning, its itinerary, cannot be reconstructed by interrogating the boatmen: they will not be able to tell how and why we were skipping from junk to junk.

Poetic discourse is a carpet fabric containing a plethora of textile warps differing from one another only in the process of coloration, only in the partitura of the perpetually changing commands of the instrumental signaling system.

It is an extremely durable carpet, woven out of fluid: a carpet in which the currents of the Ganges, taken as a fabric theme, do not mix with the samples of the Nile or the Euphrates, but remain multicolored, in braids, figures, and ornaments — not in patterns, though, for a pattern is the equivalent of paraphrase. Ornament is good precisely because it preserves traces of its origin like a piece of nature enacted. Whether the piece is animal, vegetable, steppe, Scythian or Egyptian, indigenous or barbarian, it is always speaking, seeing, acting.

Ornament is stanzaic. Pattern is of the line.

The poetic hunger of the old Italians is magnificent, their

youthful animal appetite for harmony, their sensual lust after rhyme—*il disio!*

The mouth works, the smile nudges the line of verse, cleverly and gaily the lips redden, the tongue trustingly presses itself against the palate.

The inner form of the verse is inseparable from the countless changes of expression flitting across the face of the narrator who speaks and feels emotion.

The art of speech distorts our face in precisely this way; it disrupts its calm, destroys its mask...

When I began to study Italian and had barely familiarized myself with its phonetics and prosody, I suddenly understood that the center of gravity of my speech efforts had been moved closer to my lips, to the outer parts of my mouth. The tip of the tongue suddenly turned out to have the seat of honor. The sound rushed toward the locking of the teeth. And something else that struck me was the infantile aspect of Italian phonetics, its beautiful childlike quality, its closeness to infant babbling, to some kind of eternal Dadaism.

> E consolando, usava l'idioma
> Che prima i padri e le madri trastulla;
> ...Favoleggiava con la sua famiglia
> De'Troiani, de Fiesole, e di Roma.
>
> (*Paradisio,* 15.122–26)

Would you like to become acquainted with the dictionary of Italian rhymes? Take the entire Italian dictionary and leaf through it as you will...Here every word rhymes. Every word begs to enter into *concordanza.*

The abundance of marriageable endings is fantastic. The Italian verb increases in strength toward its end and only comes to life in the ending. Each word rushes to burst forth, to fly from the lips, to run away, to clear a place for the others.

When it became necessary to trace the circumference of a time for which a millennium is less than a wink of an eyelash, Dante introduced infantile "trans-sense" language into his astronomical, concordant, profoundly public, homiletic lexicon.

Dante's creation is above all the entrance of the Italian language of his day onto the world stage, its entrance as a totality, as a system.

The most Dadaist of the Romance languages moves forward to take the first place among nations.

II

We must give some examples of Dante's rhythms. People know nothing about this, but they must be shown. Whoever says, "Dante is sculptural," is influenced by the impoverished definitions of that great European. Dante's poetry partakes of all the forms of energy known to modern science. Unity of light, sound, and matter form its inner nature. Above all, the reading of Dante is an endless labor, for the more we succeed, the further we are from our goal. If the first reading brings on only shortness of breath and healthy fatigue, then equip yourself for subsequent readings with a pair of indestructible Swiss hobnailed boots. In all seriousness the question arises: how many shoe soles, how many oxhide soles, how many sandals did Alighieri wear out during the course of his poetic work, wandering the goat paths of Italy.

Both the *Inferno* and, in particular, the *Purgatorio* glorify the human gait, the measure and rhythm of walking, the footstep and its form. The step, linked with breathing and saturated with thought, Dante understood as the beginning of prosody. To indicate walking he utilizes a multitude of varied and charming turns of phrase.

In Dante philosophy and poetry are constantly on the go, perpetually on their feet. Even a stop is but a variety of accumulated movement: a platform for conversations is created by Alpine conditions. The metrical foot is the inhalation and exhalation of the step. Each step draws a conclusion, invigorates, syllogizes.

Education is schooling in the swiftest possible associations. You grasp them on the wing, you are sensitive to allusions — therein lies Dante's favorite form of praise.

The way Dante understands it, the teacher is younger than the pupil, for he "runs faster."

> When he turned aside he appeared to me
> like one of those runners who chase each other
> over the green meadows around Verona,
> and his physique was such that
> he struck me as belonging to the host of winners, not to
> the losers...

The metaphor's rejuvenating power brings the educated old man, Brunetto Latini, back to us in the guise of a youthful victor at a Veronese track meet.

What is Dantean erudition?

Aristotle, like a double-winged butterfly, is edged with the Arabian border of Averroes.

> Averoìs, che il gran comento feo

> (*Inferno*, 4.144)

Here the Arab Averroes accompanies the Greek Aristotle.

They are both components of the same drawing. They can both find room on the membrane of a single wing. The conclusion of canto 4 of the *Inferno* is truly an orgy of quotations. I find here a pure and unalloyed demonstration of Dante's keyboard of references.

A keyboard stroll around the entire horizon of Antiquity. Some Chopin polonaise in which an armed Caesar with a gryphon's eyes dances alongside Democritus, who had just finished splitting matter into atoms.

A quotation is not an excerpt. A quotation is a cicada. Its natural state is that of unceasing sound. Having once seized hold of the air, it will not let it go. Erudition is far from being equivalent to a keyboard of references for the latter comprises the very essence of education.

By this I mean that a composition is formed not as a result of accumulated particulars, but due to the fact that one detail after another is torn away from the object, leaves it, darts out, or is chipped away from the system to go out into a new functional space or dimension, but each time at a strictly regulated moment and under circumstances which are sufficiently ripe and unique.

We do not know things themselves; on the other hand, we are highly sensitive to the facts of their existence. Thus, in reading Dante's cantos we receive communiqués, as it were, from the battlefield and from that data make superb guesses as to how the sounds of the symphony of war are struggling with each other, although each bulletin taken by itself merely indicates some slight shift of the flags for strategic purposes or some minor changes in the timbre of the cannonade.

Hence, the thing emerges as an integral whole as a result of the simple differentiating impulse which transfixed it. Not for one instant does it retain any identity with itself. If a physicist, having once broken down an atomic nucleus, should desire to put it back together again, he would resemble the partisans of descriptive and explanatory poetry for whom Dante represents an eternal plague and a threat.

If we could learn to hear Dante, we would hear the ripening of the clarinet and the trombone, we would hear the transformation of the viola into a violin and the lengthening of the valve on the French horn. And we would be able to hear the formation around the lute and the theorbo of the nebulous nucleus of the future homophonic three-part orchestra.

Furthermore, if we could hear Dante, we would be unexpectedly plunged into a power flow, known now in its totality as a "composition," now in its particularity as a "metaphor," now in its indirectness as a "simile," that power flow which gives birth to attributes so that they may return to it, enriching it with their own melting and, having barely achieved the first joy of becoming, they immediately lose their primogeniture in merging with the matter which is rushing in among the thoughts and washing against them.

The beginning of canto 10 of the *Inferno*. Dante urges us into the inner blindness of the compositional clot:

> We now climbed up the narrow
> path between the craggy
> wall and the martyrs — my teacher
> and I right at his back...

All our efforts are directed toward the struggle against the density and darkness of the place. Illuminated shapes cut through it like teeth. Here strength of character is as essential as a torch in a cave.

Dante never enters into a single combat with his material

without having first prepared an organ to seize it, without having armed himself with some instrument for measuring concrete time as it drips or melts. In poetry, where everything is measure and everything derives from measure, revolves about it and for its sake, instruments of measure are tools of a special kind, performing an especially active function. Here the trembling hand of the compass not only indulges the magnetic storm, but makes it itself.

And thus we can see that the dialogue of canto 10 of the *Inferno* is magnetized by the forms of verb tenses: the perfective and imperfective past, the subjunctive past, even the present and the future are all categorically and authoritatively presented in the tenth canto.

The entire canto is constructed on several verbal thrusts which leap boldly out of the text. Here the table of conjugations opens like a fencing tournament, and we literally hear how the verbs mark time.

First thrust:

> La gente che per li sepolcri giace
> Potrebbesi veder?...

"May I be permitted to see those people laid in open graves?" Second thrust:

> ...Volgiti: che fai?

The horror of the present tense is given here, some kind of *terror praesentis*. Here the unalloyed present is taken as a sign introduced to ward off evil. The present tense, completely isolated from both the future and the past, is conjugated like pure fear, like danger.

Three nuances of the past tense (which has absolved itself of any responsibility for what has already occurred) are given in the following tercet:

> I fixed my eyes on him,
> And he drew himself up to his full height,
> As if his great disdain could disparage Hell.

And then, like a mighty tuba, the past tense explodes in Farinata's question:

> …Chi fuor li maggior tui? —

"Who were your forefathers?"
How that auxiliary verb is stretched out here, that little truncated *fuor* instead of *furon!* Wasn't it through the lengthening of a valve that the French horn was formed?

Next comes a slip of the tongue in the form of the past perfect. This slip felled the elder Cavalcanti: from Alighieri, a comrade and contemporary of his son, the poet Guido Cavalcanti, still thriving at the time he heard something — it little matters what — about his son using the fatal past perfect: *ebbe*.

And how astonishing that precisely this slip of the tongue opens the way for the main stream of the dialogue: Cavalcanti fades away like an oboe or clarinet, having played its part, while Farinata, like a deliberate chess player, continues his interrupted move, and renews the attack:

> "E se," continuando al primo detto,
>   "S'egli han quell'arte," disse, "male appresa,
>   Ciò mi tormenta più che questo letto."

The dialogue in the tenth canto of the *Inferno* is an unanticipated explicator of the situation. It flows out all by itself from the interstices of the rivers.

All useful information of an encyclopedic nature turns out to have been already communicated in the opening lines of the canto. Slowly but surely the amplitude of the conversation broadens; mass scenes and crowd images are obliquely introduced.

When Farinata rises up contemptuous of Hell, like a great nobleman who somehow landed in jail, the pendulum of the conversation is already swinging across the full diameter of the gloomy plain now invaded by flames.

The scandal in literature is a concept going much further back than Dostoevsky; however, in the thirteenth century and in Dante's writings it was much more powerful. Dante collides with Farinata in this undesirable and dangerous encounter just as Dostoevsky's rogues run into their tormentors in the most inopportune places. A voice floats forward; it remains unclear to whom it belongs. It becomes more and more difficult for the reader to conduct the expanding canto. This voice—the first theme of Farinata—is the minor Dantean *arioso* of the suppliant type—extremely typical of the *Inferno*:

> O Tuscan, who travels alive through
> this fiery city and speaks so
> eloquently! Do not refuse to
> stop for a moment...Through
> your speech I recognized you
> as a citizen of that noble
> region to which I, alas! was
> too much of a burden...

Dante is a poor man. Dante is an internal *raznochinets*, the descendant of an ancient Roman family. Courtesy is not at all characteristic of him, rather something distinctly the opposite. One would have to be a blind mole not to notice that throughout the *Divina Commedia* Dante does not know how to behave, does not know how to act, what to say, how to bow. I am not imagining this; I take it from the numerous admissions of Alighieri himself, scattered throughout the *Divina Commedia*.

The inner anxiety and painful, troubled gaucheries which accompany each step of the diffident man, as if his upbringing were somehow insufficient, the man untutored in the ways of applying his inner experience or of objectifying it in etiquette, the tormented and downtrodden man—such are the qualities which both provide the poem with all its charm, with all its drama, and serve as its background source, its psychological foundation.

If Dante had been sent forth alone, without his *dolce padre*, without Virgil, scandal would have inevitably erupted at the very start, and we would have had the most grotesque buffoonery rather than a journey amongst the torments and sights of the underworld!

The gaucheries averted by Virgil serve to systematically amend and redirect the course of the poem. The *Divina Commedia* takes us into the inner laboratory of Dante's spiritual qualities. What for us appears as an irreproachable Capuchin and a so-called aquiline profile was, from within, an awkwardness surmounted by agony, a purely Pushkinian, *Kammerjunker* struggle for social dignity and a recognized social position for the poet. The shade which frightens children and old women took fright itself, and Alighieri suffered fever and chills: all the way from miraculous bouts of self-esteem to feelings of utter worthlessness.

Dante's fame has up to now been the greatest obstacle to understanding him and to a profound study of his work, and this situation shall continue for a long time to come. His lapidary quality is no more than a product of the enormous inner imbalance which expressed itself in dream executions, in imagined encounters, in elegant retorts prepared in advance and fostered on bile, aimed at destroying his enemy once and for all and invoking the final triumph.

How often did the kindest of fathers, the preceptor, reasonable man, and guardian snub the internal *raznochinets* of the fourteenth century who found it such agony to be a part of the social hierarchy, while Boccaccio, practically his contemporary, delighted in the same social system, plunged into it, gamboled about in it?

"*Che fai?*" (What are you doing?) sounds literally like a teacher's cry: you've lost your mind!... Then the sounds of the organ come to the rescue, drowning out the shame and concealing the embarrassment.

It is absolutely false to perceive Dante's poem as some extended single-line narrative or even as having but a single voice. Long before Bach and at a time when large monumental organs were not yet being built and only the modest embryonic prototypes of the future wonders existed, when the leading instrument for voice accompaniment was still the zither, Alighieri constructed in verbal space an infinitely powerful organ and already delighted in all its conceivable stops, inflated its bellows, and roared and cooed through all its pipes.

Come avesse lo inferno in gran dispitto

(*Inferno*, 10.36)

is the line which gave birth to the entire European tradition of demonism and Byronism. Meanwhile, instead of raising his sculpture on a pedestal as Hugo, for instance, might have done, Dante envelops it in a sordine, wraps it round with gray twilight, and conceals it at the very bottom of a sack of mute sounds.

It is presented in the diminuendo stop, it falls to the ground out of the window of the hearing.

In other words, its phonetic light is turned off. The gray shadows have blended.

The *Divina Commedia* does not so much take up the reader's time as augment it, as if it were a musical piece being performed.

As it becomes longer, the poem moves further away from its end, and the very end itself approaches unexpectedly and sounds like the beginning.

The structure of the Dantean monologue, built like the stop mechanism of an organ, can be well understood by making use of an analogy with rock strata whose purity has been destroyed by the intrusion of foreign bodies.

Granular admixtures and veins of lava indicate a single fault or catastrophe as the common source of the formation.

Dante's poetry is formed and colored in precisely this geological manner. Its material structure is infinitely more significant than its celebrated sculptural quality. Imagine a monument of granite or marble whose symbolic function is intended not to represent a horse or a rider, but to reveal the inner structure of the marble or granite itself. In other words, imagine a granite monument erected in honor of granite, as if to reveal its very idea. Having grasped this, you will then be able to understand quite clearly just how form and content are related in Dante's work.

Any unit of poetic speech, be it a line, a stanza, or an entire lyrical composition, must be regarded as a single word. For instance, when we enunciate the word "sun," we do not toss out an already prepared meaning—this would be tantamount to semantic abortion—rather we are experiencing a peculiar cycle. Any given word is a bundle, and meaning sticks out of it in various directions, not aspiring toward any single official point. In pronouncing the word "sun," we are, as it were, undertaking an enormous journey to which we are so accustomed that we travel in our sleep. What distinguishes poetry from automatic speech is that it rouses us and shakes us into wakefulness in the middle of a word. Then it turns out that the word is much longer than we thought, and we remember that to speak means to be forever on the road.

The semantic cycles of Dantean cantos are constructed in such a way that what begins, for example, as "honey" (*med*), ends up as "bronze" (*med'*), what begins as "a dog's bark" (*lai*), ends up as "ice" (*led*).

Dante, when he feels the need, calls eyelids "the lips of the eye." This is when ice crystals of frozen tears hang from the lashes and form a shield which prevents weeping.

> Gli occhi lor, ch'eran pria pur dentro molli,
> Gocciar su per le labbra...

> (*Inferno*, 32.46–47)

Thus, suffering crosses the sense organs, producing hybrids, and bringing about the labial eye.

There is not just one form in Dante, but a multitude of forms. One is squeezed out of another and only by convention can one be inserted into another.

He himself says:

> Io premerei di mio concetto il suco—

> (*Inferno*, 32.4)

"I would squeeze the juice out of my idea, out of my conception"—that is, he considers form as the thing which is squeezed out, not as that which serves as a covering. In this way, strange as it may seem, form is squeezed out of the content-conception which, as it were, envelops the form. Such is Dante's precise thought. But whatever it may be, we cannot squeeze something out of anything except a wet sponge or rag. Try as we may to twist the conception even into a plait, we will never squeeze any form out of it unless it is already a form itself. In other words, any process involving the creation of form in poetry presupposes lines, periods, or cycles of sound forms, as is the case with individually pronounced semantic units.

A scientific description of Dante's *Commedia*, taken as a flow, as a current, would inevitably assume the look of a treatise on metamorphoses, and would aspire to penetrate the multitudinous states of poetic matter, just as a doctor in making his diagnosis listens to the multitudinous unity of the organism. Literary criticism would then approach the method of living medicine.

[...]

V

Dante's drafts, of course, have not come down to us. There is no opportunity for us to work on the history of his text. But it does not follow, of course, that there were no inkstained manuscripts or that the text hatched out full grown like Leda out of the egg or Pallas Athena out of the head of Zeus. But the unfortunate interval of six centuries plus the quite excusable fact of the absence of rough drafts have played a dirty trick on us. For how many centuries have people been talking and writing about Dante as if he had expressed his thoughts directly on official paper?

Dante's laboratory? That does not concern us! What can ignorant piety have to do with that? Dante is discussed as if he had the completed whole before his eyes even before he had begun work and as if he had utilized the technique of moulage, first casting in plaster, then in bronze. At best, he is handed a chisel and allowed to carve or, as they love to call it, "to sculpt." However, one small detail is forgotten: the chisel only removes the excess, and a sculptor's draft leaves no material traces (something the public admires). The stages of a sculptor's work correspond to the writer's series of drafts.

Rough drafts are never destroyed.

There are no ready-made things in poetry, in the plastic arts, or in art in general.

Our habit of grammatical thinking hinders us here — putting the concept of art in the nominative case. We subordinate the very process of creation to the purposeful prepositional case, and we reason like some robot with a lead heart, who having swung about as required in a variety of directions, and having endured various jolts as he answered the questionnaire — about what? about whom? by whom and by what? — finally established himself in the Buddhist, schoolboy calm of the nominative case. Meanwhile, a finished thing is just as subject to the oblique cases as to the nominative case. Moreover, our entire study of syntax is the most powerful survival of scholasticism and, by being in philosophy, in epistemology, it is put in its proper subordinate position, and completely overwhelmed by mathematics which has its own independent, original syntax. In the study of art this scholasticism of syntax still reigns supreme, causing colossal damage by the hour.

Precisely those who are furthest from Dante's method in

European poetry and, bluntly speaking, in polar opposition to him, go by the name Parnassians: Heredia, Leconte de Lisle. Baudelaire is much closer. Verlaine is still closer, but the closest of all the French poets is Arthur Rimbaud. Dante is by his very nature one who shakes up meaning and destroys the integrity of the image. The composition of his cantos resembles an airline schedule or the indefatigable flights of carrier pigeons.

Thus the safety of the rough draft is the statute assuring preservation of the power behind the literary work. In order to arrive on target one has to accept and take into account winds blowing in a somewhat different direction. Exactly the same law applies in tacking a sailboat.

Let us remember that Dante Alighieri lived during the heyday of sailing ships and that sailing was a highly developed art. Let us not reject out of hand the fact that he contemplated models of tacking and the maneuvering of sailing vessels. He was a student of this most evasive and plastic sport known to man since his earliest days.

Here I would like to point out one of the remarkable peculiarities of Dante's psyche: he was terrified of the direct answer, perhaps conditioned by the political situation in that extremely dangerous, enigmatic, and criminal century.

While as a whole the *Divina Commedia* (as we have already stated) is a questionnaire with answers, each of Dante's direct responses is literally hatched out, now with the aid of his midwife, Virgil, now with the help of his nurse, Beatrice, and so on.

The *Inferno*, canto 16. The conversation is conducted with that intense passion reserved for the prison visit: the need to utilize, at whatever cost, the tiny snatches of a meeting. Three eminent Florentines conduct an inquiry. About what? About Florence, of course. Their knees tremble with impatience, and they are terrified of hearing the truth. The answer, lapidary and cruel, is received in the form of a cry. At this, even Dante's chin quivers, although he made a desperate effort to control himself, and he tosses back his head, and all this is presented in no more nor less than the author's stage direction:

Così gridai colla faccia levata

(Inferno, 16.76)

Sometimes Dante is able to describe a phenomenon so that not the slightest trace of it remains. To do this he uses a device which I would like to call the Heraclitean metaphor; it so strongly emphasizes the fluidity of the phenomenon and cancels it out with such a flourish, that direct contemplation, after the metaphor has completed its work, is essentially left with nothing to sustain it. I have already taken the opportunity several times to state that Dante's metaphorical devices exceed our conception of composition inasmuch as our critical studies, fettered by the syntactic mode of thinking, are powerless before them.

> When the peasant, climbing up the hill
> During the season when the being who illuminates the
>   world,
> Is least reticent to show his face to us,
> And the water midges yield their place to the
>   mosquitoes,
> Sees the dancing fireflies in the hollow,
> In the same spot, perhaps, where he labored as a reaper
>   or plowman —
> So with little tongues of flame the eighth circle
>   gleamed,
> Completely visible from the heights where I had
>   climbed;

And as the one who took his revenge with the aid of
    bears,
Upon seeing the departing Chariot of Elijah,
When the team of horses tore away into the heavens,
Stared as best he could but could make out nothing
Except one single flame
Wasting away, like a small cloud rising in the sky —
So the tongue-like flame filled the chinks in the tombs,
Appropriating the wealth of the graves as their profit,
While enveloped in each flame a sinner was
    concealed.

                        (*Inferno*, 26.25–42)

If your head is not spinning from this miraculous ascent, worthy of Sebastian Bach's organ music, then try to indicate where the first and second members of the comparison are to be found, what is compared with what, and where the primary and secondary explanatory elements are located.

An impressionistic preparatory introduction awaits the reader in a whole series of Dante's cantos. Its purpose is to present in the form of a scattered alphabet, in the form of a leaping, sparkling, well-splashed alphabet the very elements which, in accord with the laws of the transformability of poetic material, will be united into formulas of meaning.

Thus, in this introduction, we see the extraordinarily light, glittering Heraclitean dance of the summer midges which prepares us to apprehend the serious and tragic speech of Odysseus.

Canto 26 of the *Inferno* is the most oriented toward sailing of all Dante's compositions, the most given to tacking, and by far the best at maneuvering. It has no equals in versatility, evasiveness, Florentine diplomacy, and Greek cunning.

Two basic parts are distinguishable in this canto: the luminous, impressionistic preparatory introduction and the well-balanced, dramatic tale, which Odysseus tells about his last voyage, about his journey out into the deeps of the Atlantic and his terrible death under the stars of an alien hemisphere. In the free flow of its thought this canto comes very close to improvisation. But if you listen more attentively, you will see that the poet is improvising inwardly in his beloved, secret Greek, using only the phonetics and the fabric of his native Italian idiom to carry out his purpose.

If you give a child a thousand rubles and then suggest that he make a choice of keeping either the coins or the banknotes, he will of course choose the coins, and in this way you can retrieve the entire sum by giving him some small change. Exactly the same experience has befallen European literary criticism which nailed Dante to the landscape of Hell familiar from the engravings. No one has yet approached Dante with a geologist's hammer to ascertain the crystalline structure of his rock, to study its phenocryst, its smokiness, or its patterning, or to judge it as rock crystal subject to the most varied of nature's accidents.

Our criticism tells us: distance the phenomenon and I will deal with it and absorb it. "Holding something at a distance" (Lomonosov's expression) and cognoscibility are almost identical for our criticism.

Dante has images of parting and farewell. It is most difficult to descend through the valleys of his verses of parting.

We have still not succeeded in tearing ourselves away from that Tuscan peasant admiring the phosphorescent dance of the fireflies, nor in closing our eyes to the impressionistic dazzle of Elijah's chariot as it fades away into the clouds before the pyre of Eteocles has been cited, Penelope named, the Trojan horse flashed by, Demosthenes lent Odysseus his republican eloquence, and the ship of old age fitted out.

Old age, in Dante's conception of the term, means, above all, breadth of vision, heightened capacity, and universal interests. In Odysseus's canto the earth is already round.

It is a canto concerned with the composition of human blood which contains in itself the salt of the ocean. The beginning of the voyage is located in the system of blood vessels. The blood is planetary, solar and salty...

With all the convolutions of his brain Dante's Odysseus despises sclerosis just as Farinata despised Hell.

Is it possible that
we are born merely to enjoy
animal comforts and
that we will not devote
the remaining portion of our
vanishing senses to an act
of boldness — to Westward
sailing, beyond the Gates of
Hercules, where the world
unpopulated, continues on?

The metabolism of the planet itself takes place in the blood, and the Atlantic sucks in Odysseus, swallowing up his wooden ship.

It is inconceivable to read Dante's cantos without directing them toward contemporaneity. They were created for that purpose. They are missiles for capturing the future. They demand commentary in the *futurum*.

For Dante time is the content of history understood as a simple synchronic act; and vice-versa: the contents of history are the joint containing of time by its associates, competitors, and co-discoverers.

Dante is an antimodernist. His contemporaneity is continuous, incalculable, and inexhaustible.

That is why Odysseus's speech, as convex as the lens of a magnifying glass, may be turned toward the war of the Greeks and Persians as well as toward Columbus's discovery of America, the bold experiments of Paracelsus, and the world empire of Charles V.

Canto 26, dedicated to Odysseus and Diomed, is a marvelous introduction to the anatomy of Dante's eye, so perfectly adjusted alone for the revelation of the structure of future time. Dante had the visual accommodation of predatory birds, but it was unadjusted to focusing in a narrow radius: his hunting grounds were too large.

The words of the proud Farinata may be applied to Dante himself:

> Noi veggiam, come quei ch'ha mala luce.
>
> *(Inferno,* 10.100)

That is, we, the souls of sinners, are capable of seeing and distinguishing only the distant future, but for this we have a special gift. We become absolutely blind as soon as the doors to the future slam shut before us. And in this respect we resemble those who struggle with the twilight, and, in discerning distant objects, fail to make out what is close by.

In canto 26, dance is strongly expressed as the origin of the rhythms of the *terza rima.* Here one is struck by the extraordinary light-heartedness of the rhythm. The meter is organized according to waltz time:

E se già fosse, non saria per tempo.
Così foss' ei, da che pure esser dee;
Chè più mi graverà com' più m'attempo.

(Inferno, 26.10–12)

It is difficult for us as foreigners to penetrate the ultimate secret of foreign poetry. We cannot be judges, we cannot have the last word. But it seems to me that it is precisely here that we find the enchanting pliability of the Italian language which only the ear of a native Italian can perceive completely.

Here I am quoting Marina Tsvetaeva, who once mentioned the "pliability of the Russian language…"

If you attentively watch the mouth of an accomplished poetry reader, it will seem as if he were giving a lesson to deaf-mutes, that is, he works with the aim of being understood even without sounds, articulating each vowel with pedagogical clarity. And thus it is enough to see how canto 26 sounds in order to hear it. I would say that in this canto the vowels are anxious and twitching.

The waltz is primarily a dance of undulation. Nothing even remotely resembling it was possible in Hellenic or Egyptian culture. (I am indebted to Spengler for this juxtaposition.) The very foundation of the waltz is the purely European passion for periodic undulating movements, the very same close listening to sound and light waves found in all our theory of sound and light, in all our scientific study of matter, in all our poetry and music.

[…]

IX

The *Inferno* is a pawnshop in which all the countries and cities known to Dante were left unredeemed. This extremely powerful construct of the infernal circles has a framework. It cannot be conveyed in the form of a crater. It cannot be portrayed on a relief map. Hell hangs suspended on the wire of urban egoism.

It is incorrect to think of the *Inferno* as something with three dimensions, as some combination of enormous circuses, of deserts with scorching sands, of stinking swamps, of Babylonian capitals with mosques burning red-hot. Hell contains nothing inside itself and has no dimensions; like an epidemic, an infectious disease, or the plague, it spreads like a contagion, even though it is not spatial.

Love of the city, passion for the city, hatred for the city — these serve as the materials of the *Inferno*. The rings of Hell are no more than Saturn's circles of emigration. To the exile his sole, forbidden, and irretrievably lost city is scattered everywhere — he is surrounded by it. I would like that the *Inferno* is surrounded by Florence. Dante's Italian cities — Pisa, Florence, Lucca, Verona — these precious civic planets, are drawn out into monstrous rings, stretched into belts, restored to a nebulous, gasiform state.

The anti-landscape nature of the *Inferno* forms, as it were, the conditions of its graphic character.

Imagine Foucault's grandiose experiment carried out not with one pendulum, but with a multitude of pendulums all swinging past one another. Here space exists only insofar as it is a receptacle for amplitudes. To make Dante's images more precise is as unthinkable as listing the names of all the individuals who participated in the migration of peoples.

Just as the Flemish between
Wissant and Bruges, protecting
themselves from the sea's floodtide,
erect dikes to push the sea back;
and just as the Paduans construct
embankments along the shores of
the Brenta to assure the safety of
their cities and castles in
the expectation of spring with its
melting snows on the Chiarentana
[part of the snowy Alps] — so these
dams were built, though not so
monumental, almost despite the engineer...

(*Inferno,* 15.4–12)

Here the moons of the polynomial pendulum swing from Bruges to Padua, teaching a course in European geography, lecturing on the art of engineering, on the techniques of urban safety, on the organization of public works, and on the significance of the Alpine watershed for the Italian state.

What have we, who crawl on our knees before a line of verse, preserved from these riches? Where are its godfathers, where are its enthusiasts? What will become of our poetry which lags so disgracefully behind science?

It is terrifying to think that the blinding explosions of contemporary physics and kinetics were used 600 years before their thunder sounded. Indeed, words do not suffice to brand the shameful, barbarous indifference shown toward them by the pitiful compositors of clichéd thought.

Poetic speech creates its own instruments on the move and cancels them out without halting.

Of all our arts painting alone, and in particular modern

French painting, has not yet ceased to hear Dante. This is the painting which elongates the bodies of horses as they approach the finish line at the hippodrome.

Whenever a metaphor raises the vegetable colors of existence to an articulate impulse, I gratefully remember Dante. We describe the very thing that cannot be described. That is, nature's text comes to a standstill, but we have unlearned how to describe the single thing which, by its structure, yields to poetic representation, that is, the impulses, intentions and amplitudes of fluctuation.

Ptolemy has returned via the back door. Giordano Bruno was burned in vain!...

While still in the womb our creations become known to everyone, but Dante's multinomial, multi-sailed, and kinetically kindled comparisons preserve to this day the charm of the as-yet-unsaid.

His "reflexology of speech" is astonishing—a science, still not completely established, of the spontaneous psycho-physiological influence of the word on those who are conversing, on the audience surrounding them, and on the speaker himself, as well as on the means by which he communicates his urge to speak, that is, by which he signals with a light his sudden desire to express himself.

Here he comes closest to approaching the wave theory of sound and light, determining their relationship.

> Just as an animal covered
> with a cloth grows nervous and
> irritable, only the moving
> folds of the material indicating
> his displeasure, so the first
> created soul [Adam's] expressed

to me through the covering
[light] the extent of its
pleasure and sense of joy in
answering my question...

(*Paradisio*, 26.97–102)

In the third part of the *Commedia* (the *Paradiso*), I see a genuine kinetic ballet. Here we see every possible kind of luminous figure and dance, down to the tapping of heels at a wedding celebration.

Four torches glowed before me,
and the nearest one suddenly came
to life and grew as rosy as if Jupiter
and Mars were suddenly
transformed into birds and were
exchanging feathers.

(*Paradisio*, 27.10–15)

Isn't it strange that a man who is preparing to speak should arm himself with a tautly strung bow, a full supply of feathered arrows, prepare mirrors and convex lenses, and squint at the stars like a tailor threading a needle?...

I devised this composite quotation, merging various passages from the *Commedia*, in order to best exhibit the characteristics of the speech-preparatory moves of Dante's poetry.

Speech preparation is even more within his sphere than articulation, that is, than speech itself.

Remember Virgil's marvelous supplication to the wiliest of the Greeks.

It is completely suffused with the softness of Italian diphthongs.

These are the writhing, ingratiating, and sputtering tongues
of small unprotected oil lamps, muttering about the greasy
wick...

> O voi, che siete due entro ad un foco,
>   S'io meritai di voi, mentre ch'io vissi,
>   S'io meritai di voi assai o poco...
>
> (*Inferno*, 26.79–81)

Dante ascertains the origin, fate, and character of a man ac-
cording to his voice, just as the medicine of his day diagnosed a
man's health according to the color of his urine.

[...]

XI

Let us return once more to the question of Dante's colors.

The interior of mineral rock, the Aladdin-like space con-
cealed within, the lantern-like, lamp-like, chandelier-like sus-
pension of piscine rooms deposited within, is the best key to
understanding the coloration of the *Commedia*.

The most beautiful organic commentary to Dante is pro-
vided by a mineralogical collection.

I permit myself a small autobiographical confession. Black
Sea pebbles tossed up on shore by the rising tide helped me
immensely when the conception of this conversation was tak-
ing shape. I openly consulted with chalcedony, cornelians, gyp-
sum crystals, spar, quartz, and so on. It was thus that I came to
understand that mineral rock is something like a diary of the
weather, like a meteorological blood clot. Rock is nothing more
than weather itself, excluded from atmospheric space and ban-

ished to functional space. In order to understand this you must imagine that all geological changes and displacements can be completely decomposed into elements of weather. In this sense, meteorology is more fundamental than mineralogy, for it embraces it, washes over it, ages it, and gives it meaning. The fascinating pages which Novalis devotes to miners and mining make concrete the interconnection between mineral rock and culture. This interconnection is illuminated out of rock — weather in both the formation of culture and in the formation of mineral rock.

Mineral rock is an impressionistic diary of weather accumulated by millions of natural disasters; however, it is not only of the past, it is of the future: it contains periodicity. It is an Aladdin's lamp penetrating the geological twilight of future ages.

Having combined the uncombinable, Dante altered the structure of time or, perhaps, to the contrary, he was forced to a glossolalia of facts, to a synchronism of events, names, and traditions severed by centuries, precisely because he had heard the overtones of time.

Dante's method is anachronistic — and Homer, who emerges with his sword at his side in the company of Virgil, Horace, and Lucan from the dim shadows of the Orphic choirs, where the four of them while away a tearless eternity together in literary discussion, is its best expression . . .

Indices of the standing still of time in Dante's work are not only the round astronomical bodies, but positively all things and all personalities. Everything mechanical is alien to him. He is disgusted by the idea of causality: such prophecies are suited only for bedding down swine.

Faccian le bestie Fiesolane strame

Di lor medesme, e non tocchin la pianta,
S'alcuna surge ancor nel lor letame...

(*Inferno*, 15.73–75)

I would answer the direct question, "What is a Dantean metaphor?" saying, "I don't know," because a metaphor can be defined only metaphorically, and this can be substantiated scientifically. But it seems to me that Dante's metaphor designates the standing-still of time. Its roots are not to be found in the little word "how," but in the word "when." His *quando* sounds like *come*. Ovid's rumbling was far more congenial to him than Virgil's French elegance.

Again and again I find myself turning to the reader and begging him to "imagine" something: that is, I must invoke analogy, having in mind but a single goal: to fill in the deficiency of our system of definition.

Hence, just try to imagine that Patriarch Abraham and King David, the entire tribe of Israel including Isaac, Jacob, and all their kin, as well as Rachel, for whom Jacob endured so much, have entered a singing and roaring organ, as if it were a house with its door left ajar, and have concealed themselves within.

And, imagine that even earlier, our forefather Adam with his son Abel, old Noah, and Moses, the lawgiver and the law-abiding, had also entered...

Trasseci l'ombra del primo parente,
    D'Abèl suo figlio, e quella di Noè,
    Di Moisè legista e ubbidente;
Abraàm patriarca, e Davìd re,
    Israèl con lo padre e co' suoi nati,
    E con Rachele, per cui tanto fe'...

(*Inferno*, 4.55–60)

Following this, the organ acquires the capacity to move—all its pipes and bellows become extraordinarily agitated, when suddenly, in a frenzied rage, it begins to move backward.

If the halls of the Hermitage were suddenly to go mad, if the paintings of all the schools and great masters were suddenly to break loose from their nails, and merge with one another, intermingle and fill the air of the rooms with a Futurist roar and an agitated frenzy of color, we would then have something resembling Dante's *Commedia*.

To wrest Dante from the grip of schoolroom rhetoric would be to render a major service to the history of European culture. I hope that centuries of labor will not be required for this, but only joint international endeavors which will succeed in creating an original anti-commentary to the work of generations of scholastics, creeping philologists, and pseudo-biographers. Insufficient respect for the poetic material which can be grasped only through performance, only through the flight of the conductor's baton—this was the reason for the universal blindness to Dante, to the greatest master and manager of this material, to the greatest conductor of European art, who forestalled for many centuries the formation of an orchestra adequate (to what?)—to the integral of the conductor's baton...

The calligraphic composition realized through means of improvisation—such, approximately, is the formula of a Dantean impulse, taken simultaneously as flight and as something finished. His similes are articulated impulses.

The most complex structural passages of the poem are performed on the fife, like a bird's mating call. The fife is nearly always sent forth to scout ahead.

Here I have in mind Dante's introductions, released by him as if at random, as if they were trial balloons.

Quando si parte il gioco della zara,
  Colui che perde si riman dolente,
  Ripetendo le volte, e tristo impara;
Con l'altro se ne va tutta la gente:
  Qual vi dinanzi, e qual di retro il prende,
  E qual da lato gli si reca a mente.
Ei non s'arresta, e questo e quello intende;
  A cui porge la man più non fa pressa;
  E così dalla calca si difende.

(Purgatorio, 6.1–9)

When the dice game is ended, the loser in cheerless
solitude replays the game, despondently throwing the
dice. The whole group tags along after the lucky gam-
bler; one runs up ahead, one pulls at him from behind,
one curries favor at his side, reminding him of himself.
But fortune's favorite walks right on, listening to all
alike, and with a hand-shake for each, he frees himself
from his importunate followers...

And there goes the "street" song of the *Purgatorio* (with its
throngs of importunate Florentine souls demanding above all,
gossip, secondly, protection, and thirdly, gossip again), enticed
by the call of the genre, resounding on the typical Flemish fife
which, only three hundred years hence, would become wall
paintings.

Another curious consideration arises. The commentary (ex-
planatory) is integral to the very structure of the *Commedia*. The
miracle-ship left the shipyard with barnacles adhering to its hull.
The commentary derives from street talk, from rumor, from Flo-
rentine slander passing from mouth to mouth. The commen-

tary is inevitable like the halcyon circling about Batyushkov's ship.

> ... There now, look: it's old Marzzuco...
> How well he held up at his son's
> funeral! A remarkably staunch old man...
> But have you heard, Pietro de la
> Borgia's head was cut off for no
> reason whatsoever—he was as clean
> as a piece of glass...
> Some woman's evil hand was
> involved here...O yes, by the way,
> there he goes himself—let's go
> up and ask him...

Poetic material does not have a voice. It does not paint with bright colors, nor does it explain itself in words. It is devoid of form just as it is devoid of content for the simple reason that it exists only in performance. The finished poem is no more than a calligraphic product, the inevitable result of the impulse to perform. If a pen is dipped in an inkwell, then the resultant thing is no more than a set of letters fully commensurate with the inkwell.

In talking about Dante it is more appropriate to bear in mind the creation of impulses than the creation of forms: impulses pertaining to textiles, sailing, scholasticism, meteorology, engineering, municipal concerns, handicrafts, and industry, as well as other things; the list could be extended to infinity.

In other words, syntax confuses us. All nominative cases must be replaced by the case indicating direction, by the dative. This is the law of transmutable and convertible poetic material existing only in the impulse to perform.

... Here everything is turned inside out: the noun appears as the predicate and not the subject of the sentence. I should hope that in the future Dante scholarship will study the coordination of the impulse and the text.

—*translated by Jane Gary Harris and Constance Link*

from The Noise of Time

[…]

The person who had bellowed for a cabby was V. V. Gippius, a teacher of literature, who taught children not literature but the far more interesting science of literary spite. Why did he puff himself up in front of the children? Surely children have no need of the sting of pride, the reptilian hiss of the literary anecdote?

Even then I knew that there gather around literature its witnesses, the members, so to speak, of its household — take, just for example, the Pushkinists and so on. Later I got to know some of them. How vapid they were in comparison with V. V.!

He differed from the other witnesses of literature precisely in this malign astonishment. He had a kind of feral relationship to literature, as if it were the only source of animal warmth. He warmed himself against literature, he rubbed against it with his fur, the ruddy bristle of his hair and his unshaven cheeks. He was a Romulus who hated his wolf mother and, hating her, taught others to love her.

To arrive at V. V.'s place almost inevitably meant to wake him up. Crushing an old copy of *The Scales* or *Northern Flowers* or *The Scorpion*, he would sleep on the hard divan in his study, poisoned by Sologub, wounded by Bryusov, recalling in his sleep Sluchevsky's savage poetry, his poem "Execution in Geneva," the comrade of Konevskoy and Dobrolyubov, those belligerent young monks of early Symbolism.

The hibernation of V. V. was a literary protest, something like a continuation of the policy of the old *Scales* and *Scorpion*. Awakened, he would puff himself up and begin asking about this and that with a malign little smile. But his real conversation consisted of a simple picking over of literary names and books with a kind of animal greed, with a mad but noble envy.

He was inclined to worry about his health and of all diseases he most feared tonsillitis, which prevents one from talking.

It was, nevertheless, in the energy and articulation of his speech that one found all the strength of his personality. He was unconsciously attracted to the sibilant and hissing sounds and to "t" in word endings. To put it in learned terms: a predilection for the dentals and palatals.

Inspired by the happy example of V. V. I still conceive of early Symbolism as a dense thicket of these *shch* sounds. "Nado mnoj orly, orly govorjashchie" (Above my head eagles, eagles speaking). Thus my teacher gave his preference to the patriarchal and warlike consonants of pain and attack, insult and self-defense. For the first time I felt the joy of the outward disharmony of Russian speech when V. V. took it into his head to read to us children the *Firebird* of Fet. "Na suku izvilistom i chudnom" (On the sinuous, miraculous branch): it was as if snakes were hanging above the school desks, a whole forest of sibilant snakes. The hibernation of V. V. frightened and attracted me.

But surely literature is not a bear sucking its paws, not a heavy sleep on the study sofa after work? I would come to him to wake up the beast of literature. To listen to him growl, to watch him toss and turn. I would come to my teacher of "Russian" at home. The whole savor of the thing lay in that coming to him "at home." Even now it is difficult for me to free myself from the notion that I was then at literature's own house. Never again was literature to be a house, an apartment, a family where red-haired little boys slept side by side in their netted cribs.

Beginning as early as Radishchev and Novikov, V. V. had established personal relations with Russian writers, splenetic and loving liaisons filled with noble enviousness, jealousy, with jocular disrespect, grievous unfairness — as is customary between the members of one family.

An intellectual builds the temple of literature with immovable idols. Korolenko, for example, who wrote so much about the Komi, seems to me to have turned himself into a little tin god of the Komi. V. V. taught that one should build literature not as a temple but as a gens. What he prized in literature was the patriarchal, paternal principle of culture.

How good is it that I managed to love not the priestly flame of the ikon lamp but the ruddy little flame of literary (V. V. G.) spite!

The judgments of V. V. continue to hold me in their power down to the present day. The grand tour which I made with him through the patriarchate of Russian literature from the Novikov-Radishchev period all the way to the Konevits of early Sybolism, has remained the only one. After that, I merely "read a bit."

In place of a necktie there dangled a piece of string. His short neck, subject to tonsillitis, moved nervously in the colored, unstarched collar. From his larynx were torn sibilant, gurgling sounds: the belligerent *shch* and *t*.

It seemed as though this person was forever suffering the final agony, belligerent and passionate. Something of the death agony was in his very nature, and this tortured and agitated him, nourishing the drying roots of his spiritual being.

By the way, something like the following conversation was a commonplace in the Symbolist milieu:

"How do you do, Ivan Ivanovich?"

"Oh, all right, Pyotr Petrovich. I live in the hour of my death."

V. V. loved poems in which there were such energetic and happy rhymes as *plamen'* (flame) — *kamen'* (stone), *ljubov'* (love) — *krov'* (blood), *plot'* (flesh) — *Gospod'* (Lord).

His vocabulary was, without his being conscious of it, controlled by two words: *bytie* (existence) and *plamen'* (flame). If the entire Russian language were given over to his keeping, I seriously think that he would, out of carelessness, burn it up, destroy the whole Russian lexicon to the glory of *bytie* and *plamen'*. The literature of the century was well born. Its house was a full cup. At the broad open table the guests sat with Walsingham. New guests, throwing off their fur coats, came in out of the cold. The little blue flames on the punch reminded the new arrivals of pride, friendship, and death. Around the table flew the request which, it seemed, was always being uttered for the last time — "Sing, Mary" — the anguished request of the last banquet.

But not less dear to me than the beautiful girl who sang that shrill Scottish song was the one who, in a hoarse voice worn out with talk, asked her for the song.

If I had a vision of Konstantin Leontev yelling for a cabby on that snow-covered street of the Vasili Island it was only because he of all Russian writers is most given to handling time in lumps. He feels centuries as he feels the weather, and he shouts at them.

He might have shouted, "Oh, fine, what a splendid century we have!" — something like "A nice dry day it turned out!" Only it didn't turn out that way! He was struck dumb. The hard frost burned his throat, and the peremptory shout at the century froze like a column of mercury.

Looking back at the entire nineteenth century of Russian culture — shattered, finished, unrepeatable, which no one must repeat, which no one dares repeat — I wish to hail the century, as one would hail settled weather, and I see in it the unity lent it by the measureless cold which welded decades together into one day, one night, one profound winter, within which the terrible State glowed, like a stove, with ice.

And in this wintry period of Russian history, literature, taken at large, strikes me as something patrician, which puts me out of countenance: with trembling I lift the film of waxed paper above the winter cap of the writer. No one is to blame in this and there is nothing to be ashamed of. A beast must not be ashamed of its furry hide. Night furred him. Winter clothed him. Literature is a beast. The furriers—night and winter.

—translated by Clarence Brown

from Alagez, *from* Journey to Armenia

Which tense do you want to live in?
— I want to live in the imperative of the future passive participle — in the "what ought to be."
I feel like breathing that way. That's what I like. There exists such a thing as mounted, bandit-band, equestrian honor. That's why I like the fine Latin "gerundive" — that verb on horseback.

Yes, the Latin genius, when it was young and greedy, created that form of imperative verbal traction as the prototype of our whole culture, and it was not the only thing that "ought to be" but the thing that "ought to be praised" — *laudatura est* — the thing we like…

The above was a conversation that I carried on with myself as I rode on horseback among the natural boundaries, the nomads' territories, and the gigantic pastures of Alagez.

In Erevan Alagez stood there before my eyes like "hello" and "good-bye." I saw its snowy crown melt from one day to the next and in good weather, especially in the morning. I saw its dyed slopes crunch like dry toast.

And I felt myself drawn to it over the mulberry trees and the earthen roofs of the houses.

— translated by Clarence Brown

IV DANIIL KHARMS

(1905–1942)

*He managed to do what almost no one else could —
write the so-called prose of the twentieth century.
Kharms's prose is the real prose of the twentieth century because in
his writing the character exits the house and flies away.*

— ANNA AKHMATOVA

*Daniil Kharms, poet and dramatist, whose attention is
concentrated, not on a static figure, but on the collision of a
number of objects, on their interrelationships. At the moment of
action, the object assumes new concrete traits full of real meaning.
The action, turned inside out, in its new appearance still keeps a
classical touch and at the same time represents a broad sweep
of the Oberiu world view.*

— FROM THE OBERIU MANIFESTO, AROUND 1926

The Beginning of a Beautiful Summer Day (A Symphony)

The rooster had hardly crowed when Timofey jumped out of his window onto the roof and frightened every pedestrian on the street at that hour. Khariton the peasant stopped, picked up a stone and threw it at Timonfey. Tmofey disappeared. "Very Smart!" laughed the human herd and somcone named Zubov run full speed and rammed his head into a wall. "Oh!" exclaimed a woman with a swollen cheek. But Komarov gave her a quick slap and the woman run howling to the doorway. Fetelushin walked past and laughed. "Hello little ball of fat!" Komarov walked up to him, and hit Fetelushin in the stomach. Fetelushin leaned against the wall started to hiccup. Romashkin tried to spit from the balcony on Fetelushin's head. At this point, a few doors down, a big-nosed woman was beating her kid with a trough. A fat, young mother was rubbing her pretty little girl's face against the brick wall. A pretty little dog broke its hind leg, and was rolling around on the sidewalk. A little boy was eating some sort of a revolting thing from a spittoon. At the grocery, there was a long line for sugar. The women yelled and hit one another with bags. The peasant Khariton, having drank some methanol, stood in front of the women, his trousers undone, and said bad words.

Thus began a beautiful summer day.

—translated by Katie Farris and Ilya Kaminsky

Symphony #2

Anton Mikhailovich spat, said "gosh," spat again, said "gosh" again, spat again, said "gosh" again, and left. To hell with him. Let me tell you about Ilya Pavlovich.

Ilya Pavlovich was born in 1893 in Constantinople. When he was a small boy, his family moved to Petersburg, where he graduated from a German school on Kirochnaya Street. Then he worked in some kind of a store, then he did something else, and right before the revolution he immigrated. To hell with him. Let me tell you about Anna Ignatievna.

It's not that easy to talk about Anna Ignatievna. First of all, I know almost nothing about her. Secondly, I have just fallen off the chair and have forgotten what I was about to say. Let me tell you about myself.

I'm tall, not unintelligent; I dress elegantly and tastefully; I don't drink, don't gamble, but I do like ladies. And ladies don't avoid me. No, they even like it when I go out with them. Seraphima Izmailovna has been inviting me to her place, and Zinaida Yakovlevna has mentioned that she is always happy to see me.

I did have a funny incident with Marina Petrovna that I'd like to tell you about. Quite an ordinary thing, but still rather funny, since, because of me, Marina Petrovna turned completely bald, like a palm of a hand. This is how it happened: once I came to visit Marina Petrovna, and—bang!—she turned bald. And that was that.

—*translated by Valzhyna Mort*

INCIDENTS

One day Orlov had too many mashed peas and died. And Krylov, hearing about this, died too. But Spridonov died for no reason. And Spridonov's wife fell off a kitchen cabinet and also died. And Spridonov's children drowned in a pond. And Spridonov's grandmother took to the bottle and hit the road. And Mikhailov ceased combing his hair and got ill. And Kruglov sketched a grandama with a whip and went crazy. And Perehvostov received four hundred rubles by wire and became so uptight that they fired him from work.

Good people, they are all my good people, these citizens— but they can't keep their two feet on the ground.

—*translated by Katie Farris and Ilya Kaminsky*

A Fairytale

There once was a man by the name of Semyonov.
And Semyonov went out for a walk and lost his handkerchief.
And Semyonov started looking for a handkerchief and lost
　　his hat.
And looking for a hat, he lost his jacket.
He began to look for a jacket and lost boots.
—Yes—said Semyonov—this *is* a loss—I shall go home.
Semyonov began walking home—and he got lost.
—No—said Semyonov—I'd rather sit. And he sat down.
And he sat on a stone, and fell asleep.

—translated by Katie Farris and Ilya Kaminsky

Old Ladies Are Flying

An old lady fell out of the window, because she was too
curious. She fell out of the window, and was smashed
to pieces.
Another old lady stared down at the remains of one who was
smashed, she stared at them, out of her excessive
curiosity, and also fell out of the window, and smashed.
Then the third old lady fell out of the window, then the fourth
did, then the fifth.
When the sixth old lady fell out of the window, I got bored
watching them and went to Maltsevitsky Bazaar where,
it was announced, they gave woven shawls to the
blind.

—*translated by Katie Farris and Ilya Kaminsky*

Something about Pushkin

It's hard to say something about Pushkin to a person who doesn't know anything about him. Pushkin is a great poet. Napoleon is not as great as Pushkin. Bismarck compared to Pushkin is a nobody. And the Alexanders, First, Second, and Third, are just little kids compared to Pushkin. In fact, compared to Pushkin, all people are little kids, except Gogol. Compared to him, Pushkin is a little kid.

And so, instead of writing about Pushkin, I would rather write about Gogol.

Although, Gogol is so great that not a thing can be written about him, so I'll write about Pushkin after all.

Yet, after Gogol, it's a shame to have to write about Pushkin. But you can't write anything about Gogol. So I'd rather not write anything about anyone.

—*translated by Matvei Yankelevich with Eugene Ostashevsky*

GOGOL & PUSHKIN

GOGOL (*falls onto the stage from behind the curtains and lies still*).

PUSHKIN (*walks out, trips on Gogol and falls*): What the devil! Could it be Gogol!

GOGOL (*getting up*): What a filthy, no-good...! Won't let you alone. (*Walks, trips on Pushkin and falls.*) Could it really be Pushkin I tripped on!

PUSHKIN (*getting up*): Not a moment's peace! (*Walks, trips on Gogol and falls.*) What the devil! It couldn't be — Gogol again!

GOGOL (*getting up*): Always something going wrong! (*Walks, trips on Pushkin and falls.*) What filthy, no-good...! On Pushkin again!

PUSHKIN (*getting up*): Foolery! Foolery all over the place! (*Walks, trips over Gogol and falls.*) What the devil! Gogol again!

GOGOL (*getting up*): This is mockery, through and through! (*Walks, trips on Pushkin and falls.*) Pushkin again!

PUSHKIN (*getting up*): What the devil! Truly the devil! (*Walks, trips on Gogol and falls.*) On Gogol!

GOGOL (*getting up*): Filthy-good-for-nothings! (*Walks, trips over Pushkin and falls.*) On Pushkin!

PUSHKIN (*getting up*): What the devil! (*Walks, trips over Gogol and falls behind the curtains.*) Gogol!

GOGOL (*getting up*): Filthy good-for-nothings! (*Walks off stage.*)

From offstage the voice of Gogol is heard: "Pushkin!"

CURTAIN.

— *translated by Matvei Yankelevich*

[Dear Nikandr Andreyevich,]

Dear

Nikandr Andreyevich,
I received your letter and understood right away that it was from you. First I thought, what if it's not from you, but as soon as I opened it I knew it was from you, but I almost thought that it wasn't from you. I am glad that you have long been married because when a person marries the one whom he wanted to marry that means he has achieved that which he wanted. And so I am very glad that you got married because when a man marries someone he wanted to marry that means that he got what he wanted. Yesterday I received your letter and right away I thought that this letter was from you, but then I thought it seemed that it wasn't from you, but I unsealed it and saw it was certainly from you. You did very well to write me. At first you didn't write to me and then suddenly you did write, although earlier, before you didn't write me for some time you also wrote to me. As soon as I received your letter I decided right away that it was from you and that's why I'm very glad that you had already married. Because if a man wants to get married then he must get married no matter what. That's why I am so very glad that you finally married precisely the one you wanted to marry. And you did very well to write me. I was overjoyed when I saw your letter and right away I thought it was from you. Although, to tell the truth, while I was opening it a thought flashed through my mind that it was not from you, but then in the end I decided that it was from you. Thanks for writing. I am grateful to you for this and very happy for you. Perhaps you can't imagine why I am so happy for you, but I'll tell you straight away that I am happy for you because, because you got married and married precisely the

person you wanted to marry. And, you know, it is very good to marry precisely the person you want to marry because precisely then you get what you wanted. And that is precisely the reason that I am so happy for you. And I am also happy that you wrote me a letter. Even from afar I knew that the letter was from you, but when I took it in my hands I thought: and what if it's not from you? And then I thought: no, of course it is from you. I myself am opening the letter and at the same thinking: from you or not from you? From you or not from you? And then, when I opened it I could clearly see that it was from you. I was overjoyed and decided I would also write you a letter. I have lots to tell you, but I literally don't have the time. What I had time to tell you, I have told you in this letter, and the rest I will write you later because now I have no time left at all. At the least it's good that you wrote me a letter. Now I know that you've long been married. I knew, too, from previous letters, that you got married, and now I see it again: it's completely true, you got married. And I am very happy that you got married and wrote me a letter. As soon as I saw your letter, I knew that you had gotten married again. Well, I thought, it's good that you got married again and wrote me a letter about it. Now write to me and tell me, who is your new wife and how did it all happen. Relay my greetings to your new wife.

Daniil Kharms

—*translated by Matvei Yankelevich*

V ANDREI BELY

(1880–1934)

*I watched the others. Most kept within the boundaries of an
enviable self-esteem. All felt themselves to be names, thought of
themselves as poets. Bely alone was listening with complete self-
abandon, carried far, far away by the joy that regrets nothing
because on the heights where it is at home there is nothing other
than sacrifice and the eternal readiness for it.*

—BORIS PASTERNAK

*Imagine yourself a group of people who would wish to renew the
tradition of listening to literature during a meal and would invite a
reader, and trying hard the reader would bring
Andrei Bely's "Petersburg," and there he starts reading, and
something unimaginable happens: one person is choking on
his food, another is eating fish with a knife, another
has burned himself with a mustard. It's impossible
to imagine such a process, such work, such an endeavor,
that could have been accompanied by Bely's prose.*

—OSIP MANDELSTAM

PUSHKIN AND GOGOL

In the history of Russian prose, Gogol merits a place alongside Tolstoy and Dostoevsky—even above them, for he came first. And as far as our great poets are concerned, the prose of Pushkin and Lermontov, although beautiful, remains peripheral to their work as a whole. Pushkin's prose is limpid and restrained; it shows what could be done with the language by a classically educated stylist eager to apply the techniques of a seemingly alien culture to the literature of his "homeland." Pushkin's poetry and prose do not overlap. Do not look for lyrical and dramatic qualities in his prose, which is magnificent, witty, but somehow... "prosaic" (notice that in the narrative poems "Poltava" and "The Bronze Horseman," Pushkin constructs his imagery differently). In the poetic mode he is at home: frivolous jests and dramatic confessions fly from his pen with equal adroitness. One almost perceives a lack of form in his works, so unconstrained is he by the demands of plot. In this lies his mastery of literary form.

Pushkin approached the genre of the short story as a problem to be solved. Imagine that a man given to effusions of feeling is torn from his circle of friends and suddenly summoned away on urgent business. He enters a room full of strangers to discourse on a matter that he has subjected to scrupulous study, stunning everyone with the aplomb of his irreproachable expressions, in a diplomatic idiom from which he remains dispassionately distant. This describes Pushkin's cool phrasing. In his lyrics he is affably ingenuous; in his prose he is closed. In his lyrics the reader is his friend; in his prose the reader is an outsider. What has changed is not his audience but the acoustics of the room: the living room is now a formal reception area. Thus the method of exposition in "The Queen of Spades" is distinct from that in "The Bronze Horseman."

Lermontov, in setting before us the character and narrator Pechorin, is both more colorful and more intimate in his prose. But he, too, passes in silence along those places of the text where in his verses he shows candor.

Not so with Gogol.

Gogol invested the scope of lyric poetry, communicated rhythmically (in rhythms from which Pushkin's prose distances itself), into prose, forcing his taut lines laden with assonances and alliterations to vibrate like strings. Before Gogol, efforts to this end had won no laurels: Karamzin's lyricism has grown cold; Marlinsky is entirely dispensable. Yet after a hundred years, Gogol still surprises and excites us. And this is testimony to his victory—a virtual revolution in Russian verbal art.

Dead Souls constitutes a complete epic cycle, one which expands the boundaries of the literary epic. The epic cycles of antiquity preserve traces of prepoetical, syncretic forms that did not survive in the literary epics of later times. Similarly, in the modern period prior to Gogol there were no epic poems in prose; literary epics possessed no breadth of scope. Gogol cast the epic into prose form and the spirit of the epoch into poetry. He drew attention to the epic as a form distinct from epic poems. In fact, Gogol is the prose epic itself, in so far as Russian vernacular language instilled life into "mere literature" through prose: the pretentious "style" of the petty nobleman reduced to the ways of the bourgeoisie, the stilted phrase of the clerk, and the course and colorful language of the seminary student—all of these elements are seasoned with local folk dialects and mixed into a literary form. Pushkin had advised writers to study Russian among priests' wives, the bakers of communion bread. And from precisely this linguistic source Gogol drew forth indescribably sonorous nuances. Where there had been regional and provisional languages, there arose the "language of languages," supple in its nuanced transitions from one dialect to another. And the new language burned life into our greatest prose classics. The very concept of "prose" was reborn, so that Russian literature became foremost in the world. Gogol was the impetus.

Gogol's creations share this peculiarity: analysis proves that their plot, purpose, and style are immanent to one another. Meaning is colorful and shaded, color is meaningful; finer points of technique are conditioned by the author's cast — his *style* — of mind. One sees how form and content are engendered by the form-content process. Social content sets the process in motion. Form and content are, in turn, products of the process and bear its imprint, which resembles the traces of volcanic energy on a rock jutting out from the bowels of the earth. Gogol loved comparisons to volcanoes. "Asia was a people-spewing volcano," he says. "The Terrible Vengeance" contains a myth of an extinct volcano as a great, earth-shaking corpse.

A convulsion of unknown origin distorts the creative process in Gogol. His consciousness, limited by the disintegration of the social stratum that spawned him, brings to mind an extinct volcano, and his "dead souls" — ash and magma. As he rationalizes, Gogol crumbles like ash. As he acts creatively, he perceives a jolt from the earth's molten core; and through this perception he recorded the passions of his "blind" heroes, endowing them with a spasmodic gesture torn, as it were, from the congealed pools in which they ossify. This is the effect of the "electric shock" that Gogol dreamed about when he was writing *The Inspector General*. The gestural jolt at the play's end is possible because his "heroes" — products — were not distinct from the author of this diastrophic process — of which he was so frightened, straining to read in it a mandate to some holy mission. Gogol was unable to translate social demand into an intelligible moral language.

A disconnection between the phases of hearing, of taking and making, and of returning, forms the nerve center of his creative work from *Evenings on a Farm Near Dikanka* (*Evenings*) to the second volume of *Dead Souls*, which, as it burned and scattered its ashes, became emblematic of its author's creative process. The semi-conscious nature of the first phase has its correlate in the twisted hyper-consciousness of the final period. Gogol's products quake within him as they do within the process; and he, who is the process, quakes within them. Hence the atomistic dynamic of gestural contortions produced by the characters of *The Inspector General* and *Dead Souls*. The imbalance of forces which constitute the process is immanent to the imbalance of form and content in Gogol's works. In this immanence, the imbalance itself becomes a special kind of equilibrium, the opposite of Pushkinian equilibrium.

In Pushkin this equilibrium yields a positive result: the multiplication of the plus of form by the plus of content. Gogol's positive is the product of two negatives. His contemporaries, marveling at the colorful content of his creations, drew attention to his stylistic weaknesses, which hinted at a virtual inability to write in Russian—and they were in part correct. But the daring victories in rhythm, the evocative power, which set Gogol alongside the greatest stylists of world literature, remained outside even Pushkin's field of vision. The "plus" of content was hitched securely to the "minus" of form. Conversely, some of our contemporaries, devoting more rigorous attention to questions of form, marvel at this aspect of Gogol's work to such an extent that they ascribe to it alone what seems to result from the power of his content. Professor Eikhenbaum crowns a fine analysis of literary devices in "The Overcoat" with a reduction of the compassionate shudder that Akaky Akakievich's cry evokes in us ("Leave me alone! Why do you insult me?") to a mere principle of style. In what seemed to Pushkin a negative quality (form, technique), Professor Eikhenbaum discovers the greates positive aspect. But the content of Gogol's tale suffers as a result. The depth of plot, to take "The Nose" as another example, which criticism has yet to explore for its social content, is reduced to the cheap and once-current "noseological" puns of the beginning of the nine-teenth century.

Yet there is no smoke without fire. In Gogol's writings the "plus" is attained by multiplying an apparent minus of form by an apparent minus of content. This is because in Gogol, form and content are the result of a dialectic that switches pluses for minuses and vice versa. From *Evenings* to *Dead Souls*, form and content flow back and forth in a form-content process. By the final period, the sonorous devices of *Evenings* have degenerated into a self-destructive tendentiousness, the significance of which opens, as it were, from the back door rather than the front.

Pushkin's prose works are self-enclosed. The author sets each new piece before us like a finished statuette, proceeding then to the next. But Gogol is overgrown with the fruits of his creativ-ity, like an unkempt creature that refuses to cut its nails — as if trimming them would threaten its autonomy. And curling out toward the reader, they can never reach completion because they owe their completeness not to themselves but to the whole of the parent organism, which is the creative process. In this process Gogol's creative output merged with him, just as its sig-nificance changed for him as he came to view it from other per-spectives. This explains the crossings-out, the new redactions, the perpetually unfinished fragments, and the various incarna-tions of characters and themes from one tale to another. These tendencies finally spun into a never-ending tragedy: what Gogol had animated he could not reanimate — not at his new level of consciousness. He excluded *Evenings* from the projected edition of his collected works and twice committed *Dead Souls* to flames.

The generative process in Gogol is similar to the circulation of blood which feeds separate organs. Blood courses through each organ but is not innate to any one. The imbalance of form and content remind us of the ceaseless argument of the roots and branches in Krylov's fable. First one, then the other appears to dominate. It is like a pulse, rising and falling. Integrity derives from the style of the rhythm, which is perfectly embodied in no single place.

In Pushkin's works it is form that accounts for the unity of form and content; in Gogol's it is content. Pushkinian form is the closure of the work. Pushkin in this sense is an Eleatic, enclosing the existence of the work within a circle. Gogolian content comprises the entire creative process, of which the notional unity of the projected volumes of *Dead Souls* has become a symbol. In his sundering of form, in his breaking of the circle that encloses the existence of the single work, Gogol is a Heraclitean seized by a fiery vortex in which, indeed, he burned just like his *Dead Souls* as the rapacious self-consciousness of his elemental creativity recognized itself in his ego, where it was extinguished.

The stereotypical sentence of Pushkin is short. It is separated from contiguous sentences by periods. The structure is: subject, qualifier, predicate, period. Phrasal constructions are well-tempered in the manner of Bach. In Gogol the sentence explodes and scatters, sending out fragments of subordinate clauses which depend on the main clause and co-depend on one another. The equilibrium between noun, adjective, and verb is destroyed. Instead of "1+1+1," for example, we get "3+1+5": "[H]e glanced…at the *pages*, at the *peasants* who…used to

work, plow, get drunk, haul, cheat" (two nouns, five verbs); or
"...coarsely, rudely, roughly, shoddily, badly..." (five adverbs),
etc. For the Gogolian sentence, contemporary rhetoric (e.g.,
"*when...,when...,when...,then...*") was also uncharacteristic.
During the Gothic era of Karamzin the main clause was borne
aloft on the subordinate "when..., when" pattern as if on lancet
arches. Gogol tore apart the Karamzin era: series of subordinate
clauses became subsidiary main clauses; and their composition
resulted in a whole made up of repetitions.

Instead of Pushkin's Doric sentence and the Gothic sen-
tence of Karamzin, we have an asymmetrical baroque structure
surrounded by a colonnade of repetitions begging to be parsed
and united by arches of introductory phrases with appended ex-
clamations—somewhat like ornamental stucco moldings. But
the terse Pushkinian sentence, as a component of style, also has
a place here, like the hollow indentations between high-relief
attachments. For example: [T]he sky only reddens on one side.
And it already grows dim. In the field it grows colder" ("St. John's
Eve"). Even Karamzinian phrasing has a place, such as in the
tale "Rome."

The very foundation of Gogol's discursive style uproots the
norm. It signals the imbalance of a sentence that sparkles with
daring neologisms, which in Pushkin are *still* rare, and with the
gravity of archaisms, which in Pushkin are *already* rare. The
verbal inventory for each stylist is strikingly original. Pushkin's
lexicon is that of a highly educated member of the intelligentsia,
who at one point had a better command of French than of Rus-
sian but who took pains (through his fathers and forefathers) to
weave a Gallic smoothness of speech into our literary language,
to give it a Russian intonation, and in so doing to enrich it.
These efforts were crowned with complete success, resulting in
achievements that have lasted a century without one grammati-

cal or stylistic offense. For all of this Pushkin can claim credit. He maintained that he wrote more properly than he spoke, but that he spoke more properly than Gogol wrote.

In Pushkin's literary prose you will not encounter the colloquial expressions that glimmer throughout his correspondence. In Gogol's prose, the way that several lexicons intersect to produce syntactical puzzles gives the impression that the author had studied Dahl's dictionary prior to its compilation. From the mosaic of regional and class jargons he extracted new sounds from the language. Pushkin's style had drawn a balance from the most outstanding Russian stylists since Kantemir and Lomonosov, resulting in a Russian language that did not have to resort to unwieldy Church Slavonicisms. The Pushkinian sentence is inextricably rooted in the eighteenth century. Flowering in the nineteenth century, it nonetheless points "backward." The Gogolian sentence inaugurates a new age, the fruits of which we reap even today in the works of Mayakovsky, Khlebnikov, and the proletarian poets and prose writers.

Gogol is a new Trediakovsky, who nourishes the future of Russian literature as it strives to reveal a new, collective Pushkin. This "Potebnist" before Potebnia laughed at the guardians of linguistic purity who sought to squeeze language into grammar, and who scoffed as they heard…"from Professor (so-and-so)," a Ukranian, apparently, who has imperfect command of "Muscovite" grammar and who mentally translates into Russian from his native dialect, a fact which his biographers have proven; "a Ukranian who writes 'send *after* the artist' (instead of '*for*')" [*"poslat'* po *khudozhniku"* (instead of "*za*")]. Gogol proves that a revolution in language can manage without grammatical properties, because true literary language represents a "language of languages," in the potency of rhythms and in the glimmering of sound, or in the acts of life ablaze, and not at all in rules.

Sound-painting, transforming into a painting of language, is a flame seized from an erupting volcano.

Shocks and fiery reflections ("sweet sounds") are not unknown to Pushkin's poetry, but his poet's code consciously extinguished them in his prose. And our contemporary currents such as *zaum'* will run a course set by the deep waters of Gogolism.

The shattering potency of the Russian language, the grammar of which Gogol had not mastered, results from the shattered equilibrium of the sentence together with the plot contained within the sentence; one side pours into form, the other blends with the process, which is not exhausted in the finished products and which does not burn out even after the individual work has been printed. This explains Gogol's crossings-out, new redactions, and ultimately his incineration of the primary text.

—translated by Christopher Colbath

Gogol and Mayakovsky

Gogol's presence is discernible in diverse areas of our multifaceted literature. After running his course among his contemporaries, he began to influence the literature of our time. As early as Sologub we can detect a response to Gogol's manner, his rhythm, his distribution of words. In Blok the feminine image that Gogol perceived is reanimated. In Bely we find that verbal patterns, to say nothing of Gogolian devices, are assimilated into the Gogolian complex and that Gogol's manner of writing (e.g., a door "slits open" [*oshchelilas'*] (a Gogolian expression); "the street bared its teeth with shovels' iron laughter" [*ulitsa oskalilas' zheleznym smekhom lopat*]) is exaggerated.

Gogol's influence then ran its course in symbolism and began to work in futurism. His description of the city exhibits a preurbanist urbanism. In Paris he is "struck...by the glare of the streets, the disorder of roofs, the thickness of chimneys, the unarchitectural, unbroken masses of houses pasted with a thick raggedness of stones, the ugliness of naked...side street walls...the crowd of gold letters which crawls on the walls, on the roofs...on the chimneys, the bright transparency of the lower floors...made of mirrored glass...Paris...a mouth, a fountain casting sparks of news...fashions...petty...laws...The enchanted pile flared up...houses...became transparent," etc. ("Rome").

Who among preurbanist writers took such an approach to the city? It had its beginnings in Verhaeren and made our eyes see things anew; that is how Gogol looked at Paris, Rome, and Nevsky Prospect—with eyes seizing masses of buildings and crowds of dismembered colors in the streets. His ear could already distinguish the "wails of music" simultaneously "on the banks of the Seine, the Neva, the Thames, the Moscow…inside the walls of Algiers," anticipating radios and loudspeakers. Here is Rome (a scrap of street): in the windows "ham, sausage…lemons and leaves turned into a mosaic and composed a *plafond*; circles…of cheeses lying one atop the other, became columnar; out of bacon, white as snow, were cast…statues…groups…of biblical scenes which…the viewer might take for alabaster" ("Rome"). Indeed, under the windows K. D. W. we have "a playing crowd of walls, terraces, and cupolas"; "arches of waterways seemed to stand in the air as if glued to the sky" ("Rome"). It is characteristic for Gogol to see the "crowd of walls" as playing in the way that we see it from a streetcar: with houses jumping, opening and closing our perspective: "the sidewalk was borne along…carriages with trotting horses seemed immobile, the bridge strained and broke…on an arch, a house stood roof downwards, a booth careened at you" ("Nevsky Prospect"). This might well be the foreshortening of the painter Annenkov. Gogol even approaches the daring of futurist writing, which young artists in their break with the "World of Art" so recently used for shock value: "in a stream…light reached" the puddle [*svet dosiagnul…strueiu* do luzhi] (*Dead Souls*). The verb "reached" [*dosiagnul*] denotes the eye's perception — a futurist perception. "The watchman's halberd together with the gold words of the sign…shone…on…the eyelash" ("Nevsky Prospect"); "objects got mixed up…mustaches…seemed stuck to foreheads above the eyes, and the nose…was completely absent" (*Dead Souls*); "pincers stretched out…from his eyes" ("The Terrible Vengeance"). Just try to draw one of these descriptions. Somov groans, just as applause is heard from…Tatlin. Try to stage these actions. The Moscow Art Theater groups (the second as well as the first) refused; but Meyerhold took the dare!

It is typical for urbanists and constructivists to turn toward the apparatus and away from nature. Gogol's urbanistic pathos led him to renounce nature, with which he had been in love: "the savage ugliness of the Swiss Alps…made for a terrifying…sight" to the protagonist of "Rome." The futurist characteristically compares an archway to a mouth; and in Gogol we find "a mouth the size of the archway at Headquarters." Through Gogol the symbolists justifiably desired to contrast themselves to Kuprin. The authors of "A Trap for Judges" justifiably felt obliged to draw a distinction between themselves and the symbolists: the golden signs shook in a giant tear [*slezishche*] which Mayakovsky had dragged around in his unforgettable drama, "Vladimir Mayakovsky."

Mayakovsky revived Gogolian hyperbolism, taking it to a higher level. Then later he set about squaring and cubing it. Mayakovsky's "giant hyperbole" [*giperbolishcha*] is a beast with no precedent. Mayakovsky domesticated it. Not by chance does he admit: "The most monstrous hyperbole…is tender." Hyperbole is "the world's wet nurse."

Gogol's hyperbolism stretches adjectives to the superlative degree. He props up the superlative with verbal prefixes ("*pre*," "*raz-*," "*nai-*," — all of which denote or can easily denote the superlative) and adverbs like "exceedingly," "extremely," "splendidly," "well," "highly," etc., only to eschew precise definition: "No pen can describe it!" This is why after "daughter most dearest to me" there is the flood of inexpressive qualifiers on the order of unheard-of, unprecedented, unbearable, unportrayable. Eventually Gogol's hyperbolism crashes. Failing to reach "seventh heaven," it beats its head against the rhetorical ceiling of a "third or fourth" heaven. The rhetoric of volume 2 of *Dead Souls*, lacking the right means, attempts to elevate hyperbole to "high" heaven on a lady's sleeve that resembles a hot air balloon ("Nevsky Prospect"). Gogol's hyperbole grows into a mouth that resembles an archway and into trousers the width of the sea ("Taras Bulba"). Then it is a heavyset lady carrying watermelons...in her skirt ("The Tale of How Ivan Ivanovich Quarreled with Ivan Nikiforovich"). The sweat of her labors is a rhetoric from which Russian authors, holding their noses, rushed toward the positive degree. Their flight is like contemporary philosophers' escape from the lofty but whiffling category to the dissection of frogs (they had had enough of "oxen"). The positive degree revealed its beauty in the works of Leo Tolstoy and in the refined miniatures of Chekhov, only to degenerate suddenly into dwarfish phalanxes of "mini-Tolstoys" and "micro-Chekhovs."

Herein lay the reason for the symbolists' endeavor to turn back toward the free use of hyperbole. But it was in futurism that hyperbole's "armed uprising" was won in the field. And Mayakovsky was the drum major, overtaking and bypassing Gogol's hyperbole with its nostrils, spectacles, and mouths which recall "the wheels of the commissar's chaise" ("A May Night, or The Drowned Maiden"), or the "archway at Headquarters" ("The Nose"). One can "pour water by the bucketful" into the Gogolian nostril. It is imagery like this that binds Mayakovsky to Gogol.

A master of the grotesque, Mayakovsky also evinces Gogol's eschewal of definition ("the pen can't describe it"), so that, having uncovered the void of "no" and "not," he can pierce it with his needle, which exceeds in height even the "enema tube" the size of a tower, dragged around Roman alleyways by Gogol ("Rome"). Mayakovsky yanked even Gogol's rhetoric by the whiskers.

Mayakovsky also seizes upon Gogol's typical hyperboles, such as *"mountains* of pots," [gory *gorshkov*] ("The Sorochintsy Fair"), *"masses* of leaves" [massy *list'ev*] ("The Sorochintsy Fair"), *"bane* of witches" [ved'm *gibel*] ("The Lost Dispatch"), for salvage material: "the *mush* of applause" [kasha *rukoples-kanii*], "*lava* of attacks" [lava *atak*], "*jaws* of glows" [zevy *zarev*], "*wind* of shots" [veter *iader*], "*seven feet* of shredded human meat" [na sazhen' *chelovech'ego miasa nashinkovano*]. "My every movement...an *inexplicable* miracle" recalls Gogol's refusal to define the heavens; "*seven feet* of meat" resembles the crunch of feathers in *Dead Souls*: the cart drives over dry land [*po sushniaku*] at seven feet (*Dead Souls*).

And Mayakovsky latches onto Gogol's numerical hyperbole ("like...*fifteen* guys" [kak...piatnadtsat' *khloptsev*], "like a *thousand* mills" [budto tysiacha *mel'nits*], "a *million* hats" [million...*shapok*]): "*hundred-mile* cliffs" [stoverstnye *skaly*], "*hundred-legged* ham" [stonogii *okorok*] (recall the "statues" of bacon), "*hundred-feathered* lady" [stoperaia *dama*] (the "unprecedented" feather in Paris), "*hundred-housed* uproar" [stodomyi *sodom*]; "arise...as *a thousand* Lazaruses" [vstan'te...tysiachami *Lazarei*].

We find the same hyperbolic perception of the sun ("instead of the moon...the sun," pumpkins "made of gold," "blows...of sun rays," etc.): "golden-pawed" [*zolotolapyi*], "golden-bodied" [*zolototelyi*], "the sun's palm on my head" [*solntsa ladon' na golove moei*], "he turned"—like Ivan Nikiforovich—"first his back, then his belly to the sun" [*vvorachival...solntsu to spinu, to puzo*]; "every little girl has more of the sun on her pinkie fingernail than before on the whole globe" [u *kazhdoi devochki na nogte mizintsa solntsa bol'she, chem ran'she na vsem zemnom share*].

The furthest limit of Gogol's hyperbole is reached. Then there is its ascent in the manifesto "The Ascension of Vladimir Vladimirovich Mayakovsky," where, striding through the heavens, which were "inexplicable" for Gogol, Mayakovsky "in sweeping steps crumples miles of streets" [versty ulits vzmak-

hami shagov mial]; "only the water towers are my interlocutors" [*odni vodokachki mne sobesedniki*]; "stomach grew before my eyes like in thousands of magnifying glasses" [*zhivot ros v glazakh, kak v tysachakh lup*]; "with a dormer window…the roofs caught what I threw in their ears" [*oknom slukhovym…lovili kryshi, chto broshu v ushi ia*]; "ladies rushed away from me like a rocket" [*dam'e ot menia raketoi sharakhalos'*]; "I would redeem all with my love" [*ia vsekh by v liubvi moei vykupal*]; "I kiss into you fiery lips of streetlights" [*v tebia vsteluiu ognennye guby fonarei'*]; "your name…is baked on a lip torn out by a shot" [*tvoe imia…zapeksheesia na vydrannoi iadrom gube*]. One recoils from these kisses that hit like a bullet in the mouth; as a result of which: "eyes on your face were dug out as two pits of graves" [*iamami dvukh mogil vyrylis' na tvoem litse glaza*]; or: "tearing from the meridians of the atlas of archways, the golden mouth of francs, dollars, rubles, crowns, marks rings" [*rvias' iz meridianov atlasa arok, zvenit zolotoi rot frankov, dollarov, rublei, kron, marok*]; "a legion of Galileos crawls along the stars in the eyes of telescopes" [*legion Galileev elozit po zvezdam v glaza teleskopov*]. The long poem "War and the World" is a hyperbole that bares its fangs at Gogol's hyperbole in order to swallow it and grow fat on its juices: "in all water-pipes oozed out a reddish brown slush" [*vo vsekh vodoprovodakh sochilas' ryzhaia zhizha*]. "Continents" hang like "carcasses on bayonets" [*tushami na shtykakh materiki*].

Gogol's hyperbole, which did not grow into an ox, evaporates into a steam of rhetoric after splitting into smeared, frogskin-like scraps. And then there is Mayakovsky, who inflates and roams and skips about the seven heavens, blinding us with the sparks from his horseshoe-hyperbole: "The day opened in such a way that Andersen's fairy tales crawled about at its feet like puppies"

[*Den' otkrylas' takoi, chto skazki Andersena shchenkami polzali u nego v nogakh*]; "gangs of cannons...on a forest glade...peacefully nibble the grass" [*pushek shaiki...na luzhaike...mirno shchipliut travu*]. That mocker of hyperbole, Prutkov, would faint, done in by a veritable cannon shot of hyperbole which has been reequipped to compose a new dithyramb. "Junker Schmidt" is not writing the doggerel—Prutkov himself wants to shoot himself with a revolver. What is he to do, when we take seriously both "of whom I yell" [*o kom oru ia*] and "quarterton Ludwigs" [*Liudoviki-desiatipudoviki*]; "brothel after brothel darted around like six-floored fauns in a dance" [*shestietazhnymi favnami rinulis' v pliaske publichnyi dom za publichnym domom*]; "covered like meat in down and cotton, cities crawl down to sweat on each other, shaking with the creak of beds" [*vyvalias' miasami v pukhe i vate, spolzutsia drug na druga potet' gorada, sodrogaia skripom krovatei*]; "burning from curiosity" before this picture "the stars' eyes crawl out of their orbits" [*vygoraia ot liubopytstva...zvezd glaza povylezali iz orbit*]; and suddenly: "from my right eye I pull out...a budding grove" [*iz pravogo glaza vynu...tsvetushchuiu roshcha*].

Flailing [*prutkami*] Prutkov to death with his hyperboles, Mayakovsky sticks his arm down to extract a "*grove*" from Gogol's eye—and up to that point rhetorical vacuity endeavored to fill itself in this eye with an ugly formlessness: "we summon with the call!" [*vozzovem zovom!*]. Now we heed the rhetoric: "with nails of words pounded into the paper" [*gvozdiami slov pribit k bumage*]; "hang your ears on the nail of attention" [*poves' ushi na gvozd' vnimaniia*], for both "the artillery citadel of the head can be destroyed by all artillery" [*vsemi artilleriiami gromimaia tsitadel' golovy*] and "noseless Taglioni in a ballet of skeletons" [*baleta skeletov beznosaia Tal'oni*] (the dance of Death) mark a rhetoric fiercely tamed and drilled for artistic effect: the rhetoric of the poster. Not in the use of hyperbole alone does Mayakovsky's language recall Gogol's. In stressing the importance of the sounds of words, which Gogol did not fully understand, Khlebnikov and the futurists rejected the pat division into archaisms and neologisms and claimed their right to create their own words, which make up the nervous system of the language; the nerve-wracking critic cannot pick out the nerve from this kind of word. In the studies of Wundt, Vossler, in the grammar of Lomonosov, in the lexical riches of Dahl, and not just in the articles of Iakubinsky, Brik, Tynianov, do we find the charter of liberty given to *"zaum"* [trans-rational language], which was introduced into prose in the nineteenth century by...Gogol. Materials for Dahl's dictionary reveal the distant future, for they show how any prefix may be attached to a word root, as well as any ending. Dahl's conclusions led to the realization that the true dictionary in language is the ear that directs the articulation of language.

Gogol was anticipating and putting into practice Dahl's dictionary when he used words like "u-*khlopotalsia*" (instead of "*za-*") [took pains] ("Marriage"), "s-*pestrit'sia*" (instead of "*za*") [become colorful], "is-*konfuzit*" [to embarrass], "ras-*svetliat*" [shine all over]. He took liberties in appending both prefixes and endings around a word root, anticipating...the futurists. Mayakovsky has the Gogolian expressions: "smashlilis' *glazki*" [eyes took on a shine], "*izlaskat*" [caress to death], "*okarkan*" [showered with croaking]. And we find what Iosif Mandelshtam calls the "Ukrainian" device of prefixing words with "*vy*," which was introduced into our language by Gogol. Gogol has "vy-*metnut' nogami*" [throw out his legs] ("The Enchanted Place"), "vy-*b'etsia serdtse*" [pounding heart out of the chest] ("The Terrible Vengeance"), "vy-*znachilas' priroda*" [nature appeared] (*Dead Souls*), "vy-*sidet' vraga*" [unseat the enemy] ("Taras Bulba"). Mayakovsky, who was no Ukrainian, is a great user of "*vy-*": "*vyzariu*" [I will shine forth], "*vyzhuiut*" [they will chew], "*vykosilas'*" [look out at], "*vyzolachivaite*" [turn gold], "*vyvertelsia*" [turned around], "*vypestrennyi*" [varicolored], "*vyfrantiv*" [all dressed up], "*vylaskat*" [caress], "*vyshchemit'*" [pinch], "*vyzlit'*" [anger], ad infinitum! Madame Gippius—oh, cover your powdered face in shame, you who prided yourself on *your* word, "*vyiavit*" [expose]; Mayakovsky and Gogol drown you out with their "*vyk's*" (the issue is not the word but the principle).

Gogol and Mayakovsky do the same with word endings. Gogol has "*oglokh*-lyi" [for *oglokhshii*, gone deaf], "*raznogolosnyi*" [for *raznogolosyi*, discordant] ("The Terrible Vengeance"), "*mord*-atyi" [for *mordastyi*, large-muzzled] (*Dead Souls*), "*rechivyi*" [for *rechistyi*, garrulous] ("Rome"), "*rogozh*-ennyi" [for *rogovoi*, horned] ("The Tale of How Ivan Ivanovich Quarreled with Ivan Nikiforovich"). Mayakovsky has "*losha*-zhii" [horse's], "*stodomyi*" [hundred-housed], "*masso*-miasyi" [masses of meat], "*liud'e*," "*dam'e*" [neologistic collective nouns for "people" and "women"], etc.

Mayakovsky plays around with verbs at will: "*sekundy* bystrilis*" [the seconds sped up], "razhzhuzhennyi *ulei*" [buzzing beehive] (from the verb "*razhzhuzhit'*"), "*okarkan*" [showered with croaking], "*skukozhit'sia*" [live a dull life]. This pattern follows Gogol, who has "*barklai-de-tol'evskoe*" [Barclay de Tolly-like] (*Dead Souls*), "*atuknut*" [attack], "*kustit'sia*" [grow side-shoots], "*shapkat'sia*" [be hat-like], "*obravnodushit*" [take courage], "*omnogoliudit*" [make crowded], "*obinostrannit*" [make foreign], "*omedvedit'*" [render bear-like], "*naimenit*" [name], etc.

Now here is a novelty: "*okaloshit'*" [to make galoshes-like]!

Just fifteen years ago Severianin was given an award for this galoshes business, to the chagrin of criticism's old maids. It is better to say *"ia tebia ulalakaiu"* [I will ooh-la-la you] (there is such a word—blush, Gornfel'ds!). One can say *"skhvativ palku, otpalkaiu palkoi"* [having grabbed my cane, I will cane you with my cane]; and this will be no bolder than word-sounds like *"ukha s finterleiami"* or *"Popopuz"* (Popopu-), *"Makogonenko"* (kovo-ko). In Gogol the nickname "squawks" through a "crow's mouth"; but the sunset itself comes crashing toward Mayakovsky, having "grown a fat belly by the dawn," guzzling a little tea.

Mayakovsky and Gogol made a racket over the heads of self-respecting writers, squawking loudly through their "crows' mouths"; Gogol had already sniffed out the "dogs" of *zaum'*. He did not "eat" them up whole. Mayakovsky, who devoured a "dog" from the table of *"dyr-bul-shchur"* that fed Kruchenykh, poured forth floods of the "distantish" [*dalekovatykh*] comparisons foreseen by Lomonosov.

However strange it may be, Vladimir Mayakovsky, having had a taste of *zaum'*, from across distant centuries knocks on the door of ancient traditions, presenting his visiting card to his forefather, Homer, on which is written the Homeric inscription: "curly-headed mage" [kudrogolovyi *volkhv*], "verse-fingered" [*strokoperstnyi*]. This antiquarian tendency, which Turgenev, of course, despised, unites him with Gogol, who has "two-oared" [*dvukhrul'nyi*] and "gray-forelocked," among other expressions that leap out of ages past. This futurist's and prefuturist's tribute to the great forefather depends on the colorful ability to harmonize according to the *rododaktylos*. Gogol's consonance with Mayakovsky is touching, as is Mayakovky's...with Gogol. Both hold their heads high, in order to see centuries ahead and centuries back. Both despise purist, prissy, peevish souls, semi-passéists and semi-modernists, "not so much fattened up on Homer, but not entirely thin either," like the Turgenevs, Dymovs, who, for whatever Zhirmunskification they might have undergone, failed to reach a stature as high as the belly button of those writers—lower, in fact.

—*translated by Christopher Colbath*

from THE DRAMATIC SYMPHONY, Part One

1. In the hall there was singing. A clean-shaven youth in a tail-
coat played the piano.

2. He jigged on the edge of his stool, with hands raised over
the keys, and elbows bearing the whole weight of his body.

3. This was the accepted thing.

4. A good-natured military man from the General Staff with
silver aiguillettes played the guitar, keeping time with his
soft, lacquered boots, nodding his graying head to right and
left.

5. So they pleasantly amused themselves. The Kingdom of
Heaven appeared to have come down to earth.

—translated by Roger and Angela Keys

from THE DRAMATIC SYMPHONY, Part Three

1. In the next room it was dark. This was where Varya was.

2. Her eyes streamed with tears. She was biting a tiny handkerchief.

3. She dropped the handkerchief onto the back of the armchair and went out into the garden.

4. And the handkerchief showed white on the back of the armchair, as if it were someone's face, ominous and deathly pale.

5. But nobody was there.

—translated by Roger and Angela Keys

from THE DRAMATIC SYMPHONY, Part Four

1. On that white day a certain person was talking to the old woman, Mertvago, and listening to the intimate songs of the snow-storm.

2. Through the window you could see the snow-covered courtyard, and hanging down from the edges of the roofs were gigantic icicles.

3. It was a person neither old, nor young, but *passive* and *knowing*, and in his conversation with the old woman he was expressing his dissatisfaction with the behavior of the Moscow mystics.

4. He said that disappointment awaited them, because they had chosen the false path.

5. Regretful and melancholy, he stared with clouded gaze at the pale snow twisting and whirling, as it hid the icicles from view.

6. He seemed to be saying to himself: "Well, there you are, Lord! They are *unable to see themselves!*"

7. But old woman Mertvago did not want to understand this intimate fairy-tale of his and advised him to make a complaint.

—translated by Roger and Angela Keys

VI VLADIMIR MAYAKOVSKY

(1893–1930)

*He would sit in a chair as though it were the saddle of
a motorcycle, bend forward, cut and rapidly swallow a Wiener
schnitzel, play cards with sidelong glances, not turning his head,
majestically stroll along the Kuznetsky, drone out, like bits of
the liturgy, dully and nasally, specially profound lines of his own
and others' verse: he scowled, grew, traveled, appeared in public,
and in a depth behind all this, as behind the upright stance of
a skater going at full speed, one perpetually glimpsed
the one day preceding all his days…*

—Boris Pasternak

*Mayakovsky revived Gogolian hyperbolism, taking it to a
higher level. Then later he set about squaring and cubing it.
Mayakovsky's "giant hyperbole" is a beast with no precedent.
Mayakovsky domesticated it. Not by chance does he admit:
"The most monstrous hyperbole…is tender."
Hyperbole is "the world's wet nurse."*

—Andrei Bely

from THE CLOUD IN TROUSERS

A TETRAPTYCH

Your thought,
musing on a sodden brain
like a boated lackey on a greasy couch,
I'll taunt with a bloody morsel of heart;
and satiate my insolent, caustic contempt.

No gray hairs streak my soul,
no grandfatherly fondness there!
I shake the world with the might of my voice,
and walk — handsome,
twentytwoyearold.

Tender souls!
You play your love on a fiddle,
and the crude club their love on a drum.
But you cannot turn yourselves inside out,
like me, and be just bare lips!

Come and be lessoned —
prim officiates of the angelic league,
lisping in drawing-room cambric.

You, too, who leaf your lips like a cook
turns the pages of a cookery book.

If you wish,
I shall rage on raw meat;

or, as the sky changes its hue,
if you wish,
I shall grow irreproachably tender:
not a man, but a cloud in trousers!

I deny the existence of blossoming Nice!
Again in song I glorify
men as crumpled as hospital beds,
and women as battered as proverbs.

[...]

—translated by Max Hayward and George Reavey

They Don't Understand a Thing

I walk into the barber's and whisper:
"Be so kind, comb my ears."
The smooth barber begins to grow pine needles, —
his face droops, like a pear.
"Red-haired idiot!
Nut!"
He tosses saliva, he yells, he squeals,
and for a lo-o-o-ong
time someone's head in a crowd
giggles
like an old radish.

—translated by Katie Farris and Ilya Kaminsky

from I, MYSELF

Bad habits

Summer. An amazing number of guests. Birthdays have accumulated. Father brags about my memory. For each birthday I have to learn a poem. I remember the one I learned especially for Dad's birthday:

> There was once a time before a crowd of
> Congeneric hills...

"Congeneric" irritated me. Who this was, I didn't know, but in life he never bothered introducing himself to me. Later, I found out that this was "poetic" and began to quietly detest it.

[...]

The first book

Some *Agafia of the Aviary*. If more books like this had come my way—would have stopped reading entirely. Thankfully, the second one was *Don Quixote*. Now that's a book! I made a wooden sword and some armor and attacked everything in sight.

[...]

1905

Other things to do than study. Got F's. Graduated to the fourth year only because my head got bashed in with a rock (got into a fight by the Rion)—on the makeup examinations they took pity on me. For me, the revolution started like this: My friend, the priest's cook, Isidor, jumped from joy, barefoot onto the stove—they'd killed General Alihanov. Georgia's "pacifier." Protests and mutinies began. I also went. Good. Absorb it chromatically—the anarchists in black, the Socialist-Revolutionaries in red, the Social Democrats in blue, the federalists in all the other colors.

1906

Father died. Pricked his finger (sewing book bindings). Blood poisoning. Since then can't stand pins. Prosperity ended. After Father's funeral with had three rubles. Feverishly and instinctively sold all of our tables and chairs. Moved toward Moscow. Why? We didn't know anyone there.

[...]

11 months of Butyrki

(a Moscow prison)

The most important time for me. After three years of theory and its practical application—I threw myself into literature.

Read all the newest stuff. Symbolists—Bely, Balmont. Piqued by innovations in form. But it was foreign to me. Themes, images not from my own life. Tried to write as well, but about other things—impossible. It turned out maudlin and trite. Something like:

> In gold and purple the forests were dressed,
> The sun on the church tops played

I awaited: but days got lost in months.
Hundreds of languishing days.

Filled a whole notebook with this sort of thing. A thank-you to the guards—they took it away at my release. Otherwise I would have published it! Having read all the contemporaries, I collapsed onto the classics. Byron, Shakespeare, Tolstoy. The last book—*Anna Karenina*. Didn't finish it. They called me at night and told me to gather my things. Still don't know what ended up happening to those Karenins. I was released. Was supposed to (according to the secret police) do three years in Truchansk. My father's friend, Mahmudbekov, interceded for me in Karlov.

While doing time, I was tried for the first offense—guilty, but I was a minor. Released under police surveillance and parental supervision.

This so-called dilemma

All worked up when released. Those whom I'd read are so-called greats. But it's not at all hard to write better than them. I already have the right attitude toward life. I just need experience in art. Where do I get it? I'm completely ignorant. I need to go through serious schooling. And I'd been expelled from high school, even from Stroganovsky. If I were to remain in the Party—I'd have to become an outlaw. As an outlaw, it seemed to me, I wouldn't be able to complete my studies. Perspective—spend my whole life writing leaflets, laying out thoughts from books that were correct, but not my own inventions. If one were to shake out of me everything I'd read, what would be left? Marxist method. But did this weapon not fall into a child's hands? It's easy to handle when equipped only with your own thoughts. But what do you do when confronted with an enemy? Since, after all, I can't actually write better than Bely. He knew how to get his jollies— "I sent a pineapple up into the sky," as I'm whining— "a hundred languishing days." The other Party members are lucky. They at least had university. (I held higher education—I didn't know what it was yet—in high regard back then!) What contrast could I create to the old aesthetic that was burying me? Wouldn't the revolution demand serious schooling? I dropped by Medvedev's, a friend from the Party. Want to make Socialist art. Seriozha laughed for a long time: "You haven't got the guts."

I think that he underrated my guts.

I ended Party work. Sat down to my studies.

Beginning of mastery

Thought—I can't write poetry. My attempts were pitiful. Began painting. Studied with Zhukovsky. Painted little silver tea sets with some ladies. After a year, figured out I was making handicrafts. Went to Kelin. Realist. A good draftsman. Best teacher. Firm. Adjusting.

Requirement— mastery, Holbein. Had no patience for prettiness.

Respected the work of poet Sasha Chornoy. Happy with the anti-aestheticism.

The last school

Got into the School of Painting, Sculpture, and Architecture: the only place that accepted you without a certificate of good conduct. Worked well.

Surprised: imitators were encouraged and innovators were bullied. My revolutionary instinct put me behind the bullied ones.

David Burliuk

Burliuk appeared at the school. Had an arrogant air about him. Lorgnette. Frock coat. Walks around humming. I began picking on him. We almost came to blows.

In the smoking room

Social event. Concert. Rachmaninov. *Isle of the Dead*. Ditched it because of the unbearably melodic boredom. A minute later so did Burliuk. We both had a good laugh about it. We left to go for a walk together.

Memorable night

A conversation. From the Rachmaninov boredom, we went on to academic boredom, and then from academic boredom to all the other classic boredoms. David has the anger of a master that has surpassed his contemporaries, I have the pathos of a Socialist, knowing the inevitability of the collapse of old ways. Russian Futurism was born.

Next

I made a poem during that day. That is—fragments. Bad ones. Published nowhere. Night. Sretensky Boulevard. Read lines of it to Burliuk, adding that they were from a friend of mine. David stopped. Looked me over. Barked: "But you wrote this yourself.

You are a genius." Applying such a grandiose and undeserved epithet to me made me giddy. I immersed myself fully in poetry. That evening, completely unexpectedly, I became a poet.

Burliuk's strangeness

Already that morning. Burliuk, introducing me to someone, announced: "You don't know? My brilliant friend. The famous poet Mayakovsky." I gave him a shove, but Burliuk was undeterred. He even growled at me, taking a step back: "Now write. Otherwise you're going to make me look bad."

Thus daily

Had to write. And I wrote my first one (my first professional, printable one) — "Red and White," as well as others.

[…]

Things get going

Exhibits of "Jack of Diamonds." Disputes. Impassioned speeches, mine and David's. Newspapers began to fill up with Futurism. The tone wasn't all too polite. For example, they simply called me a "Son of a Bitch."

The yellow blouse

I never had any suits. Had two blouses — hideous things. There's a tried-and-true method to sprucing up any outfit — a tie. No money. Took a yellow ribbon from my sister. Tied it around myself. A huge to-do. Therefore, the most noticeable and beautiful thing about a person is…a tie. Apparently, the bigger the tie, the bigger the to-do. And, as the size of a tie has its limitations, I went about things with some cunning — I made a shirt out of ties, and a tie out of shirts.

The impression it made was irresistible.

Naturally

The board was getting indignant. Count Lvov, the director of the Institute. Suggested we stop the criticism and agitation. Refused. Council of "artists" expelled us from the school.

[…]

Called up

Drafted. Now I don't want to go to the front. Pretended to be a draftsman. Learning at night from some engineer how to draft autos. With printing, things are even worse. Soldiers are forbidden to publish. Only Brik makes me happy. Buys all my poems at 50 kopeks a line. Printed "Backbone Flute" and *Cloud*. *Cloud* came out very wispy. The censors blew on it. About six pages' worth of dotted lines.

Since then, I've despised dotted lines. And commas too.

October

To accept or not to accept? This question didn't exist for me or for the other Moscow Futurists. My revolution. Went to the Smolni Institute. Worked on anything that came my way.

—translated by Katya Apekina

from How Are Verses Made?

[. . .]

I walk along, waving my arms and mumbling almost wordlessly, now shortening my steps so as not to interrupt my mumbling, now mumbling more rapidly in time with my steps. So the rhythm is trimmed and takes shape—and rhythm is the basis for any poetic work, resounding through the whole thing. Gradually, individual words begin to ease themselves free of this dull roar.

Several words just jump away and never come back, others hold on, wriggle and squirm a dozen times over, until you can't imagine how any word will ever stay in its place (this sensation, developing with experience, is called talent). More often than not the most important word emerges first: the word that most completely conveys the meaning of the poem, or the word that underlies the rhyme. The other words come forward and take up dependent positions in relation to the most important word. When the fundamentals are already there, one has a sudden sensation that the rhythm is strained: there's some little syllable or sound missing. You begin to shape all the words anew, and the work drives you to distraction. It's like having a tooth crowned. A hundred times (or so it seems) the dentist tries a crown on the tooth, and it's the wrong size; but at last, after a hundred attempts, he presses one down, and it fits. The analogy is all the more aposite in my case, because when at last the crown fits, I (quite literally) have tears in my eyes, from pain and relief.

Where this basic dull roar of a rhythm comes from is a mystery. In my case it's all kinds of repetitions in my mind of noises, rocking motions, or in fact of any phenomena with which I can associate a sound. The sound of the sea, endlessly repeated, can provide my rhythm, or a servant who slams the door every morning, recurring and intertwining with itself, trailing through my consciousness; or even the rotation of the earth, which in my case, as in a shop of visual aids, gives way to and inextricably connects with the whistle of a high wind.

This struggle to organize movement, to organize sounds around oneself, discovering their own proper nature, their peculiarities, is one of the most important constants of the work of the poet: laying in rhythmic supplies. I don't know if the rhythm exists outside me or only inside me — more probably inside. But there must be a jolt, to awaken it; in the same way as the sound of a violin, any violin, provokes a buzz in the guts of the piano, in the same way as a bridge sways to and fro and threatens to collapse under the synchronized tread of ants.

Rhythm is the fundamental force, the fundamental energy of verse. You can't explain it, you can only talk about it as you do about magnetism or electricity. The rhythm can be the same in a lot of poems, even in the whole oeuvre of the poet, and still not make the work monotonous, because a rhythm can be so complex, so intricately shaped, that even several long poems won't exhaust its possibilities.

[. . .]

—*translated by G. M. Hyde*

from V. V. KHLEBNIKOV

[...]

Khlebnikov's poetical fame is immeasurably less than his significance.

For every hundred readers, fifty considered him simply a graphomaniac, forty read him for pleasure and were astonished that they found none, and only ten (futurist poets and philologists of the "OPOYAZ" [Society for the Study of Poetic Language]) knew and loved this Columbus, this discoverer of new poetic continents that we now populate and cultivate. Khlebnikov is not a poet for consumers—they can't read him. Khlebnikov is a poet for producers. Khlebnikov never completed any extensive and finished poetic works. The apparent finished state of his published pieces is most often the work of his friends' hands. We chose from the pile of his discarded notebooks those that seemed most valuable to us and we published them. Often the tail of one draft was pasted to an extraneous head, to Khlebnikov's cheerful astonishment. You couldn't let him have anything to do with proofs: he would cross out everything completely and give you an entirely new text.

When bringing something in for publication, Khlebnikov usually remarked, "If something isn't right, change it." When he recited his poems he would sometimes break off in the middle of a sentence and indicate simply "et cetera."

In this "etc." is the whole of Khlebnikov: he posed a poetic task, provided the means for its solution, but the use of this solution for practical purposes, this he left to others.

The story of Khlebnikov's life is worthy of his brilliant literary constructions; it is an example to real poets and a reproach to hacks.

What about Khlebnikov and poetic language?

For the so-called new poetry (our latest), and especially for the symbolists, the word is the raw material for the writing of verses (expressions of feelings and thoughts)—a raw material, the texture, resistance, and treatment of which was unknown. This raw material the new poets dealt with intuitively, first in one poem and then in another. The alliterative accidents of similar-sounding words were taken to be an internal cohesion, and to signify an unbreakable relationship. The established form of a word was considered to be permanent and some poets tried to fit it over things that went far beyond the verbal material itself.

For Khlebnikov, the word is an independent force which organizes the raw material of thoughts and feelings. Hence the delving into roots, into the source of the word, into the time when the name corresponded to things—when there were only ten root words, but new words appeared as case modifications of the root (declension of the root, according to Khlebnikov). For example, *byk* ("bull")—that which hits—*byot; bok* ("side")—the place *where* it hits. Or *lys* ("bald")—that which the forest (*les*) becomes; *los* ("elk"), *lis* ("fox")—those who live in the forest. Take Khlebnikov's lines

Lesa lysy.
Lesa obezlosili. Lesa obezlisili.

(The forests are bald/bare.
The forests are elkless. The forests are foxless.)

These lines may not be broken apart. They are an iron chain.

⟶

The word as we think of it now is a completely arbitrary thing useful for practical purposes. But a word in its proper poetic function must express a wide variety of nuances of meaning. Khlebnikov created an entire "periodic table of the word." Taking the word in its undeveloped unfamiliar forms, comparing these with the developed word, he demonstrated the necessity and inevitability of the emergence of new words.

If the existing word *plyas* ("dance") has a derivative *plyasunya* ("dancer"), then the growth of aviation, of "flying (*lyot*), ought by analogy to yield the form *letunya* ("flier"). And if the day of christening is *krestiny*, then the day of flying is, of course, *letiny*. There is, of course, no trace here of cheap Slavophile slapping together of roots. It is not important that the word *letunya* is for the present neither necessary nor established in usage. Khlebnikov is simply revealing the process of word formation.

Khlebnikov, however, is a master of verse.

I've already said that Khlebnikov did not have any finished compositions. In his last piece, *Zangezi*, for example, you clearly feel that two different variants have been published together. But in studying Khlebnikov you must take into account fragments of poems that contribute to the solution of poetic problems.

In all Khlebnikov's things you are struck by his unprecedented skill. He could not only quickly write a poem upon request (his mind worked on poetry twenty-four hours a day), but he could also give things the most unusual form. He wrote a very long poem, for instance, that's simply a palindrome; it may just as easily be read from right to left as from left to right:

Koni Topot. Inok.
No ne rech, a cheren on.

(Horses, Clapping, Monk.
But no speech, black he is.)

This, of course, is just a deliberate trick, the result of an excess of poetic inventiveness. But Khlebnikov was very little interested in trickery: he made things neither for self-display nor for the market.

Philological work brought Khlebnikov to a kind of poetry that develops a lyrical theme through variations on the root of a single word.

His best known poem, *Zaklyatie smekhom* ("Incantation by Laughter"), published in 1909, is a favorite of poets, innovators, and parodists, and of critics too:

O, zasmeytes, smekhachi,
Chto smeyutsya smekhami,
Chto smeyanstvuyut smeyalno,
O, issmeysya rassmeyalno smekh
Usmeynykh, smeyachey...

(O laugh it up you laughletes!...
That laugh with laughs.
That laugherize laughily.
O laugh it out so laughily...the laugh
Of laughish laugherators.)

Here the one word *smekh* ("laughter") yields *smeyevo*, the "country of laughter," and the sly *smeyunchiki* ("laughers"), and *smekhachi* (perhaps "laughletes")—by analogy with *silachi* ("athletes").

In comparison with Khlebnikov how verbally wretched is Balmont when he attempts to construct a poem using only the word *lyubit* ("to love"):

> Lyubite, lyubite, lyubite, lyubite,
> Bezumno lyubite, lyubite lyubov.
>
> (Love, love, love, love
> Madly love love itself.)

This is mere tautology. Mere word poverty. And this is offered as a complete definition of love! Khlebnikov once submitted for publication six pages of derivations of the root *lyub* ("love"). It couldn't be published because the provincial typographer didn't have enough of the letter "l."

—

One other thing. I intentionally omit mention of those immense works of historical fantasy that Khlebnikov wrote, since their foundation is—poetry itself.

But what of Khlebnikov's life?

His own words describe that life better than anything else:

> Segodnya snova ya poydu
> Tuda — na zhizn, na torg, na rynok,
> I voysko pesen povedu
> S priboem rynka v poedinok.

(Today again I will go there —
Into the marketplace, to life,
And a troop of songs I will lead
In single combat with the market's roar.)

I knew Khlebnikov for twelve years. He came to Moscow often, and then, except for the last days, we met daily. Khlebnikov's work never failed to amaze me. His empty room was always heaped with notebooks, paper, and scraps filled up with his minute handwriting. If there hadn't happened to occur, by chance, a publication at about this time of a collection of his pieces, and if someone had not extracted from the pile of manuscripts some publishable pages, then surely very much would have been lost. For Khlebnikov when he traveled stuffed his pillowcase with manuscripts, used them for a pillow, and then promptly lost the pillow.

Khlebnikov traveled often. The reason for these travels and their duration no one could ever hope to understand. Three years ago, after a great deal of difficulty, I succeeded in arranging a paying publication of some of his pieces (Khlebnikov had given me a rather large sheaf of confused manuscripts chosen in Prague by Jakobson, who had written a singularly excellent work on Khlebnikov). On the evening of the day we had told Khlebnikov that permission would be granted and money received, I met him on Theatrical Square. He was carrying a small suitcase.

"Where are you going?"

"South. It's spring!" and he left.

He left riding the roof of a railway coach. He was gone two years. He retreated and attacked with our army in Persia, caught typhus several times, and then last winter returned again, this time in a coach for epileptics, exhausted and ragged, wearing nothing but a hospital robe.

He brought back with him not a single line. Of what he wrote during this period I know only the poem about hunger that was published in some Crimean newspaper, and two astonishing handwritten books, *Harmonious World (Ladomir)* and *A Scratch in the Clouds (Tsarapina po nebu)*, which he had sent on earlier. *Harmonious World* was submitted to the State Publishing House, but it never succeeded in being published. Could Khlebnikov ever have beaten that wall down with his head? In practical matters Khlebnikov was an altogether disorganized person. He published not a single line on his own initiative. In his eulogy to Khlebnikov, Gorodetsky virtually attributes organizational talent to the poet: the creation of futurism, the publication of *A Slap in the Face of Public Taste (Poshchechina obshchestvennomu vkusu)*, and so forth. This is completely false. Both *The Fishpond of Judges (Sadok sudey)*, in which appeared Khlebnikov's first poems, and the *Slap* were organized by David Burliuk. In order to involve Khlebnikov in anything you almost had to catch him with a snare. Of course, impracticality is detestable if it is the whim of a rich man, but with Khlebnikov, who hardly owned even his trousers, this indifference to his own advantage took on the character of genuine asceticism, a kind of martyrdom in the name of the poetic idea.

All who knew him loved Khlebnikov. But this was the love of the strong for a strong, extremely well-educated, and witty poet. He had no one of his own capable of caring for him. When he was ill he became very demanding and suspicious of people who did not give him their full attention. A sharp phrase, accidentally uttered without any reference to him, might be exaggerated and understood as disparagement of his poetry or disregard of him personally.

In the name of preserving a just literary perspective, I consider it my certain duty to publish in my own name and, I do not doubt, in the name of my friends the poets Aseev, Burliuk, Kruchonykh, Kamensky, and Pasternak, the statement that we considered and do consider him one of our masters in the art of poetry, and a most magnificent knight in our poetic battles.

After Khlebnikov's death, there appeared in various journals and newspapers articles about him full of sympathy and understanding. I have read these articles with disgust. When will this comedy of posthumous kindness end? Where were those writers when Khlebnikov, abused by his critics, wandered about Russia alive? I know some still living who may not be his equals, but are neglected as much as he was.

Let us finally drop this reverence for hundred-year anniversaries, this honoring of posthumous publications! Let us have articles about the living! Let us have bread for the living! Let us have paper for the living!

— *translated by Judson Rosengrant*

VII VELIMIR KHLEBNIKOV

(1885–1922)

> Khlebnikov thought of language as a state, not in space,
> not in terms of geography, but rather, in time... Khlebnikov
> doesn't know what it means to be a contemporary. He is
> a citizen of the whole history, the whole system of
> language and poetry... Khlebnikov's poetry is idiotic,
> in its original, Greek, inoffensive meaning.
>
> —OSIP MANDELSTAM

> Khlebnikov's poetical fame is immeasurably less than his
> significance. For every hundred readers, fifty considered him
> simply a graphomaniac, forty read him for pleasure and were
> astonished that they found none, and only ten (futurist poets and
> philologists...) knew and loved this Columbus, this discoverer
> of new poetic continents that we now populate and cultivate.
> Khlebnikov is not a poet for consumers—they can't read him.
> Khlebnikov is a poet for producers.
>
> —VLADIMIR MAYAKOVSKY

Incantation by Laughter

Hlaha! Uthlofan, lauflings!
Hlaha! Ufhlofan, lauflings!
Who lawghen with lafe, who hlaegen lewchly,
Hlahla! Ufhlofan hlouly!
Hlaha! Hloufish lauflings lafe uf beloght lauchalorum!
Hlaha! Loufenish lauflings lafe, hlohan utlaufly!
Lawfen, lawfen,
Hloh, hlouh, hlou! Luifekin, luifekin,
Hlofeningum, hlofeningum.
Hlaha! Uthlofan, lauflings!
Hlaha! Uflofan, lauflings!

—*translated by Paul Schmidt*

THE SOLO ACTOR

While Akhmatova wept and her poems poured out over
    Tsarskoe Selo,
I unwound the enchantress' thread
and dragged myself like a drowsy corpse through a desert
where all about me impossibility lay dying:
a worn-out actor, a face-faker,
looking for a break in the wall.
But meanwhile in dark caves
the curly head of that subterranean bull
kept up its chomping, devouring men
in the smoke of insolent threats.
And wrapped in the moon's inclination
like the lated traveler in his drowsy cloak,
in dreams I leapt upon the precipice
and moved from cliff to cliff.
I moved like a blind man, until
Freedom's wind directed me,
beat me with slanting rain.
And I cut the bull's head from the hulking meat and the
    bones,
and set it upon the wall.
Like a fighter for the truth I shook it in the world's face:
Here it is! Look!
Here is that curly head the crowd once blazed for!
And with horror
I understood — no one could see me.

I would have to sow eyes.
My task was to be a sower of eyes!

—translated by Paul Schmidt

[RUSSIA, I GIVE YOU MY DIVINE...]

Russia, I give you my divine
white brain. Be me. Be Khlebnikov.
I have sunk a foundation deep in the minds
of your people, I have laid down an axis.
I have built a house on a firm foundation.
"We are Futurians."

—translated by Paul Schmidt

[THAT YOU MADE US MORTAL...]

That you made us mortal,
suit yourselves, gods.
Now we'll shoot at you
a poisoned arrow of sorrow.
We have a bow.

—*translated by Valzhyna Mort*

[ROAST MOUSE...]

Roast mouse.
Their son fixed it, went and
caught them in the field.
They lie stretched out on the table,
their long dark tails.
Today it's a decent dinner,
a real good meal!
Just a while back the housewife would shudder
and holler, smash the pitcher to smithereens
if she found a mouse drowned in the cream.
But now, how silent and peaceful.
Dead mice for dinner
stretched out on the table,
dangling dark tails.

—translated by Paul Schmidt

[THE LICE HAD BLIND FAITH, AND THEY PRAYED TO ME...]

The lice had blind faith, and they prayed to me.
Every morning they would congregate on my clothes,
every morning I visited punishment upon them
and listened to them crackle and die.

But they kept on returning again and again
in a quiet worshipful wave.

—translated by Paul Schmidt

from ON POETRY

People say a poem must be understandable. Like a sign on the street, which carries the clear and simple words "For Sale." But a street sign is not exactly a poem. Though it is understandable. On the other hand, what about spells and incantations, what we call magic words, the sacred language of paganism, words like "shagadam, magadam, vigadam, pitz, patz, patzu"—they are rows of mere syllables that the intellect can make no sense of, and they form a kind of beyonsense language in folk speech. Nevertheless an enormous power over mankind is attributed to these incomprehensible words and magic spells, and direct influence upon the fate of man. They contain powerful magic. They claim the power of controlling good and evil and swaying the hearts of lovers. The prayers of many nations are written in a language incomprehensible to those who pray. Does a Hindu understand the Vedas? Russians do not understand Old Church Slavonic. Neither do Poles and Czechs understand Latin. But a prayer written in Latin works just as powerfully as the sign in the street. In the same way, the language of magic spells and incantations rejects judgments made by everyday common sense.

Its strange wisdom may be broken down into the truths contained in separate sounds: *sh, m, v,* etc. We do not yet understand these sounds. We confess that honestly. But there is no doubt that these sound sequences constitute a series of universal truths passing before the predawn of our soul. If we think of the soul as split between the government of intellect and a stormy population of feelings, then incantations and beyonsense language are appeals over the head of the government straight to the population of feelings, a direct cry to the predawn of the soul or a supreme example of the rule of the masses in the life of language and intellect, a lawful device reserved for rare occasions. Another example: Sophia Kovalevskaia owes her talent for mathematics, as she herself makes clear in her memoirs, to the fact that the walls of her nursery were covered with unusual wallpaper—pages of her uncle's book on advanced algebra. We must acknowledge that the world of mathematics is a restricted area as far as the feminine half of humanity is concerned. Kovalevskaia is one of the few mortals who has entered that world. Could a child of seven really have understood those symbols—equal signs, powers, brackets—all the magic marks of sums and subtractions? Of course not; nevertheless they exercised a decisive influence on her life, and it was under the influence of the childhood wallpaper that she became a famous mathematrix.

Similarly, the magic in a word remains magic even if it is not understood, and loses none of its power. Poems may be understandable or they may not, but they must be good, they must be real.

From the examples of the algebraic signs on the walls of Kovalevskaia's nursery that had such a decisive influence on the child's fate, and from the example of spells, it is clear that we cannot demand of all language: "be easy to understand, like the sign in the street." The speech of higher intelligence, even when it is not understandable, falls like seed into the fertile soil of the spirit and only much later, in mysterious ways, does it bring forth its shoots. Does the earth understand the writing of the seeds a farmer scatters on its surface? No. But the grain still ripens in autumn, in response to those seeds. In any case, I certainly do not maintain that every incomprehensible piece of writing is beautiful. I mean only that we must not reject a piece of writing simply because it is incomprehensible to a particular group of readers. The claim has been made that poems about labor can be created only by people who work in factories. Is this true? Isn't the nature of a poem to be found in its withdrawal from itself, from its point of contact with everyday reality? Is a poem not a light from the *I*? A poem is related to flight; in the shortest time possible its language must cover the greatest distance in images and thoughts.

[...]

There is no place to escape from the self. Inspiration always deludes itself about the poet's background. Medieval knights wrote about rustic shepherds, Lord Byron about pirates, Buddha was a king's son who wrote in praise of poverty. Or the other way around: Shakespeare was convicted of theft but wrote in the language of kings, as did Goethe, the son of a modest burgher, and their writing is devoted to portrayals of court life. The tundras of the Pechersky region have never known warfare, yet there they preserve epic songs about Vladimir and his hero knights that have long since been forgotten in the Dnieper. If we consider artistic creativity as the greatest possible deviation of the string of thought from the axis of the creator's life, as a flight from the self, then we have good reason for believing that even poems about an assembly line will be written not by someone who works on an assembly line, but by someone from beyond the factory walls. It's always the other way around: once he withdraws from the assembly line, stretching the string of his soul to the fullest length, the assembly-line poet will either pass into the world of scientific imagery, of strange scientific visions, into the future of Planet Earth, like Gastev, or into the world of basic human values, like Alexandrovsky, into the subtle life of the heart.

—translated by Paul Schmidt

from A SLAP IN THE FACE OF PUBLIC TASTE

written with David Burliuk, Aleksei Kruchenykh, and Vladimir Mayakovsky

To the Readers of our First New Unexpected.

We alone are the *face* of *our* time. Through us the horn of time blows through the art of the word.

The past is too tight. The Academy and Pushkin are less intelligible than hieroglyphics.

Throw Pushkin, Dostoyevsky, Tolstoy, etc., etc., overboard from the Ship of Modernity.

[...]

From the heights of skyscrapers we gaze down at their insignificance!

We order that poets' rights be preserved!

1. To enlarge the *scope* of the poet's vocabulary with arbitrary and derivative words (word-novelty).
2. To feel an insurmountable hatred for the language existing before their time.
3. To push with horror off their proud brow the Wreath of cheap fame you have made from bathhouse switches.
4. To stand on the rock of the word "we" amidst the sea of boos and outrage.

And if *for the time being* the filthy slogans of your "Common sense" and "good taste" are still present in our lines, these same lines *for the first time* already glimmer with the Summer Lightning of the New Coming Beauty of the Self-sufficient (self-centered) Word.

—*translated by Anna Lawton and Herbert Eagle*

[LET THEM READ ON MY GRAVESTONE...]

Let them read on my gravestone: He wrestled with the notion of species and freed himself from its hold. He saw no distinction between human and animal species and stood for the extension to the noble animal species of the commandment and its directive: "Love thy neighbor as thyself." He called the indivisible noble animal species his "neighbors," and would point out the advantage of utilizing experiences from the past life of the most ancient species. So he supposed that it would benefit the human race to introduce into human behavior something like the system of worker bees in a hive, and he often emphasized that he saw in the concept of worker bees his own personal ideal. He raised high the banner of Galilean love, and the shadow of that banner fell on many a noble animal species. The heart, the real meat of the contemporary impulse forward of human societies, he saw not in the princely individual, but in the prince-tissue: the princely lump of human tissue confined in the calcium box of the skull. He was inspired to dream of being a prophet and a great interpreter of the prince-tissue, and of that alone. Divining its will, with a single impulse of his own flesh, blood, and bone, he dreamed of increasing the ratio ε/ρ, where ε equals the mass of prince-tissue and ρ equals the mass of peasant-tissue, as far as he personally was concerned. He dreamed of the distant future, of the earthball of the future, and his dreams were inspired when he compared the earth to a little animal of the steppe, darting from bush to bush. He discovered the true classification of the sciences, he linked time and space, he established a geometry of numbers. He discovered the Slav principle. He founded an institute for the study of the prenatal life of the child. He discovered the microbe that causes progressive paralysis. He linked and explained the fundamentals of chemistry in space. Enough, let a page be devoted to him, and indeed not one alone.

He was such a child he imagined that six came after five, and seven after six. He used even to dare think that as a general rule wherever we have one and then one more, we also have three, and five, and seven, and infinity — ∞.

Of course, he never thrust his opinion on anyone else, he considered it belonged to him personally, and he recognized that the most sacred and holiest of all rights was to be able to hold a contrary opinion.

On the five-and-more senses.

Five aspects, there are five of them, but that's not enough. Why not simply say: there is only one, but a great one?

Pattern of points, when will you fill up the white spaces, when will you populate the vacant slots?

There is a certain muchness, a manifold with an unspecified number of dimensions incessantly altering its shape, which in relation to our five senses stands in the same position as a continuous two-dimensional space stands in relation to a triangle, a circle, an ovoid, a rectangle.

That is, just as a triangle, a circle, an octagon are parts of a plane, so our senses of hearing, seeing, taste, and smell are parts, accidental lapses of this one great, extended manifold.

It has raised its lion's head and looks at us, but its mouth is sealed.

Furthermore, just as by the continuous alteration of a circle one may obtain a triangle, and the triangle may be continually altered to form an octagon, and just as from a sphere in three-dimensional space through continuous variation one can obtain an egg, an apple, a horn, a barrel, just so there exist certain quantities, independent variables, which as they change transform the senses of the various classes—for example, sound and sight or smell—one into the other.

Thus by changing certain existing values, the blue color of a cornflower (I mean the pure sensation as such) can be continuously varied through areas of disjunction we humans are unaware of and be transformed into the sound of a cuckoo's call or a child's crying; it *becomes* them.

During this process of continuous variation, it forms a certain one-dimensional manifold, all of whose points, except those close to the first and last, belong to a region of unknown sensations, as if they come from another world.

Surely such a manifold has at least once illuminated the mind of a dying man, flashing like a lightning bolt that links two swollen clouds, linking two orders of experience in the inflamed consciousness of a diseased brain.

Perhaps at the moment just before death, when all is haste, when everything in fear and panic abandons itself to flight, rushes headlong, leaps all barriers, abandons hope of saving the whole, the sum total of many personal lives, and is concerned for itself alone, when what happens in a man's head resembles what happens in a city inundated by hungry waves of molten lava, perhaps at that moment just before death in a terrifying rush in every human head there occurs just such a filling up of gaps and ditches, such destruction of forms and fixed boundaries. And perhaps in every human consciousness, in just such a terrifying rush, a sensation that belongs to one order, A, is transformed into a sensation of a different order, B, and only then, after it has become B, does that sensation slow down and become graspable, the way we can distinguish the spokes of a wheel only when the speed of its revolution drops below a certain limit. The speeds at which the sensations move across that unknown space are selected in such a way that the sensations most closely connected, positively or negatively, with the safety of the whole being move most slowly, and may thus be examined with precision, in the greatest detail. Those sensations which have the least to do with matters of survival pass more rapidly and the consciousness is unable to dwell upon them.

— translated by Paul Schmidt

VIII ANNA AKHMATOVA

(1899–1966)

*When in the first poem of her first book, the young Akhmatova
conveys the confusion of love in the lines: 'I drew my left hand
glove / Onto my right hand —' she conveys at one blow all
feminine and all lyric confusion (all the confusion of the
empirical!), immortalizing with one flourish of the pen that
ancient nervous gesture of woman and of poet who at life's great
moments forget right and left—not only of glove, but of hand, and
of country of the world, suddenly losing all their certainty. Through
a patient and even penetrating precision of detail, something
bigger than an emotional state is affirmed and symbolized—a
whole structure of the mind...The woman, the whole poet is in
these two lines; the whole Akhmatova, unique,
unrepeatable, inimitable...*

—MARINA TSVETAEVA

*Akhmatova transformed you into Homo sapiens with just the tone
of her voice or the turn of her head...In conversation with her, or
simply drinking tea or vodka with her, you became a Christian, a
human being in the Christian sense of that word, faster than by
reading the appropriate texts or attending church. The poet's
role in society largely comes down to just this.*

—JOSEPH BRODSKY

[HE LIKED THREE THINGS ...]

He liked three things:
white peacocks, evensong,
and washed-out maps of America.

He didn't like it when children cried.
He didn't like raspberry jam with tea,
and women's hysterics.

...And I was his wife.

—translated by Valzhyna Mort

from Wild Honey Is a Smell of Freedom

Wild honey has a scent — of freedom.
Dust — a scent of sunshine.
And a girl's mouth — of violets.

But gold — nothing.
Water — like mignonette.
And like apple — love.
But we have learned that

blood smells only of blood.

— translated by Ilya Kaminsky and Katie Farris

On the Road

Though this land is not my own
I will never forget it,
or the waters of its ocean,
fresh and delicately icy.

Sand on the bottom is whiter than chalk,
and the air drunk, like wine.
Late sun lays bare
the rosy limbs of the pine trees.

And the sun goes down in waves of ether
in such a way that I can't tell
if the day is ending, or the world,
or if the secret of secrets is within me again.

—translated by Jane Kenyon with Vera Sandomirsk

VORONEZH

—for Osip Mandelstam

Before me stands a frozen town,
glass walls, glass trees, glass snow.
Into this glass I hesitantly step.
The painted sleigh is skidding in the snow.
Above me, over Voronezh — crows,
and poplars. And the sky is sea green,
washed, blurry, all in sun-dust.
And the old battle of Kulikovo still
swells the hills of this triumphant land.
Above our heads, poplars chime
as if with cups raised to our jubilation
by a thousand guests at some wedding.

But in the room of the banished poet
fear and the muse stand watch by turn,
and the night that knows no dawn
is nearing.

—a version by Ilya Kaminsky, Katie Farris, and Valzhyna Mort

When a Man Dies, His Portraits Change

When a man dies,
his portraits change.
Different eyes stare at us, lips
stir in a stranger's smile.
I noticed this, returning
from a funeral of a poet.
Since then I often checked it,
and my theory has been confirmed.

—translated by Katie Farris and Ilya Kaminsky

from REQUIEM, 1935–1940

> No foreign sky protected me,
> no stranger's wing shielded my face.
> I stand as witness to the common lot,
> survivor of that time, that place.

—1961

Instead of a preface

In the terrible years of the Yezhov terror I spent seventeen months waiting in line outside the prison in Leningrad. One day somebody in the crowd identified me. Standing behind me was a woman, with lips blue from the cold, who had, of course, never heard me called by name before. Now she started out of the torpor common to us all and asked me in a whisper (everyone whispered there):

"Can you describe this?"

And I said: "I can."

Then something like a smile passed fleetingly over what had once been her face.

—*translated by Stanley Kunitz with Max Hayward*

PUSHKIN'S *Stone Guest*

I

As is well known, Pushkin was revered by his contemporaries in the early period of his literary career (when *The Prisoner of the Caucasus, The Fountain of Bakhchisaray*, and the early lyrics came out); his literary career developed quickly and brilliantly. And then, sometime around 1830, the readers and critics forsook Pushkin. The reason for this lies first and foremost in Pushkin himself. He had changed. Instead of *The Prisoner of the Caucasus*, he was writing *The Little House in Kolomna*, instead of *The Fountain of Bakhchisaray—The Little Tragedies*, and later *The Golden Cockerel* and *The Bronze Horseman*. His contemporaries were perplexed; his enemies and those who envied him rejoiced. His friends kept mum. Pushkin himself writes in 1830:

> There are both almanacs and journals
> Where precepts are reprised to us,
> Where nowadays they abuse me so,
> And where I would encounter such madrigals
> About myself from time to time.

In precisely what way and how did Pushkin change?

In the preface proposed for the eighth and ninth chapters of *Eugene Onegin* (1830), Pushkin polemicizes with the critics: "The age may move forward," but "poetry stays in one and the same place... Its means and ends are one and the same."

In that same year, however, in the drafts of an article about

Baratynsky, Pushkin depicts the relationship between the poet and the reader in an entirely different way:

> The concepts and feelings of the eighteen-year-old poet are still near and dear to everyone; young readers understand him and are delighted to recognize their own feelings and thoughts, which are clearly expressed, alive, and harmonious in his works. But as the years go by and the youthful poet reaches manhood, his talent grows, his understanding becomes greater, his feelings change. His songs are no longer the same. But the readers are the same and have only become more coldhearted and indifferent toward the poetry of life. The poet grows apart from them, and little by little withdraws entirely. He creates for himself, and if his works are still published from time to time, he encounters coldness or inattention, and he finds an echo of his sounds only in the hearts of a few admirers of poetry, who, like himself, are secluded and forgotten by the world.

It is odd that it has still not been noted anywhere that it was Baratynsky himself who suggested this idea to Pushkin in a letter in 1828, where he explains the failure of *Onegin* this way:

> I think that a poet in Russia can hope for great success only with his first immature experiments. All the young people, who find in him what are virtually their own feelings and thoughts, brilliantly expressed, are on his side. The poet develops, writes with greater deliberation and profundity, but the officers are bored with

him, and the brigadiers do not accept him, because after all his poetry is not prose. Don't take these reflections as referring to yourself; they are general ones.

Just how Pushkin developed Baratynsky's idea is evident from a comparison of these two citations. Thus, it is not so much that poetry is static, as that the reader does not keep pace with the poet. All of Pushkin's contemporaries enthusiastically recognized themselves in the hero of *The Prisoner of the Caucasus*, but who would agree to recognize himself in Eugene from *The Bronze Horseman?*

II

The Little Tragedies can be numbered among those of Pushkin's mature works that not only his contemporaries, but even the poet's friends did not know. There is perhaps no single work of world poetry in which such formidable moral questions are presented so sharply and complexly as Pushkin's *Little Tragedies*. The complexity is so great at times that, when combined with the breathtaking conciseness, the sense is almost obscured, which invites various interpretations (for example, the denouement of *The Stone Guest*).

I believe that Pushkin himself provides an explanation for this in his note about Musset (October 24, 1830), where he commends the author of *Contes d'Espagne et d'Italie* for the absence of moralizing and in general advises against "tacking on a moral admonition to everything." This observation in part provides a key to understanding the supposedly humorous ending of *The Little House in Kolomna* (October 9, 1830):

"Have you at least some moral admonition?"
"No...well, perhaps...I'll think, with your
permission...Here is a moral for you..."

This is followed by a parody on a moral ending, clearly meant
as a challenge: "Nothing more fine / Can be squeezed out of
this plain tale of mine."

It is understandable that many of the standard ways of rep-
resenting passions were closed to a poet who had thus posed
the question about moralizing. Everything above is particularly
relevant to *The Stone Guest*, which nevertheless represents an
adaptation of the universal theme of retribution; and Pushkin's
predecessors did not hesitate to moralize when dealing with this
theme.

Pushkin takes a different path. He needs to convince the
reader from the very first lines, and without resorting to explicit
moralizing, that the hero must perish. The fact that *The Stone
Guest* is a tragedy of retribution for Pushkin is proven by the very
title he has chosen (*The Stone Guest*, not *Don Juan*). Therefore,
all the dramatis personae—Laura, Leporello, Don Carlos, and
Doña Anna—act only so as to prepare and hasten the death of
Don Juan. The hero himself tirelessly pleads for the same:

All's for the best. Unlucky enough to kill
Don Carlos, taking refuge as a monk
Within these cloisters...

But Leporello says:

That's the style.
Now let's enjoy ourselves. Forget the dead.

Pushkin scholarship has shown us how Pushkin's Don Juan resembles his predecessors. And it makes sense for us to determine now in what way he is original.

It is characteristic of Pushkin that Don Juan's wealth is referred to only once, and in passing, whereas this is an essential theme for da Ponte and Molière. Pushkin's Juan is neither da Ponte's rich man, who wants "to revel in his money," nor Molière's doleful raisonneur, who deceives his creditors. Pushkin's Juan is a Spanish grandee whom the king would not fail to recognize if he encountered him on the street. Reading *The Stone Guest* attentively, we make an unexpected discovery: Don Juan is a poet. Laura sings his verses that have been set to music; and even Juan calls himself an "Improvisor of Love Songs."

This draws him nearer to the basic Pushkin hero. Charsky, repeating one of Pushkin's favorite thoughts, says in *The Egyptian Nights*: "Our poets do not enjoy the patronage of gentlemen, our poets are themselves gentlemen..." As far as I know, no one else has thought to make his Don Juan a poet.

The situation at the tragedy's denouement is itself very close to Pushkin. In the 1820s Pushkin was tormented by the dream of a secret return from exile. That is precisely why Pushkin transferred the action from Seville (where it was set in the drafts — Seville is Don Juan's city of long standing) to Madrid: he needed the capital. Pushkin, through Don Juan, says of the king:

> Send me away again.
> I don't suppose I'll have my head chopped off.
> I'm not accused of crime against the State.

Read "political prisoner," on whom the death penalty is customarily imposed for an unauthorized return from exile. His friends said something of the sort to Pushkin himself when he wanted to return to Petersburg from Mikhailovskoye. And apropos of this, Pushkin's Leporello, turning to his lord, exclaims: "Well, then, you should *have stayed in safety.*"

Pushkin, it is true, does not put his Don Juan into the same ridiculous and shameful situation of every other Don Juan—no amorous Elvira pursues him and no jealous Mazetto intends to beat him; he doesn't even disguise himself as a servant to seduce the housemaid (as in Mozart's opera); he is a hero to the end, but this combination of cold cruelty and childish carelessness produces an incredible impression. Hence, Pushkin's Don Juan, despite his elegance and worldly manners, is far more terrifying than his predecessors.

Both heroines note this, each in her own way: Doña Anna— "You are a real demon"; Laura—"Ruffian, fiend."

If Laura perhaps is simply scolding, then the word "demon" on the lips of Doña Anna produces just the impression that Don Juan must make, in accordance with the author's conception.

In contrast to other Don Juans, who treat all women absolutely the same way, Pushkin's Juan addresses each of the three very different women with different words.

The hero of *The Stone Guest* scolds his servant in the same way as both Mozart's and Molière's Don Juans, but the buffoonish scene in the opera's finale—the gluttony of servant and master—would, for example, be absolutely impossible in Pushkin's tragedy.

Pushkin originally wanted to emphasize the circumstances surrounding Juan's proposal to meet with the Commendador's widow near his statue, but then Leporello's indignant remark: "Atop a husband's grave...he is shameless; *it will turn out badly for him!*" seemed to smack too much of moralizing to Pushkin, and he left it to the reader to guess where the meetings take place.

In neither the final text nor in the drafts of *The Stone Guest* is there even a single word of explanation for the cause of the duel between Don Juan and the Commendador. This is odd. I dare say that the reason for this unexplained omission is as follows: in all the works preceding Pushkin's (save Molière's, where, in contrast to *The Stone Guest*, the Commendador is presented as an entirely abstract figure, not linked to the action in any way), the Commendador perishes defending the honor of his daughter, Doña Anna. Pushkin made Doña Anna the Commendador's wife, not his daughter, and he himself informs us that Juan has never seen her before. The former cause falls by the wayside, but Pushkin did not want to devise a new one that would distract the reader's attention from what was most important. He emphasizes only the Commendador was killed in a duel

When we two met behind the Escorial...

and not in a scandalous nocturnal fight (in which even Doña Anna takes part), which would not have been in keeping with Juan's character.

If the scene of Juan's declaration to Doña Anna can be traced to Shakespeare's *Richard III*, we must remember that Richard is a consummate villain and not a professional seducer; he is motivated by political considerations, not at all from amorous ones, as he explains to the onlookers then and there.

Pushkin thereby wished to say that thoughtlessness can lead his Juan to act like a villain, although he is only a society rake.

Second, to my mind a more significant link with Shakespeare that has gone unnoticed can be found in the closing scene of the tragedy *The Stone Guest*:

Doña Anna
How did you dare
Come here? If someone recognized you — death.

In the draft:

People could recognize you.

Juliet
How cam'st thou hither, tell me, and wherefore?...
And the place death, considering who thou art,
If any of my kinsmen find thee here...
(*Romeo and Juliet*, Act II, scene 2)

Even the scene of inviting the statue, the only one that follows tradition, reveals the real abyss between Pushkin's Don Juan and his prototypes. Pushkin has transformed the inappropriate prank of the Mozartian and Molièrian Don Juans, evoked and motivated by the fact that he read an insulting inscription on the monument, into demonic bravado. Instead of the absurd and traditional invitation to dine offered to the statue, we see something unparaled:

My good Commendador, tomorrow evening
Come to your widow's house — I shall be there —
And will you stand outside the door on guard?
You'll come?

That is, Juan speaks to the statue as to a lucky rival.

Pushkin retained his hero's reputation as an atheist, a reputation proceeding from *l'Ateista fulminado* (the hero of a religious drama presented in churches and monasteries).

Depraved and *godless* scoundrel named Don Juan
    (the monk)
Your Don Juan is a *godless* scoundrel (Don Carlos)
Don Juan is described to you as being without
    conscience, *without faith* (Don Juan himself)
I have heard you are a *godless* libertine (Doña Anna)

Accusations of atheism were a usual refrain in the young Pushkin's life.

On the other hand, Pushkin completely banished from his tragedy another feature typical of Don Juans—the wanderings. It suffices to recall Mozart's *Don Giovanni* and Leporello's celebrated aria—the catalogue of conquests (641 in Italy, 231 in Germany, 100 in France, 91 in Turkey, and in Spain, a neat 1,003). Pushkin's grandee (his exile excepted, it goes without saying) leads a completely settled metropolitan way of life in Madrid, where every "tipsy fiddler or strolling gypsywoman" would recognize him.

III

Pushkin's Don Juan does not do or say anything that any contemporary of Pushkin's would not have done or said, aside from what is necessary to preserve the Spanish local color ("I'll take him out concealed beneath my cloak / And put him at a crossroads"). This is precisely how Dalti, the hero of Musset's *Portia*, deals with the corpse of his rival, which is found the next day "*le front sur le pavé*" ("face down on the road").

Laura's guests (obviously Madrid's golden youth—Don Juan's friends) are more like members of the Green Lamp, dining with some celebrity of that time, such as Kolosova, and discussing art, than like noble Spaniards of whatever era. But the author of *The Stone Guest* knows that this presents no danger for him. He is confident that his brief description of the night will create a brilliant and unforgettable impression that this is Spain, Madrid, the South:

> Come out upon the balcony. How clear
> The sky; the air is warm and still—the evening
> Wafts us the scent of lemon boughs and laurel;
> The moon shines bright upon the deep dark blue —

Juan sports with Laura like a Petersburg rake with an actress; he recalls Iñez, whom he has ruined, in a melancholy way; he praises the stern spirit of the Commendador, whom he has killed; and he seduces Doña Anna according to all the rules of "Adolphian" worldly strategy. Then something mysterious happens that is not fully explicated. Don Juan's final exclamation, when there can be no question of pretense:

> I die—My end has come—O, Doña Anna!

convinces us that he has truly been reborn during his meeting with Doña Anna, and indeed the entire tragedy operates on the premise that at this moment he loved and was happy, but instead of salvation, from which he was but a step away, comes death. Let us note one more detail: "Leave her," says the statute. This means that Juan flings himself at Doña Anna; it means that he sees only her at this terrible moment.

Indeed, if Don Carlos had killed Don Juan, we would not have had a tragedy, but something on the order of *Les Marrons du feu*, which Pushkin so admired in 1830 for its absence of moralizing and where the Don Juanian hero (*"Mais c'est du don Juan"*) perishes accidentally and senselessly. Pushkin's Don Juan perishes neither accidentally nor senselessly. The Commendador's statue is a symbol of retribution, but if it had carried Don Juan away while still in the cemetery, then we would have had not so much a tragedy as a theater of horrors or *l'Ateista fulminado* of medieval mystery plays. Juan is not afraid of death. We see that he is not in the least frightened of Don Carlos's sword and does not give even a second thought to the possibility of his own death. That is why Pushkin needed the duel with Don Carlos: to show Don Juan as he really is. At the finale of the tragedy we see him in a completely different way. And it is not at all a matter of whether the statue is an otherworldly phenomenon: the nod in the scene at the cemetery is also an otherworldly phenomenon, one to which Don Juan does not pay proper attention, however. Juan is not afraid of death or punishment after death, but of the loss of happiness. Hence his last words: "O, Doña Anna!" And Pushkin places him in the only situation (according to Pushkin) in which death terrifies his hero. And we suddenly recognize something we know full well. Pushkin himself provides a motivated and comprehensive explanation for the tragedy's denouement. *The Stone Guest* is dated November 4, 1830, and in mid-October, Pushkin wrote "The Shot," the autobiographical character of which no one disputes. Silvio, the hero of "The Shot," says: "What use is there for me, thought I, to deprive him of life, when he in no way values it? A wicked thought came to mind (. . .) Let's see if he'll accept death as indifferently on the eve of his wedding as he once did when he was eating cherries!" We may conclude from this that Pushkin believed death to be terrible only if there was happiness. This is exactly how Juan responds to Doña Anna's question: "And have you loved me long?"

> How long or lately
> I cannot say. But *since that love began*
> *I've learned the price of every passing moment,*
> *And what it means to speak of Happiness.*

That is, he learned the price of every passing moment when he became happy. In both "The Shot" and *The Stone Guest*, the woman whom the hero loves is present at the moment of reckoning, contrary to the Don Juan tradition. In Mozart, for example, only the buffoonish Leporello is present, in Molière — Sganarel.

The problem of happiness troubled Pushkin greatly at this time (1830). "As far as happiness is concerned, I am an atheist; I don't believe in it," he wrote to P. A. Osipova the day after finishing *The Stone Guest* (the original is in French); "The devil himself tricked me into raving about happiness as if I had been created for it" — Pushkin's letter to Pletnyov; "Ah, what a cursed trick happiness is!" — to Vyazemsky (original in French). It would be simple to cite a whole series of such quotations, and one can even say, at the risk of seeming paradoxical, that Pushkin was as afraid of happiness as others are afraid of sorrow. And inasmuch as he was always expecting trouble of all sorts, he was uneasy in the face of happiness, that is to say, in the face of the loss of happiness.

IV

But that's not all. In addition to analogies with the autobiographical "The Shot," we should cite quotations from Pushkin's correspondence. The first is from a letter to his future mother-in-law, N. I. Goncharova (April 5, 1830): "I pictured in my mind the errors of my early youth; they were distressing enough just taken by themselves, but calumny has intensified them even more; unfortunately, the rumors about them have been wide-spread" (original in French). How close this is to Don Juan's confession:

> Maybe, report is not entirely false,
> Maybe, upon a tried and weary conscience
> There lies a weight of evil. Long was I
> A model pupil of debauchery...

And: "Poor thing! She is so young, so innocent, but he is such a frivolous, such an *immoral* man" (autobiographical fragment, May 13, 1830). Here "immoral," of course, is an extenuation of "debauched." And this is just what the voice of rumor communicates.

In that same year, Pushkin addresses the very same question in a poem that was not published during his lifetime, "At moments when your graceful form...":

> Too keenly mindful in your heart
> Of past betrayal's doleful mention...
> I curse the cunning machinations
> That were my sinful youth's delight...

All of Doña Anna's rejoinders are implied in this verse. Pushkin, who had just gotten married, writes to Pletnyov: "I am...happy...Ths state is so new for me that it seems I have been reborn"; compare with *The Stone Guest*: "My inmost being has changed." Juan says of the Commendador: "He...enjoys the bliss of *Heaven!*"; compare with Pushkin's letter to A. P. Kern: "How is it possible to be your husband? I cannot picture such a thing for myself, just as I cannot picture heaven" (original in French).

In *Eugene Onegin*, Pushkin promises that when he depicts declarations of love, he will recall:

The language of impassioned pining
Will I renew, and love's reply,
The like of which in days gone by
Came to me as I lay reclining
At a dear beauty's feet...

The similarity of these citations speaks not so much to the autobiographical quality of *The Stone Guest* as to the lyrical source of this tragedy.

V

If Pushkin did not publish *The Covetous Knight* for six years, afraid, as was then said, of "applications [to himself]," then we can assume the same of *The Stone Guest*, which he did not publish at all. (I shall note in passing that *The Feast at the Time of the Plague* was published in 1832, that is, almost immediately after it was written, and this is not because *The Feast* is a simple translation.) However that may be, *The Stone Guest* is the only one of *The Little Tragedies* not published in Pushkin's lifetime. It is easy to see that something that we can unearth now only with the very greatest difficulty was, in Pushkin's mind, floating right on the surface. He had invested too much of himself in *The Stone Guest* and treated it like several of his lyric poems, which remained in manuscript regardless of their quality. In his mature period, Pushkin was not at all inclined to expose "the wounds of his conscience" before the world (to which, to a certain extent, every lyric poet is condemned), and I dare say that *The Stone Guest* was not printed for the very same reason that Pushkin's contemporaries did not read until after his death the conclusion of "Remembrance," "No, no, those fierce delights I do not treasure," and "At moments when your graceful form," and not for the same reason that *The Bronze Horseman* remained in manuscript. Besides all the parallels I have cited, the lyrical source of *The Stone Guest* can be established by a connection with, on one hand, "The Shot" (the problem of happiness) and, on the other, with *The Water Sprite*, which is recounted in brief (as indeed befits a prehistory) in Juan's recollection of Iñez. Juan's rendezvous with Iñez takes place at the cemetery of the Saint Anthony Monastery (as is clear from the draft):

> Wait: that is Saint Anthony's Monastery —
> And the monastery cemetery...
> Oh, I remember everything. You used to come here...

Like the prince in *The Water Sprite*, Juan recognizes the place and recalls a woman he had ruined. In both works she is the daughter of a miller. And it is no accident that Juan says to his servant: "Just go to the village, you know, that one where the mill is." Later he calls the place the cursed *venta* (bazaar). The final wording of these lines partially erased this similarity, but now that the drafts have been studied, there is no doubt that Pushkin's tragedy begins with an obscured mention of the crime of a hero whom fate brings to the very same place where this crime was perpetrated and where he perpetrates a new crime. Everything has been predetermined by this, and the shade of poor Iñez plays a much greater role in *The Stone Guest* than has customarily been thought.

VI

The preceding remarks concern the Don Juan line of the tragedy *The Stone Guest*. But this work obviously has another line as well—that of the Commendatore. Pushkin breaks completely with tradition here as well. In Mozart, da Ponte's Don Juan does not want to be reminded of the Commendatore to such an extent that when Leporello asks permission to say something, his master answers: "All right, if you don't talk about the Commendatore."

But Pushkin's hero talks almost non-stop about the Commendatore.

And what is even more important is the fact that, both in the legend and in all its literary adaptations, the statue makes an appearance in order to appeal to Juan's conscience, so that he will repent of his sins. This would not make sense in Pushkin's tragedy, because Juan confesses without being coerced:

> My inmost being has changed—in love with you
> I am in love with virtue, and at last
> On trembling knees I humbly bend before it.

The Commendatore arrives at the moment of the "cold, peaceful kiss" to take his wife away from Juan. All other authors depict the Commendatore as a decrepit old man and an insulted father. In Pushkin, he is a jealous husband ("And I heard that the deceased was a jealous man. He kept Doña Anna under lock and key"), and it does not follow from this that he is an old man. Juan says:

> Don't torment my
> Heart, Doña Anna, with the passionate mention
> Of your spouse —

to which Doña Anna protests: "How jealous you are."

We have every right to regard the Commendatore as one of the characters in the tragedy *The Stone Guest*. He has a biography, a personality, and he takes part in the action. We even know what he looks like: "he was small, thin." He had married a beauty who did not love him and was able through his love to be worthy of her favor and gratitude. Not a word of this is from the Don Juan tradition. The thought about his jealousy enters Don Juan's head (in the draft when he does not yet even know Doña Anna) from the first moment; and it is then that Leporello says of his master: "Atop a husband's grave...he is shameless; it will turn out badly for him!"

And Pushkin's Commendatore is more like the "incensed jealous man" of Pushkin's youthful poem "To a Young Widow," where a dead husband appears before a widow who is unfaithful to his memory (and where the deceased is also called a happy man, as in *The Stone Guest*), than like a phantom from beyond the grave who calls on the hero to renounce his impious life.

In the seventh chapter of *Eugene Onegin* Pushkin touches on the theme of jealousy from beyond the grave in connection with Lensky's grave and Olga's unfaithfulness:

> Was the despondent bard perturbed
> By the news of the betrayal?

> At least, out of the grave
> There did not rise on that sad day
> His jealous shade,
> And at the late hour dear to Hymen,
> No traces of sepulchral visitations
> Frightened the newlywed.

It is as though Pushkin were disappointed (seeking a plot where an angered and jealous shade would appear). That is why he changes the plot of Don Juan and turns the Commendatore into the husband, not the father of Doña Anna.

The moving widowed fiancée, Xenia Godunova, crying over the portrait of her dead betrothed whom she has never seen in life, says: "I will be faithful to the deceased."

Tatyana's celebrated rebuff:

> But I was pledged another's wife,
> And will be faithful all my life.

is only a pale reflection of what Xenia Godunova and Doña Anna affirm ("a widow must be faithful to the grave").

But what is even more astonishing is the fact that, in the letter cited above to N. N. Goncharova's mother (April 5, 1830), Pushkin writes: "As God is my witness, I am ready to die for her; but to die and leave her a radiant widow, free to choose a new husband for herself the next day—this thought is hell for me." And still more striking: "...should she consent to give me her hand, I would see in this merely the proof of the serene indifference of her heart" (original in French). Compare *The Stone Guest*:

> No,
> My mother gave my hand to Don Alvaro.

And further the entire situation is the same in the letter as in the tragedy.

Thus, in the tragedy *The Stone Guest*, Pushkin is chastising his young, carefree, and sinful self—and the theme of jealousy from beyond the grave (that is, the fear of it) resounds as loudly as the theme of retribution.

A careful analysis of *The Stone Guest*, therefore, leads us to the firm conviction that behind the external borrowings of names and situations, what we have in essence is not simply a new treatment of the universal Don Juan legend, but a deeply personal and original work by Pushkin, whose principal feature is determined not by the plot of the legend, but by Pushkin's own lyrical feelings, inseparably linked with his life experience. We have before us the dramatic embodiment of Pushkin's inner personality, an aesthetic revelation of what tormented and captivated the poet. In contrast to Byron, who (in Pushkin's view) "cast a one-sided glance at the world and human nature, then turned away from them and became absorbed in himself," Pushkin, proceeding from personal experience, creates finished and objective characters: he does not shut himself away from the world, but goes out into the world.

That is why self-avowals are so inconspicuous in his works and can be identified only through painstaking analysis. Responding "to every sound," Pushkin absorbed the experience of his entire generation in himself. Pushkin's lyrical richness allowed him to avoid the error he had observed in the dramatic works of Byron, who dispensed "a single component of his personality to each protagonist" and who thus reduced his work "to several petty and insignificant characters."

—translated by Janet Tucker

IX JOSEPH BRODSKY

(1940–1996)

Don't you find that Joseph is a...cat-and-a-half?

—ANNA AKHMATOVA

*There was a wonderfully undoubting quality about Joseph,
an intellectual readiness that was almost feral. Conversation
attained immediate take-off and no deceleration was possible.
Which is to say that he exemplified in life the very thing that he
most cherished in poetry—the capacity of language to go farther
and faster than expected and thereby provide an escape from
the limitations and preoccupations of the self. Verbally, he had
a lower boredom threshold than anyone I have ever known,
forever punning, rhyming, veering off and honing in,
unexpectedly raising the stakes or switching the tracks.
Words were a kind of high-octane for him,
and he loved to be propelled by them...*

—SEAMUS HEANEY

HOMAGE TO GIROLAMO MARCELLO

Once in winter I, too, sailed in
here from Egypt, believing that I'd be greeted
on the crowded quay by my wife in resplendent furs
and a tiny veiled hat. Yet I was greeted
not by her but by two small, decrepit
Pekinese with gold teeth. Their German owner
told me later that, should he be
robbed, the Pekinese might help him
to make ends meet; well, at least initially.
I was nodding and laughing.

The quay was infinite and completely
vacant. The otherworldly
winter light was turning palazzi into porcelain crockery
and the populace into those who won't
dare to touch it.
Neither veil nor, for that matter, furs
were at issue. The sole transparent
thing was the air and its pinkish laced
curtain in the hotel "Meleager and Atalanta,"
where, as far back as then, eleven years ago,
I could have surmised, I gather,
that the future already
had arrived. When a man's alone,
he's in the future — since it can manage
without the supersonic stuff,
streamlined bodies, an executed tyrant,
crumbling statues; when a man's unhappy,
that's the future.

Nowadays I don't get
on all fours any longer in the hotel
room, imitating its furniture and safeguarding
myself against my own maxims. Now to die of grief
would mean, I'm afraid, to die
belatedly, while latecomers
are unwelcome, particularly in the future.

The quay swarms with youngsters chattering in Arabic.
The veil has sprouted into a web of rumors,
dimmed later into a net of wrinkles.
And the Pekinese long ago got consumed by their canine
        Auschwitz.
No sign of the owner, either. What seems to have survived
is but water and me, since water also
has no past.

—translated by the author

To My Daughter

Give me another life, and I'll be singing
in Caffè Rafaella. Or simply sitting
there. Or standing there, as furniture in the corner,
in case that life is a bit less generous than the former.

Yet partly because no century from now on will ever manage
without caffeine or jazz, I'll sustain this damage,
and through my cracks and pores, varnish and dust all over,
observe you, in twenty years, in your full flower.

On the whole, bear in mind that I'll be around. Or rather,
that an inanimate object might be your father,
especially if the objects are older than you, or larger.
So keep an eye on them always, for they no doubt will judge
     you.

Love those things anyway, encounter or no encounter.
Besides, you may still remember a silhouette, a contour,
while I'll lose even that, along with the other luggage.
Hence, these somewhat wooden lines in our common
     language.

—written in English

from A PART OF SPEECH

You've forgotten that village lost in the rows and rows
of swamp in a pine-wooded territory where no scarecrows
ever stand in orchards: the crops aren't worth it,
and the roads are also just ditches and brushwood surface.
Old Nastasia is dead, I take it, and Pesterev, too, for sure,
and if not, he's sitting drunk in the cellar or
is making something out of the headboard of our bed:
a wicket gate, say, or some kind of shed.
And in winter they're chopping wood, and turnips is all they
　　　live on,
and a star blinks from all the smoke in the frosty heaven,
and no bride in chintz at the window, but dust's gray craft,
plus the emptiness where once we loved.

— translated by Daniel Weissbort with the author

On Love

Twice I woke up tonight and wandered to
the window. And the lights down on the street,
like pale omission points, tried to complete
the fragment of a sentence spoken through
sleep, but diminished into darkness, too.

I'd dreamt that you were pregnant, and in spite
of having lived so many years apart
I still felt guilty and my heartened palm
caressed your belly as, by the bedside,
it fumbled for my trousers and the light

switch on the wall. And with the bulb turned on
I knew that I was leaving you alone
there, in the darkness, in the dream, where calmly
you waited till I might return,
not trying to reproach or scold me

for the unnatural hiatus. For
darkness restores what light cannot repair.
There we are married, blest, we make once more
the two-backed beast and children are the fair
excuse of what we're naked for.

Some future night you will appear again.
You'll come to me, worn out and thin now, after
things in between, and I'll see son or daughter
not named as yet. This time I will restrain
my hand from groping for the switch, afraid

and feeling that I have no right
to leave you both like shadows by that sever-
ing fence of days that bar your sight,
voiceless, negated by the real light
that keeps me unattainable forever.

—*translated by Daniel Weissbort with the author*

from NATURE MORTE, SECTION X

Mary now speaks to Christ:
"Are you my son? — or God?
You are nailed to the cross.
Where lies my homeward road?

Can I pass through my gate
not having understood:
Are you dead? — or alive?
Are you my son? — or God?"

Christ speaks to her in turn:
"Whether dead or alive,
woman, it's all the same —
son or God, I am thine."

— translated by George L. Kline

LETTER TO HORACE

My dear Horace,

If what Suetonius tells us about your lining your bedroom walls with mirrors to enjoy coitus from every angle is true, you may find this letter a bit dull. On the other hand, you may be entertained by its coming to you from a part of the world whose existence you never suspected, and some two thousand years after your death, at that. Not bad for a reflection, is it?

You were almost fifty-seven, I believe, when you died in 8 BC, though you weren't aware of either C. Himself or a new millennium coming. As for myself, I am fifty-four now; my own millennium, too, has only a few years to run. Whatever new order of things the future has in store, I anticipate none of it either. So we may talk, I suppose, man to man, Horace. And I may as well begin with a locker-room kind of story.

Last night I was in bed rereading your *Odes*, and I bumped into that one to your fellow poet Rufus Valgius in which you are trying to convince him not to grieve so much over the loss of his son (according to some) or his lover (according to others). You proceed for a couple of stanzas with your exempla, telling him that So-and-so lost this person and Such-and-such another, and then you suggest to Rufus that he, as a kind of self-therapy, get engaged in praising Augustus's new triumphs. You mention several recent conquests, among them grabbing some space from the Scythians.

Actually, that must have been the Geloni; but it doesn't matter. Funny, I hadn't noticed this ode before. My people—well, in a manner of speaking—aren't mentioned that often by great poets of Roman antiquity. The Greeks are a different matter, since they rubbed shoulders with us quite a bit. But even with them we don't fare that well. A few bits in Homer (of which Strabo makes such a meal afterward!), a dozen lines in Aeschylus, not much more in Euripides. Passing references, basically; but nomads don't deserve any better. Of the Romans, I used to think, it was only poor Ovid who paid us any heed; but then he had no choice. There is practically nothing about us in Virgil, not to mention Catullus or Propertius, not to mention Lucretius. And now, lo and behold, a crumb from your table.

Perhaps, I said to myself, if I scratch him hard enough, I may find a reference to the part of the world I find myself in now. Who knows, he might have had a fantasy, a vision. In this line of work that happens.

But you never were a visionary. Quirky, unpredictable, yes—but not a visionary. To advise a grief-stricken fellow to change his tune and sing Caesar's victories—this you could do; but to imagine another land and another heaven—well, for that one should turn, I guess, to Ovid. Or wait for another millennium. On the whole, you Latin poets were bigger on reflection and rumination than on conjecture. I suppose because the empire was large enough as it was to strain one's own imagination.

So there I was, lying across my unkempt bed, in this unimaginable (for you) place, on a cold February night, some two thousand years later. The only thing I had in common with you, I thought, was the latitude and, of course, the little volume of your *Collected*, in Russian translations. At the time you wrote all this, you see, we didn't have a language. We weren't even we; we were Geloni, Getae, Budini, etc.: just bubbles in our future gene pool. So two thousand years were not for nothing, after all.

Now we can read you in our own highly inflected language, with its famous gutta-percha syntax suiting the translation of the likes of you marvelously.

Still, I am writing this to you in a language with whose alphabet you are more familiar. A lot more, I should add, than I am. Cyrillic, I am afraid, would only bewilder you even further, though you no doubt would recognize the Greek characters. Of course the distance between us is too large to worry about increasing it—or, for that matter, about trying to shrink it. But the sight of Latin letters may be of some comfort to you, no matter how bewildering their use may look.

—

So I was lying atop my bed with the little volume of your *Carmina*. The heat was on, but the cold night outside was winning. It is a small, two-storied wooden affair I live in here, and my bedroom is upstairs. As I looked at the ceiling, I could almost see cold seeping through my gambrel roof: a sort of anti-haze. No mirrors here. At a certain age one doesn't care for one's own reflection, company or no company; especially if no. That's why I wonder whether Suetonius tells the truth. Although I imagine you would be pretty sanguine about that as well. Your famous equipoise! Besides, for all this latitudinal identity, in Rome it never gets that cold. A couple of thousand years ago the climate perhaps was different; your lines, though, bear no witness to that. Anyhow, I was getting sleepy.

And I remembered a beauty I once knew in your town. She lived in Subura, in a small apartment bristling with flowerpots but redolent with the smell of the crumbling paperbacks the place was stuffed with. They were everywhere, but mostly on shelves reaching the ceiling (the ceiling, admittedly, was low).

Most of them were not hers but belonged to her neighbor across the hall, about whom I heard a lot but whom I never met. The neighbor was an old woman, a widow, who was born and spent her entire life in Libya, in Leptis Magna. She was Italian but of Jewish extraction—or maybe it was her husband who was Jewish. At any rate, when he died and when things began to heat up in Libya, the old lady sold her house, packed up her stuff, and came to Rome. Her apartment was apparently even smaller than my tender companion's, and jammed with a lifetime's accretions. So the two women, the old and the young, struck a deal whereupon the latter's bedroom began to resemble a regular second-hand-book store. What jarred with this impression wasn't so much the bed as the large, heavily framed mirror leaning somewhat precariously against a rickety bookshelf right across from the bed, and at such an angle that whenever I or my tender companion wanted to imitate you, we had to strain and crane our necks rather desperately. Otherwise the mirror would frame only more paperbacks. In the early hours it could give one an eerie feeling of being transparent.

All that happened ages ago, though something nudges me to mutter, centuries ago. In an emotional sense, that would be valid. In fact, the distance between that place in Subura and my present precincts psychologically is larger than the one between you and me. Which is to say that in neither case are "millennia" inapplicable. Or to say that, to me, your reality is practically greater than that of my private memory. Besides, the name of Leptis Magna interferes with both. I've always wanted to visit there; in fact, it became a sort of obsession with me once I began to frequent your town and Mediterranean shores in general. Well, partly because one of the floor mosaics in some bath there contains the only surviving likeness of Virgil, and a likeness done in his lifetime, at that! Or so I was told; but maybe it's in Tunisia. In Africa, anyway. When one is cold, one remembers Africa. And when it's hot, also.

—

Ah, what I wouldn't give to know what the four of you looked like! To put a face to the lyric, not to mention the epic. I would settle for a mosaic, though I'd prefer a fresco. Worse comes to worse, I would resign myself to the marbles, except that the marbles are too generic — everybody gets blond in marble — and too questionable. Somehow, you are the least of my concerns, i.e., you are the easiest to picture. If what Suetonius tells us about your appearance is indeed true — at least something in his account must be true! — and you were short and portly, then you most likely looked like Eugenio Montale or Charlie Chaplin in the *King in New York* period. The one I can't picture for the life of me is Ovid. Even Propertius is easier: skinny, sickly, obsessed with his equally skinny and sickly redhead, he is imaginable. Say, a cross between William Powell and Zbigniew Cybulski. But not Ovid, though he lasted longer than all of you. Alas, not in those parts where they carved likenesses. Or laid mosaics. Or bothered with frescoes. And if anything of the sort was done before your beloved Augustus kicked him out of Rome, then it was no doubt destroyed. So as not to offend high sensibilities. And afterward — well, afterward any slab of marble would do. As we used to say in northern Scythia — Hyperborea to you — paper can endure anything, and in your day marble was a kind of paper.

—

You think I am rambling, but I am just trying to reproduce the train of thought that took me late last night to an unusually graphic destination. It meandered a bit, for sure; but not that much. For, one way or another, I've always been thinking about you four, especially about Ovid. About Publius Ovidius Naso. And not for reasons of some particular affinity. No matter how similar my circumstances may now and then appear to his in the eyes of some beholder, I won't produce any *Metamorphoses*. Besides, twenty-two years in these parts won't rival ten in Sarmatia. Not to mention that I saw my Terza Roma crumble. I have my vanity, but it has its limits. Now that they are drawn by age, they are more palpable than before. But even as a young pup, kicked out of my home to the Polar Circle, I never fancied myself playing his double. Though then my empire looked indeed eternal, and one could roam on the ice of our many deltas all winter long.

No, I never could conjure Naso's face. Sometimes I see him played by James Mason —a hazel eye soggy with grief and mischief; at other time, though, it's Paul Newman's winter-gray stare. But, then, Naso was a very protean fellow, with Janus no doubt presiding over his lares. Did you two get along, or was the age difference too big to bother? Twenty-two years, after all. You must have known him, at least through Maecenas. Or did you just think him too frivolous, saw it coming? Was there bad blood between you? He must have thought you ridiculously loyal, true blue in a sort of quaint, self-made man's kind of way. And to you he was just a punk, an aristo, privileged from the cradle, etc. Not like you and Anthony Perkin's Virgil, practically working-class boys, only five years' difference. Or is this too much Karl Marx reading and moviegoing, Horace? Perhaps. But wait, there is more. There is Dr. Freud coming into this, too, for what sort of interpretation of dreams is it, if it's not filtered through good old Ziggy? For it was my good old subconscious the train of thought I just mentioned was taking me to, late last night, and at some speed.

———

Anyhow, Naso was greater than both of you—well, at least as far as I'm concerned. Metrically, of course, more monotonous; but so is Virgil. And so is Propertius, for all his emotional intensity. In any case, my Latin stinks; that's why I read you all in Russian. It copes with your asclepiadic verse in a far more convincing way than the language I am writing this in, for all the familiarity of the latter's alphabet. The latter just can't handle dactyls. Which were your forte. More exactly, Latin's forte. And your *Carmina* is, of course, their showcase. So I am reduced to judging the stuff by the quality of imagination. (Here's your defense, if you need one.) And on that score Naso beats you all.

All the same, I can't conjure up your faces, his especially; not even in a dream. Funny, isn't it, not to have any idea how those whom you think you know most intimately looked? For nothing is more revealing than one's use of iambs and trochees. And, by the same token, those who don't use meters are always a closed book, even if you know them physically, inside out. How did John Clare put it? "Even those whom I knew best / Are strange, nay! Stranger than the rest." At any rate, metrically, Flaccus, you were the most diverse among them. Small wonder that this huffing and puffing train took you for its engineer as it was leaving its own millennium and heading for yours, unaccustomed as it may have been to electricity. Hence I was traveling in the dark.

———

Few things are more boring than other people's dreams, unless they are nightmares or highly carnal. This one, Flaccus, was of the latter denomination. I was in some very sparsely furnished bedroom, in a bed sitting next to the sea-serpent-like, though extremely dusty, radiator. The walls were absolutely naked, but I was convinced I was in Rome. In fact, I was sure I was in Subura, in the apartment of that pretty friend of mine from days of yore. Except that she wasn't there. Neither were the paperbacks, nor the mirror. But the brown flowerpots stood absolutely intact, emitting not so much the aroma of their plants as the tint of their own clay: the whole scene was done in terra-cotta-cum-sepia tones. That's how I knew I was in Rome.

Everything was terra-cotta-cum-sepia-shaded. Even the crumpled bedsheets. Even the bodice of my affections' target. Even those looming parts of her anatomy that wouldn't have benefited from a suntan, I imagine, in your day either. The whole thing was positively monochrome; I felt that, had I been able to see myself, I would be in sepia, too. Still, there was no mirror. Imagine those Greek vases with their multifigured design running around, and you'll get the texture.

⌐

This was the most vigorous session of its kind I've ever taken part in, whether in real life or in my imagination. Such distinctions, however, should have been dispensed with already, given the character of this letter. Which is to say, I was as much impressed by my stamina as by my concupiscence. Given my age, not to mention my cardiovascular predicament, this distinction is worth sustaining, dream or no dream. Admittedly, the target of my affections—a target long since reached—was markedly younger than I, but not by a huge margin. The body in question seemed in its late thirties, bony, yet supple and of great elasticity. Still, its most exacting aspect was its tremendous agility, wholly devoted to the single purpose of escaping the banality of bed. To condense the entire endeavor into one cameo, my target's upper torso would be plunged into the narrow, one-foot-wide trough between the bed and the radiator, with the tanless rump and me atop it floating at the mattress's brink. The bodice's laced hem would do as foam.

Throughout all this I didn't see her face. For the above-implied reasons. All I knew about her was that she was from Leptis Magna, although I have no idea how I learned this. There was no sound track to this session, nor do I believe we exchanged two words. If we did, that was before I became cognizant of the process, and the words must have been in Latin: I have a faint sense of some obstacle regarding our communication. Still, all along I seem to have known, or else managed to surmise in advance, that there was something of Ingrid Thulin in the bone structure of her face. Perhaps I espied this when, submerged as she was under the bed, her right hand now and then, in an awkward backward motion, groped for the warm coils of that dusty radiator.

When I woke up the next—i.e., this—morning, my bedroom was dreadfully cold. A mealy, revolting daylight was arriving through both windows like some kind of dust. Perhaps dust is indeed daylight's leftover; well, this shouldn't be ruled out. Momentarily, I shut my eyes; but the room in Subura was gone. Its only evidence lingered in the dark under my blanket where daylight couldn't reach, but clearly not for long. Next to me, opened in the middle, was your book.

No doubt it's you whom I should thank for this dream, Flaccus. Now, the hand jerkily trying to clutch the radiator could of course stand for the straining and craning in days of yore, as that pretty friend of mine or I tried to catch a glimpse of ourselves in that gilded mirror. But I rather doubt it—two torsos can't shrink into one limb; no subconscious is that economical. No, I believe that hand somehow echoed the general motion of your verse, its utter unpredictability and, with this, the inevitable stretching— nay, straining—of your syntax in translation. As a result, practically every line of yours is surprising. This is not a compliment, though; just an observation. In our line of work, tricks, naturally, are de rigueur. And the standard ratio is something like one little miracle per stanza. If a poet is exceptionally good, he may come up with a couple. With you, practically each line is an adventure; sometimes there are several in one line. Of course, some of this has to do with having you in translation. But I suspect that in your native Latin, too, your readers seldom knew what the next word was going to be. It's like constantly walking on broken glass or something: on the mental— oral?—version of broken glass, limping and leaping. Or like that hand clutching the radiator: there was something distinctly logaoedic about its bursts and withdrawals. But, then, next to me I had your *Carmina*.

Had it been your *Epodes* or *Epistles*, not to mention *Satires* or, for that matter, *Ars Poetica*, the dream I am sure would have been different. That is, it would perhaps have been as carnal, but a good deal less memorable. For it's only in the *Carmina* that you are metrically enterprising, Flaccus. The rest is practically all done in couplets; the rest is bye-bye to asclepiads and Sapphics and hello to downright hexameters. The rest is not that twitching hand but the radiator itself, with its rhythmic coils like nothing more than elegiac couplets. Make this radiator stand on end and it will look like anything by Virgil. Or by Propertius. Or by Ovid. Or by you, save your *Carmina*.

It will look like any page of Latin poetry. It will look like — should I use the hateful word — text.

‹—›

Well, I thought, what if it *was* Latin poetry? And what if that hand was simply trying to turn the page? And my efforts vis-à-vis that sepia-shaded body simply stood for my reading of a body of Latin poetry? If only because I still — even in a dream! — couldn't make out her face. As for that glimpse of her Ingrid Thulin features that I caught as she was straining to turn the page, it had most likely to do with the Virgil played in my mind by Tony Perkins. Because he and Ingrid Thulin have sort of similar cheekbones; also since Virgil is the one I've read most of all. Since he has penned more lines than anybody. Well, I've never counted, but it sure feels that way, thanks to the *Aeneid*. Though I, for one, by far prefer his *Bucolics* or *Georgics* to his epic.

I'll tell you why later. The truth of the matter, however, is that I honestly don't know whether I espied those cheekbones first and learned that my sepia-shaded target was from Leptis Magna second, or vice versa. For I'd seen a reproduction of that floor-mosaic likeness some time before. And I believed it was from Leptis Magna. I can't recall why or where. On the frontispiece of some Russian edition, perhaps? Or maybe it was a postcard. Main thing, it was from Leptis Magna and done in Virgil's lifetime, or shortly thereafter. So what I beheld in my dream was a somewhat familiar sight; the sensation itself wasn't so much that of beholding as that of recognition. Never mind the armpit muscle and the breast bustling in the bodice.

Or precisely because of that: because, in Latin, poetry is feminine. That's good for allegory, and what's good for allegory is good for the subconscious. And if the target of my affections stood—lay down, rather—for a body of Latin poetry, its high cheekbones could just as well resemble Virgil's, regardless of his own sexual preferences, if only because the body in my dream was from Leptis Magna. First, because Leptis Magna is a ruin, and every bedroom endeavor resembles a ruin, what with sheets, pillows, and the prone and jumbled limbs themselves. Second, because the very name "Leptis Magna" always struck me as being feminine, like Latin poetry, not to mention what I suppose it literally means. Which is, a great offering. Although my Latin stinks. But be that as it may, what is Latin poetry after all if not a great offering? Except that my reading, as you no doubt would charge, only ruins it. Well, hence this dream.

—

Let's avoid murky waters, Flaccus; let's not saddle ourselves with exploring whether dream can be reciprocal. Let me hope at least you won't proceed in a similar fashion about my own scribblings should you ever get acquainted with them. You won't pun about pen and penis, will you? And why shouldn't you get acquainted with my stuff quite apart from this letter. Reciprocity or no reciprocity, I see no reason why you, so capable of messing up my dreams, won't take the next step and interfere with my reality.

You do, as it is; if anything, my writing you this letter is the proof. But beyond that, you know full well that I've written to you, in a manner of speaking, before. Since everything I've written is, technically, addressed to you: you personally, as well as the rest of you. Because when one writes verse, one's most immediate audience is not one's own contemporaries, let alone posterity, but one's predecessors. Those who gave one a language, those who gave one forms. Frankly, you know that far better than I. Who wrote those asclepiadics, Sapphics, hexameters, and Alcaics, and who were their addressees? Caesar? Maecenas? Rufus? Varus? Lydias and Glycerias? Fat lot they knew about or cared for trochees and dactyls! And you were not aiming at me, either. No, you were appealing to Asclepiades, to Alcaeus and Sappho, to Homer himself. You wanted to be appreciated by them, first of all. For where is Caesar? Obviously in his palace or smiting the Scythians. And Maecenas is in his villa. Ditto Rufus and Varus. And Lydia is with a client and Glyceria is out of town. Whereas your beloved Greeks are right here, in your head, or should I say in your heart, for you no doubt knew them by heart. They were your best audience, since you could summon them at any moment. It's they you were trying to impress most of all. Never mind the foreign language. In fact, it's easier to impress them in Latin: in Greek, you wouldn't have the mother tongue's latitude. And they were talking back to you. They were saying, Yeah, we're impressed. That's why your lines are so twisted with enjambments and qualifiers, that's why your argument is always so unpredictable. That's why you advise your grief-stricken pal to praise Augustus's triumphs.

So if you could do this to them, why can't I do that to you? The language difference at least is here; so one condition is being met. One way or the other, I've been responding to you, especially when I use iambic trimeters. And now I am following this up with a letter. Who knows, I may yet summon you here, you may yet materialize in the end even more than you've done already in my verses. For all I know, logaoedics with dactyls beat any old séance as a means of conjuring. In our line of work, this sort of thing is called pastiche. Once the beat of a classic enters one's system, its spirit moves in, too. And you are a classic, Flaccus, aren't you, in more ways than one, which alone would be complex enough.

And ultimately who else is there in this world one can talk to without revulsion, especially if one is of a misanthropic disposition by nurture. It is for this reason, not vanity, that I hope you get acquainted with my iambs and trochees in some netherworldly manner. Stranger things have happened, and my pen at least has done its bit to that end. I'd much rather, of course, talk to Naso to Propertius, but with you I have more in common metrically. They stuck to elegiac couplets and hexameters; I seldom use those. So it's between you and me here, presumptuous as this may sound to everybody. But not to you. "All the literati keep / An imaginary friend," says Auden. Why should I be an exception?

At the very least, I can sit myself down in front of my mirror and talk to it. That would be fairly close, although I don't believe that you looked like me. But when it comes to the human appearance, nature, in the final analysis, doesn't have that many options. What are they? A pair of eyes, a mouth, a nose, an oval. For all their diversity, in two thousand years nature is bound to repeat itself. Even a God will. So I could easily claim that that face in the mirror is ultimately yours, that you are me. Who is there to check, and in what way? As conjuring tricks go, this might do. But I am afraid I am going too far: I'll never write myself a letter. Even if I were truly your look-alike. So stay faceless, Flaccus, stay unconjured. This way, you may last for two millennia more. Otherwise, each time I mount a woman she might think that she is dealing with Horace. Well, in a sense she is, dream or no dream. Nowhere does time collapse as easily as in one's mind. That's why we so much like thinking about history, don't we? If I am right about nature's options, history is like surrounding oneself with mirrors, like living in a bordello.

Two thousand years—of what? By whose count, Flaccus? Certainly not in terms of metrics. Tetrameters are tetrameters, no matter when and no matter where. Be they in Greek, Latin, Russian, English. So are dactyls, and so are anapests. Et cetera. So two thousand years in what sense? When it comes to collapsing time, our trade, I am afraid, beats history, and smells, rather sharply, of geography. What Euterpe and Urania have in common is that both are Clio's seniors. You start talking your Rufus Valgius out of his protracted grieving by evoking the waves of Mare Caspium; even they, you write, do not remain rough forever. This means that you knew about that *mare* two thousand years ago—from some Greek author, no doubt, as your own people didn't cast their quills that wide. Herein, I suppose, lay this *mare's* first attraction for you as a Roman poet. An exotic name and, on top of that, one connoting the farthest point of your Pax Romana, if not of the known world itself. Also, a Greek one (actually, perhaps even Persian, but you could bump into it only in Greek). The main thing, though, about "Caspium" is that this word is dactylic. That's why it sits at the second line's end, where every poem's meter gets established. And you are consoling Rufus in an asclepiad.

Whereas I—I crossed that Caspium once or twice. When I was either eighteen or nineteen, or maybe twenty. When—I am tempted to say—you were in Athens, learning your Greek. In those days, the distance between Caspium and Hellas, not to mention Rome, was in a sense even greater than it was two thousand years ago; it was, frankly, insurmountable. So we didn't meet. The *mare* itself was smooth and shiny, near its western shorts especially. Thanks not so much to the propitious proximity to civilization as to vast oil spills, perennial in those parts. (I could say this was the real case of pouring oil upon troubled waters, but I am afraid you wouldn't catch the reference.) I was lying flat on the hot upper deck of a dirty steamer, hungry and penniless, but happy all the same, because I was participating in geography. When you are going by boat you always do. Had I read by that time your piece to Rufus, I would have realized that I was also participating in poetry. In a dactyl rather than in a sharpening horizon.

—

But in those days I wasn't that much of a reader. In those days I was working in Asia: mountain climbing and desert trekking. Prospecting for uranium, basically. You don't know what that stuff is, and I won't bore you with an explanation, Flaccus. Although "uranium" is another dactylic word. What does it feel like to learn a word you cannot use? Especially—for you—a Greek one? Awful, I suppose; like, for me, your Latin. Perhaps if I were able to operate in it confidently, I could indeed conjure you up. On the other hand, perhaps not: I'd become for you just another Latin author, and that is a recipe for hiatus.

In any case, in those days I'd read none of you, except—if my memory doesn't play tricks on me—Virgil, i.e., his epic. I remember that I didn't care for it much, partly because against that backdrop of mountains and deserts few things managed to make sense; mainly because of the epic's rather sharp smell of commission. In those days, one's nostrils were very keen for that sort of thing. Besides, I simply couldn't make out 99 percent of his exempla, which were getting in the way rather frequently. What do you expect from an eighteen-year-old from Hyperborea? I am better with this sort of thing now, but it's taken a lifetime. On the whole, it seems to me that you all were overdoing it a bit with the references; they often strike one as filler. Although euphonically of course they—the Greek ones especially—do marvels for the texture.

—

What rattled me perhaps most in the *Aeneid* was that retroactive prophecy of Anchises, when the old man predicts what has already taken place. Here, I thought, your friend went a bit too far. I don't mind the conceit, but the dead should be allowed to be more imaginative. They ought to know more than just Augustus's pedigree; after all, they are not oracles. What a waste of that stunning, mind-boggling idea about souls being entitled to a second corporeality and lapping from the river Lethe to cleanse themselves of their previous memories! To reduce them to paving the road for the reign of the current master! Why, they could become Christians, Charlemagnes, Diderots, Communists, Hegels, us! Those who will come after, mongrels and mutants, and in more ways than one! That would be a real prophecy, a real flight of fancy. Instead, he rehashes the official record and serves it as hot news. The dead are free of causality, to begin with. The knowledge available to them is that about time—all time. That much he could have learned from Lucretius; your friend was a learned man. More than that, he had a terrific metaphysical instinct, a real nose for things' spiritual lining: his souls are far less physical than Dante's. True *manes*: gaseous and unpalpable. One is tempted to say his scholasticism here is practically medieval. But that would be a put-down. Because metaphysically your future turned out to be far less imaginative than your Greek past. For what is life eternal to a soul compared with a second corporeality? What is Paradise to it after the Pythagorean promise of another body? Just unemployment.

Still, whatever his sources were—Pythagoras, Plato's *Phaedrus*, his own fancy—he blows it all for the sake of Caesar's lineage. Well, the epic was his; he had the right to do with it what he liked. But I find it, frankly, unforgivable. It's failures of imagination like these that paved the road to the triumph of monotheism. The one, I guess, is always more graspable than the many; and after that gigantic Greek-and-homemade stew of gods and heroes, this sort of longing for something more graspable, more coherent, was practically inevitable. In other words, for all his expansive gestures, your friend, my dear Flaccus, was just craving metaphysical security. And that, I am afraid, is a contradiction in terms; perhaps the chief attraction of polytheism is that it would have none of that. But I suppose the place was getting too populous to indulge in insecurity of any kind. That's why your friend pins this whole thing, metaphysics and all, on his beloved Caesar in the first place. Civil wars, I should say, do wonders for one's spiritual orientation.

—

But it's not use talking to you like that. You all loved Augustus, didn't you? Even Naso, although he apparently was more curious about Caesar's sentimental property, beyond suspicion as it habitually was, than about his territorial conquests. But then, unlike your friend, Naso was a womanizer. Among other things, that's what makes it so difficult to picture his appearance, that's why I oscillate between Paul Newman and James Mason. A womanizer is an everyman: not that it means he should be trusted any more than a pedophile. And yet his account of what transpired between Dido and Aeneas sounds a bit more convincing than that of your friend. Naso's Dido claims that Aeneas is abandoning her and Carthage in such a hurry—remember, there was a storm looming and Aeneas must have had it with storms by then, what with being tossed on the high seas for seven years—not because he heeded the call of his divine mother but because Dido was pregnant with his child. And that's why she commits suicide: because her reputation is ruined. She is a queen, after all. Naso makes his Dido even question whether Venus was indeed the mother of Aeneas, for she was the goddess of love, and departure is an odd (though not unprecedented) way to manifest this sentiment. No doubt Naso spoofs your friend here. No doubt this depiction of Aeneas is unflattering and, given the fact that the legend of Rome's Trojan origins was the official historical orthodoxy from the third century BC onward, downright unpatriotic. Equally doubtless is that Virgil never read Naso's *Heroides*; otherwise, the former's treatment of Dido in the netherworld would be less reprehensible. For he simply stashes her away, together with Sychaeus, her former husband, in some remote nook of Elysium, where the two forgive and console each other. A retired couple in an old people's home. Out of our hero's way. To spare him agony, to provide him with a prophecy. Because the latter makes better copy. Anyhow, no second corporeality for Dido's soul.

You will argue that I am applying to him the standards that took two millennia to emerge. You are a good friend, Flaccus, but it's nonsense. I am judging him by his own standards, more evident actually in the *Bucolics* and the *Georgics* than in his epic. Don't play the innocent: you all had a minimum of seven centuries of poetry behind you. Five in Greek and two in your own Latin. Remember Euripides, remember his *Alcestis*: the wedding scene's scandal of King Admetus with his parents beats anything in Dostoyevsky hands down—though you may not catch the reference. Which means it beats any psychological novel. Which is something we excelled at in Hyperborea a hundred years ago. Out there, you see, we are big on agony. Prophecy is a different matter. Which is to say, two thousand years were not in vain.

No, the standards are his, by way of the *Georgics*. Based on Lucretius and on Hesiod. In this line of work, Flaccus, there are no big secrets. Only small and guilty ones. Herein, I must add, lies their beauty. And the small and guilty secret of the *Georgics* is that their author, unlike Lucretius—and, for that matter, Hesiod—had no overriding philosophy. To say the least, he was no atomist, no epicurean. At best, I imagine, he hoped that the sum total of his lines would add up to a worldview, if he cared about such a thing in the first place. For he was a sponge, and a melancholic one at that. For him, the best—if not the only—way to understand the world was to list its contents, and if he missed anything in his *Bucolics* or in the *Georgics*, he caught up with that in his epic. He was an epic poet, indeed; an epic realist, if you will, since, speaking numerically, reality itself is quite epic. The cumulative effect of his output upon my reflective faculty has always been the sensation that this man has itemized the world, and in a rather meticulous fashion. Whether he talks of plants or planets, soils or souls, the deeds and/or destinies of the men of Rome, his close-ups are both blinding and binding; but so are things themselves, dear Flaccus, aren't they? No, your friend was no atomist, no epicurean; nor was he a stoic. If he believed in any principle, it was life's regeneration, and his *Georgics*' bees are no better than those souls chalked up for second corporeality in the *Aeneid*.

But perhaps they are better, and not so much because they don't end up buzzing "Caesar, Caesar" as because of the *Georgics*' tonality of utter detachment. Perhaps it's those days of yore

I spent roaming the mountains and deserts of Central Asia that make this tonality most appealing. Back then, I suppose, it was the impersonality of the landscape I'd find myself in that impressed itself on the cortex. Now, a lifetime later, I might blame this taste for monotony on the human vista. Underneath either one lies, of course, an inkling that detachment is the final product of many intense attachments. Or else the modern predilection for a neutral voice, so characteristic of didactic genres in your times. Or both, which is more likely still. And even if the *Georgics*' impersonal drone is nothing but a Lucretian pastiche—as I strongly suspect it is—it is still appealing. Because of its implicit objectivity and explicit similarity to the monotonous clamor of days and years; to the sound time makes as it passes. The very absence of story, the absence of characters in the *Georgics* echo, as it were, time's own perspective on any existential predicament. I even remember myself thinking back then that should time have a pen of its own and decide to compose a poem, its lines would include leaves, grass, earth, wind, sheep, horses, trees, cows, bees. But not us. Maximum, our souls.

So the standards are indeed his. And the epic, for all its splendors, as well as because of them, is a letdown as regards those standards. Plain and simple, he had a story to tell. And a story is bound to have us in it. Which is to say, those whom time dismisses. On top of that, the story wasn't his own. No, give me the *Georgics* any day. Or, should I say, any night, considering my present reading habits. Although I must confess that even in those days of yore, when the sperm count was much higher, hexameter would have left my dreams dry and uneventful. Logaoedics apparently are much more potent.

———

Two thousand years this, two thousand years that! Just imagine, Flaccus, if I'd had company last night. And imagine an—er— translation of this dream into reality. Well, half of humanity must be conceived that way, no? Wouldn't you be responsible, at least in part? Where would those two thousand years be; and wouldn't I have to call the offspring Horace? So, consider this letter a soiled sheet, if not your own by-blow.

And, by the same token, consider the part of the world I am writing to you from, the outskirts of the Pax Romana, ocean or no ocean, distance or no distance. We've got all sorts of fly-ing contraptions here to handle that, not to mention a republic with the first among equals built in, to boot. And tetrameters, as I said, are still tetrameters. They alone can take care of any millennia, to say nothing of space or of the subconscious. I've been dwelling here for twenty-two years now, and I've noticed no difference. In all likelihood, here is where I'll die. So you can take my word for it: tetrameters are still tetrameters, and so are trimeters. And so forth.

It was a flying contraption, of course, that brought me here from Hyperborea twenty-two years ago, though I can as easily put down that flight to my rhymes and meters. Except that the latter might add up to an even greater distance between me and the good old Hyperborea, as your dactylic Caspium does to the actual size of your Pax Romana. Contraptions—flying ones especially—only delay the inevitable: you gain time, but time can fool space only so far; in the end, space catches up. What are years, after all? What can they measure save the decay of one's epidermis, of one's wits? Yet the other day I was sitting in a café here with a fellow Hyperborean, and as we were chatting about our old town in the delta, it suddenly crossed my mind that should I, twenty-two years ago, have tossed a splinter of wood into that delta, it could, given the prevailing winds and currents, have crossed the ocean and reached by now the shores I am dwelling on, to witness my decay. That's how space catches up with time, my dear Flaccus; that's how one truly departs from Hyperborea.

—

Or: how one expands Pax Romana. By dreams, if necessary. Which, come to think of it, are yet another—perhaps the last—form of life's regeneration, especially if you've got no company. Also, it doesn't lead up to Caesar, beating in this sense even the bees. Although, I repeat, it's no use talking to you like this, since your sentiments toward him were in no way different from Virgil's. Nor were your methods of conveying them. You, too preach Augustus's glory over man's grief, saddling with this task not—to your considerable credit—idling souls but geography and mythology. Commendable as this is, it implies, I'm afraid, that Augustus either owns or is sponsored by both. Ah, Flaccus, you might just as well have used hexameter. Asclepiads are just too good for this stuff, too lyrical. Yes, you're right: nothing breeds snobbery better than tyranny.

Well, I suppose I am just allergic to this sort of thing. If I am not reproaching you more venomously, it is because I am not your contemporary: I am not he, because I am almost you. I've written in your meters, and in this one particularly. That, as I've said, is what makes me appreciate "Caspium," Niphaten," and "Gelanos" sitting there at the end of your lines, expanding the empire. And so do "Aquilonibus" and "Vespero," but upward. My subject matter, of course, was more humble; besides, I used rhyme. The only way to overlap with you completely would be by setting myself the task of repeating all your stanzaic patterns in this tongue or in my native Hyperborean. Or else by translating you into either. Come to think of it, such an exercise is plausible—far more so than redoing, say, Ovid's hexameters and elegiac couplets. After all, your *Collected* is not such a large book, and the *Carmina* itself is just ninety-five pieces of varying length. But I am afraid the dog's too old for new and old tricks alike; I should have thought of that earlier. We are destined to stay separated, to remain pen pals at best. Not for long, I'm afraid, but long enough, I hope, to get close to you now and then. Even if not close enough to make out your face. In other words, I am doomed to my dreams; but this doom is welcome.

＿

Because the body in question is so rum. Its greatest charm, Flaccus, is the total lack of the egocentricity that so often plagues its successors, and I daresay the Greeks also. It seldom pushes the first person singular—though that's partly the grammar. In a language so highly inflected, it's hard to zero in on one's own plight. Although Catullus managed; that's why he is loved so universally. But among you four, even with Propertius, the most ardent of all of you, that was out. And certainly with your friend, treating as he did both man and nature *sui generis*. Most of all with Naso, which, given some of his subject matter, must be what turned the Romantics against him so sharply. Still, in my proprietary (after last night) capacity, this pleases me considerably. Come to think of it, the absence of egocentricity may be a body's best defense.

＿

It is—in my day and age, in any case. Actually, of all of you, Flaccus, it is you who are perhaps the most egocentric. Which is to say, the most palpable. But that isn't so much a matter of pronouns, either: it is, again, the distinctness of your metrics. Standing out against the other guys' sprawling hexameters, they suggest some unique sensibility, a character that can be judged—while the others are largely opaque. Sort of like a solo versus the chorus. Perhaps they went for this hexametric drone precisely for reasons of humility, for purposes of camouflage. Or else they just wanted to play by the rules. And hexameter was that game's standard net; to put it differently, its terra-cotta. Of course, your logaoedics don't make you a cheat; still, they flash rather than obscure individuality. That's why for the next two thousand years practically everybody, including the Romantics, would embrace you so readily. Which rattles me, naturally—in my proprietary capacity, that is. In a manner of speaking, you were that body's tanless part, its private marble.

And with the passage of time you got whiter and whiter: more private and more desirable. Suggesting that you can be an egocentric and still handle a Caesar; that it's only a matter of equipoise. Music to so many ears! But what if your famous equipoise was just a matter of the phlegmatic temperament, easily passing for personal wisdom? Like Virgil's melancholy, say. But unlike the choleric upsurges of Propertius. And certainly unlike Naso's sanguinic endeavors. Now, here's one who paved not an inch of that highway leading to monotheism. Here's one who was short on equipoise and had no system, let alone a wisdom or a philosophy. His imagination couldn't get curbed, neither by its own insights nor by doctrine. Only by hexameter; better yet, by elegiac couplets.

Well, one way or another, he taught me practically everything, the explication of dreams included. Which begins with that of reality. Next to him, somebody like the Viennese doctor—never mind not catching the reference!—is kindergarten, child's play. And frankly, you, too. And so is Virgil. To put it bluntly, Naso insists that in this world *one thing is another*. That, in the final analysis, reality is one large rhetorical figure and you are lucky if it is just a polyptoton or a chiasmus. With him a man evolves into an object, and vice versa, with the immanent logic of grammar, like a statement sprouting a subordinate clause. With Naso the tenor is the vehicle, Flaccus, and/or the other way around, and the source of it all is the ink pot. So long as there was a drop of that dark liquid in it, he would go on—which is to say, the world would go on. Sounds like "In the beginning was the word"? Well, not to you. To him, though, this adage would not be news, and he would add that there will be a word in the end as well. Give him anything and he will extend it—or turn it inside out—which is still an extension. To him, language was a godsend; more exactly, its grammar was. More exactly still, to him the world was the language; one thing was another, and as to which was more real, it was a toss-up. In any case, if one thing was palpable, the other was bound to be also. Often in the same line, especially if it was hexameter: there is a big caesura. Failing that, in the next line; especially if it is an elegiac couplet. For measures to him were a godsend also.

He would be the first to confirm this, Flaccus, and so would you. Remember his recalling in *Tristia* how amid the storm that hit the ship taking him into exile (to my parts, roughly; to the outskirts of Hyperborea) he caught himself again composing verses? Naturally you don't. That was some sixteen years after you died. On the other hand, where is one better informed than in the netherworld? So I shouldn't worry that much about my references: you are catching them all. And meters are always meters, in the netherworld especially. Iambs and dactyls are forever, like stars and stripes. More exactly: whenever. Not to mention, wherever. Small wonder that he eventually came to compose in the local dialect. As long as vowels and consonants were there, he could go on, Pax Romana or no Pax Romana. In the end, what is a foreign tongue if not just another set of synonyms. Besides, my good old Geloni had no *écriture*. And even if they had, it would be only natural for him, the genius of metamorphosis, to mutate into an alien alphabet.

That, too, if you will, is how one expands the Pax Romana. Although that never happened. He never stepped into our genetic pool. The linguistic one was enough, though: it took practically these two thousand years for him to enter Cyrillic. Ah, but life without an alphabet has its merits! Existence can be very poignant when it's just oral. Actually, as regards *écriture*, my nomads were in no hurry. To scribble, it takes a settler: someone who's got nowhere to go. That's why civilizations blossom more readily on islands, Flaccus: take, for instance, your dear Greeks. Or in cities. What is a city if not an island surrounded by space? Anyway, if he indeed barged into the local dialect, as he tells us, it was not so much out of necessity, not in order to endear himself to the natives, but because of verse's omnivorous nature: it claims everything. Hexameter does: it is not so sprawling for nothing. And an elegiac couplet is even more so.

—

Lengthy letters are anathema everywhere, Flaccus, including in the afterlife. By now, I guess, you've quit reading, you've had enough. What with these aspersions cast on your pal and praise of Ovid practically at your expense. I continue because, as I said, who is there to talk to, anyway? Even assuming that Pythagorean fantasy about virtuous souls' second corporeality every thousand years is true, and that you've had a minimum of two opportunities so far, and now with Auden dead and the millennium having only four years to go, that quota seems to be busted. So it's back to the original you, even if by now, as I suspect, you've quit reading. In our line of work, addressing the vacuum comes with the territory. So you can't surprise me with your absence, nor can I you with my perseverance.

Besides, I have a vested interest—and you, too. There is that dream that once was your reality. By interpreting it, one gets two for the price of one. And that's what Naso is all about. For him, one thing was another; for him, I'd say, A was B. To him, a body—a girl's especially—could become—nay, *was*—a stone, a river, a bird, a tree, a sound, a star. And guess why? Because, say, a running girl with her mane undone looks in profile like a river? Or asleep on a couch, like a stone? Or, with her arms up, like a tree or a bird? Or, vanishing from sight, being theoretically everywhere, like a sound? And, triumphant or remote, like a star? Hardly. That would suffice for a good simile, while what Naso was after wasn't even a metaphor. His game was morphology, and his take was metamorphosis. When the same substance attains a different form. The main thing is the sameness of substance. And, unlike the rest of you, he managed to grasp the simple truth of us all being composed of the stuff the world is made of. Since we are of this world. So we all contain water, quartz, hydrogen, fiber, et cetera, albeit in different proportions. Which can be reshuffled. Which already have been reshuffled into that girl. Small wonder she becomes a tree. Just a shift in her cellular makeup. Anyhow, with our species, shifting from the animate to the inanimate is the trend. You know what I mean, being where you are.

———

Smaller wonder, then, that a body of Latin poetry—of its Golden Age—became the target of my relentless affection last night. Well, regard it perhaps as a last gasp of your joint Pythagorean quota. And yours was the last part to submerge: because it was less burdened with hexameters. And attribute the agility with which that body strove to escape the banality of bed to its flight from my reading you in translation. For I am accustomed to rhyme, and hexameters won't have it. And you, who came closest to it in your logaoedics, you too gravitated to hexameters: you groped for that radiator, you wanted to submerge. And for all the relentlessness of my pursuit, which stood—no pun intended— for a lifetime of reading you, the dream never turned wet, not because I am fifty-four, but precisely because all of you were rhymeless. Hence the terra-cotta sheen of that Golden Age body; hence, too, the absence of your beloved mirror, not to mention its gilded frame.

And do you know why it wasn't there? Because, as I said, I am accustomed to rhyme. And rhyme, my dear Flaccus, is itself a metamorphosis, and metamorphosis is not a mirror. Rhyme is when one thing turns into another without changing its substance, which is sound. As far as language is concerned, to say the least. It is a condensation of Naso's approach, if you will—a distillation, perhaps. Naturally he comes frightfully close to it himself in that scene with Narcissus and Echo. Frankly, closer even than you, to whom he is metrically inferior. I say "frightfully" because, had he done so, for the next two thousand years we all would have been out of business. Thank God, then, for the hexametric inertia that kept him off, in that scene in particular; thank God for that myth's own insistence on keeping eyesight and hearing apart. For that's what we've been at for the past two thousand years: grafting one onto another, fusing his vision with your meters. It is a gold mine, Flaccus, a full-time occupation, and no mirror can reflect a lifetime of reading.

—

At any rate, this should account for at least half of the body in question and its efforts to escape me. Perhaps, had my Latin stunk less, this dream would never have occurred in the first place. Well, at a certain age, it appears, one has reasons to be grateful for one's ignorance. For meters are still meters, Flaccus, and anatomy is still anatomy. One may claim to possess the whole body, even though its upper part is submerged somewhere between the mattress and the radiator: as long as this part belongs to Virgil or Propertius. It is still tanned, it is still terra-cotta, because it is still hexametric and pentametric. One may even conclude it is not a dream, since a brain can't dream about itself: most likely, it is reality—because it is a tautology.

Just because there is a word, "dream," it doesn't follow that reality has an alternative. A dream, Flaccus, is at best a momentary metamorphosis: far less lasting than that of rhyme. That's why I haven't been rhyming here—not because you wouldn't appreciate the effort. The netherworld, I presume, is a polyglot kingdom. And if I've resorted to writing at all, it is because the interpretation of a dream—of an erotic one especially—is, strictly speaking, a reading. As such, it is profoundly anti-metamorphic, for it is the undoing of a fabric: thread by thread, line by line. And its repetitive nature is its ultimate giveaway: it asks for an equation mark between the reading and the erotic endeavor itself. Which is erotic because it is repetitive. Turning pages: that's what it is; and that's what you are or should be doing now, Flaccus. Well, this is one way of conjuring you up, isnt' it? Because repetition, you see, is the primary trait of reality.

284

Someday, when I end up in your part of the netherworld, my gaseous entity will ask your gaseous entity whether you've read this letter. And if your gaseous entity should reply, No, mine won't feel offended. On the contrary, it will rejoice at this proof of reality's extension into the domain of shadows. For you've never read me to begin with. In this sense, you'll be like many people above who never read either one of us. To say the least, that's one thing that constitutes reality.

But should your gaseous entity reply, Yes, my gaseous entity will not be much worried either about having offended you with my letter, especially its smutty bits. Being a Latin author, you would be the first to appreciate an approach triggered in one by a language in which "poetry" is feminine. And as for "body," what else can one expect form a man in general, and a Hyperborean at that, not to mention the cold February night. I wouldn't even have to remind you that it was just a dream. To say the least, next to death, dream is reality.

So we may get along famously. As for the language, the realm, as I said, is most likely poly- or supra-glot. Besides, being just back from filling up your Pythagorean quota as Auden, you may still retain some English. That's perhaps how I would recognize you. Though he was a far greater poet than you, of course. But that's why you sought to assume his shape last time you were around, in reality.

Worse comes to worse, we can communicate through meters. I can tap the First Asclepiadic stanza easily, for all its dactyls. The second one also, not to mention the Sapphics. That might work; you know, like inmates in an institution. After all, meters are meters even in the netherworld, since they are time units. For this reason, they are perhaps better known now in Elysium than in the asinine world above. That's why using them feels more like communicating with the likes of you than with reality. And naturally I would like you to introduce me to Naso. For I wouldn't know him by sight, since he never assumed anyone else's shape. I guess it's his elegiacs and hexameters that conspired against this. For the past two thousand years, fewer and fewer people have tried them. Auden again? But even he rendered hexameter as two trimeters. So I wouldn't aspire to a chat with Naso. All I would ask is to take a look at him. Even among souls he should be a rarity.

I shall not bother you with the rest of the crowd. Not even with Virgil: he's been back to reality, I should say, in so many guises. Nor with Tibullus, Gallus, Varus, and the others: your Golden Age was quite populous, but Elysium is no place for affinities, and I won't be there as a tourist. As for Propertius, I think I'll look him up myself. I believe it should be relatively easy to spot him: he must feel comfortable among the *manes* in whose existence he believed so much in reality.

No, the two of you will be enough for me. One's taste sustained in the netherworld amounts to an extension of reality into the domain of shadows. I should hope I'll be able to do this, at least initially. Ah, Flaccus! Reality, like the Pax Romana, wants to expand. That's why it dreams; that's why it sticks to its guns as it dies.

— written in English

from IN A ROOM AND A HALF

[...]

I write this in English because I want to grant them a margin of freedom: the margin whose width depends on the number of those who may be willing to read this. I want Maria Volpert and Alexander Brodsky to acquire reality under "a foreign code of conscience." I want English verbs of motion to describe their movements. This won't resurrect them, but English grammar may at least prove to be a better escape route from the chimneys of the state crematorium than the Russian. To write about them in Russian would be only to further their captivity, their reduction to insignificance, resulting in mechanical annihilation. I know that one shouldn't equate the state with language but it was in Russian that two old people, shuffling through numerous state chancelleries and ministries in the hope of obtaining a permit to go abroad for a visit to see their only son before they died, were told repeatedly, for twelve years in a row, that the state considers such a visit "unpurposeful." To say the least, the repetition of this utterance proves some familiarity of the state with the Russian language. Besides, even if I had written all this in Russian, these words wouldn't see the light of day under the Russian sky. Who would read them then? A handful of émigrés whose parents either have died or will die under similar circumstances? They know this story only too well. They know what it feels like not to be allowed to see their mothers or fathers on their deathbed; the silence that follows their request for an emergency visa to attend a relative's funeral. And then it's too late, and a man or a woman puts the receiver down and walks out of the door into the foreign afternoon feeling something neither language has words for, and for which no howl will suffice, either...What could I possibly tell them? In what way could I console them? No country has mastered the art of destroying its subjects' souls as well as Russia, and no man with a pen in his hand is up to mending them; no, this is a job for the Almighty only, this is what He has all that time of His for. May English then house my dead. In Russian I am prepared to read, write verses or letters. For Maria Volpert and Alexander Brodsky, though, English offers a better semblance of afterlife, maybe the only one there is, save my very self. And as far as the latter is concerned, writing this in this language is like doing those dishes; it's therapeutic.

[...]

—*written in English*

from A POET AND PROSE

I

The tradition of dividing literature into poetry and prose dates from the beginnings of prose, since it was only in prose that such a distinction could be made. Ever since, poetry and prose have customarily been regarded as separate areas—or, better yet, spheres—of literature wholly independent of each other. To say the least, "prose poems," "rhythmical prose," and the like indicate a derivative mentality, a polarized rather than integral perception of literature as a phenomenon. Curiously enough, such a view of things has by no means been imposed upon us by criticism from without. This view is, above all, the fruit of the guild approach to literature taken by literati themselves.

The concept of equality is extrinsic to the nature of art, and the thinking of any man of letters is hierarchical. Within this hierarchy poetry occupies a higher position than prose, and the poet, in principle, is higher than the prose writer. This is true not so much because poetry is in fact older than prose, but because a poet in narrow circumstances can sit down and produce a piece; whereas in similar straits a prose writer would hardly give thought to a poem. Even if the prose writer has what it takes to write a decent verse text, he knows full well that poetry pays a lot worse, and more slowly than prose.

With few exceptions, all the more or less eminent writers of recent times have paid their dues to verse. Some, like Nabokov, for example, have tried to the very end to convince themselves and those around them that even if they were not primarily po-ets, they were poets all the same. Most of them, however, after once yielding to the temptation of poetry, never addressed themselves to it again except as readers; still, they remained deeply grateful for the lessons in laconism and harmony it taught them. In twentieth-century literature the only case of an outstanding prose writer becoming a great poet is that of Thomas Hardy. In general, however, it can be said that the prose writer without active experience in poetry is prone to prolixity and grandiloquence.

What does a writer of prose learn from poetry? The dependence of a word's specific gravity on context, focused thinking, omission of the self-evident, the dangers that lurk within an elevated state of mind. And what does the poet learn from prose? Not much: attention to detail, the use of common parlance and bureaucratese, and, in rare instances, compositional know-how (the best teacher of which is music). All three of these, however, can be gleaned from the experience of poetry itself (especially from Renaissance poetry), and theoretically—but only theoretically—a poet can get along without prose.

And only theoretically can he get along without writing prose. Need or a reviewer's ignorance, not to mention ordinary correspondence, will sooner or later force him to write in run-on lines, "like everyone else." But apart from these, a poet has other reasons, which we will attempt to examine here.

In the first place, one fine day a poet may simply get an urge to write something in prose. (The inferiority complex that the prose writer suffers vis-à-vis the poet doesn't automatically imply the poet's superiority complex vis-à-vis the prose writer. The poet often deems the latter's work much more serious than his own, which he may not even always regard as work.) Moreover, there are subjects that can be treated only in prose. A narrative involving more than three characters resists almost every poetic form except the epos. Reflections on historical themes, as well as childhood remembrances (in which the poet indulges to the same degree as ordinary mortals do), in turn look more natural in prose. *The History of the Pugachev Rebellion, The Captain's Daughter*—what could be more gratifying subjects for romantic poems! And especially in the era of Romanticism…However, what happens in the end is that the novel in verse is replaced more and more often by "verses from a novel." No one knows how much poetry loses when a poet turns to prose; it is quite certain, though, that prose profits from it greatly.

The prose works of Marina Tsvetaeva explain this better than anything else. To paraphrase Clausewitz, prose for Tsvetaeva was nothing but the continuation of poetry by other means (which, in fact, is what prose historically is). Everywhere—in her diary entries, essays on literature, fictionalized reminiscences—that is just what we encounter: the resetting of the methodology of poetic thinking into a prose text, the growth of poetry into prose. Tsvetaeva's sentence is constructed not so much in accordance with the principle of subject followed by predicate as through the use of specifically poetic technology: sound association, root rhyme, semantic enjambment, etc. That is, the reader is constantly dealing not with a linear (analytic) development but with a crystalline (synthesizing) growth of thought. Perhaps no better laboratory can be found for analyzing the psychology of poetic creation, inasmuch as all stages of the process are shown at extremely close range, verging on the starkness of caricature.

"Reading," says Tsvetaeva, "is complicity in the creative process." This most certainly is the statement of a poet; Leo Tolstoy would not have said such a thing. In this statement a sensitive or at least a reasonably alert ear can distinguish a note of despair, greatly muffled by authorial (and feminine at that) pride, coming specifically from a poet sorely fatigued by the ever-widening rift—growing with each additional line—between author and audience. And in the poet's turning to prose, that *a priori* "normal" form of communication with a reader, there is always a touch of slackening tempo, shifting gear, trying to make oneself clear, to explain things. For without complicity in the creative process there is no comprehension: what is comprehension if not complicity? As Whitman said: "Great poetry is possible only if there are great readers." In turning to prose, and dismantling almost every other word of it into component parts, Tsvetaeva shows her reader what a word, a thought, a phrase consists of; she tries, often against her own will, to draw the reader closer to her: to make him equally great.

There is still another explanation of the methodology of Tsvetaeva's prose. Since the day that the narrative genre first came into being, every form of it—short story, tale, novel—has dreaded one thing: the charge of being unconvincing. Hence either a striving for realism, or structural mannerisms. In the final analysis, every writer strives for the same thing: to regain or hold back time past or current. Toward this end a poet has at his disposal caesura, unaccented feet, dactylic endings; a prose writer has nothing of the kind. Turning to prose, Tsvetaeva quite unconsciously transfers to it the dynamics of poetic language— essentially the dynamics of song—which is in itself a form of restructured time. (If only because a verse line is short; each word in it, frequently each syllable, is subjected to a double or triple semantic burden. A multiplicity of meanings presupposes a corresponding number of attempts to comprehend, that is, several takes; and what is a *take* if not a unit of time?) Tsvetaeva, however, is not particularly concerned about how convincing the language of her prose is: whatever the topic of her narrative, its technology remains the same. Furthermore, her narrative in a strict sense is plotless and is held together mainly by the energy of monologue. But all the same, unlike professional prose writers and other poets who have resorted to prose, she does not submit to the genre's aesthetic inertia: she imposes her own technology on it, she imposes herself. This is not a result of an obsession with her own self, the belief generally held; instead it comes from an obsession with intonation, which is far more important to her than either poem or story. Verisimilitude in a narrative may be a result of complying with the genre's requirements; the same effect may also be ascribed to the timbre of the voice that does the narrating. In the latter case both the plausibility of the story line and the story line itself recede into the background of the listener's consciousness (i.e., into parentheses), as the author's dues paid to the proprieties of the genre. What stand outside the parentheses are the timbre of the voice and its intonation. To create this effect on the stage requires supplementary gestures; on paper—that is, in prose—it is achieved by the device of dramatic arrhythmia, which is most often brought about by interspersing nominative sentences among a mass of complex ones. In this alone one can see elements of borrowing from poetry. Yet Tsvetaeva, who doesn't have to borrow anything from anyone, starts with the utmost structural compactness of language and ends with it as well. The degree of linguistic expressiveness of her prose, given the minimal use of typographical means, is remarkable. Let us recall the author's stage direction describing Casanova in her play Casanova's End: "Not starlike—tsarlike." (Ne barstvenen— tsarstvenen). Let us now try to imagine what space this would have taken in Chekhov. At the same time, this is not a result of intentional economy—of paper, words, or effort—but a by-product of the poet's instinctive laconism.

Extending poetry into prose, Tsvetaeva does not obliterate the boundary existing between them in the popular consciousness; instead, she shifts it into hitherto syntactically inaccessible linguistic spheres—upward. And prose, where the danger of a stylistic dead end is much greater than in poetry, only benefits from this shift: there, in the rarefied air of her syntax, Tsvetaeva imparts to it an acceleration that leads to a change in the very notion of inertia. "Telegraphic style," "stream of consciousness," "the art of subtext," and so forth, bear no relation to the above. The works of her contemporaries, not to mention authors of subsequent decades whose production begs for such definitions, can be read seriously mainly for nostalgic reasons, or else for literary history (which is about the same) considerations. The literature created by Tsvetaeva is a literature of "supertext"; if her consciousness "streams," it follows a channel of ethics. The only way in which her style approaches the telegraphic is through her principal punctuation mark, the dash, identifying proximity of phenomena as well as leaps across the self-evident. That dash does serve one more purpose, though: it crosses out a great deal in Russian literature of the twentieth century.

[. . .]

—written in English

AFTERWORD

Through us the horn of time blows through the art of the word.

—*from* "A SLAP IN THE FACE OF PUBLIC TASTE,"
BY DAVID BURLIUK, ALEKSEI KRUCHENYKH,
VLADIMIR MAYAKOVSKY, AND
VIKTOR KHLEBNIKOV

On Two Love Poems

by Valzhyna Mort

A translator of Russian poetry is often faced with a problem of rendering not eloquence, but rather a speech impairment, a tongue-tie. Russian poets are stumblers and stutterers, masters of arrangement, mixers of high and low, researchers of the immobilized spheres of their language. They change the world order by changing the word order. Fortunately for them, Russian language is the original Russian gymnast. In the opening pages of *Conversation about Dante*, Osip Mandelstam compares the creation of poetic meaning to traversing a river crammed with Chinese junks moving simultaneously in various directions—neither a traveler nor a boatman can reconstruct the exact itinerary.

Vladimir Nabokov uses a different yet analogous metaphor to describe literary meaning-making. Here is what he writes in his book on Gogol:

> ... the prodigious artistic merit of the final result is due ... not to what is said but to how it is said—to the dazzling combination of drab parts. As in the scaling of insects the wonderful color effect may be due not to the pigment of scales but to their position and refractive power...

The writing of a poem is precisely this irrational testing of drab parts against each other until the combination is hacked, and the poet is dazzled by their arrangement, their ability to transmute, their illumination.

Let's look at Mandelstam's rhyme in his poem "Necklace": "Take from my palm, for joy, for ease, / A little honey, a little sun. That we may obey Persephone's bees." Wiman's bee-size words hum in the hives of alliterations and inner rhymes. "The string of bees" is a string of bids and a sting of bees at the same time. Every kiss is a sting that brings death, and in the end a whole necklace of tiny dead bodies has fallen over the lover's chest. In the "fur-shod" underworld of the "night's never-ending hum," the dead bees are the only reminder of the sun. Mandelstam writes this poem in 1920, his relationship with language is about to change; the poem is about to turn prophetic.

Here is a literal translation of the first tercet: "Take for joy from my palms / A little sun and a little honey, / As we have been told by Persephone's bees." As I reread the key words, *ladonej — solnca — mioda — Persephony*, I cannot help but hear the word *ladan*, frankincense. It's more than a sound trick. The scent of frankincense is closely associated with the worship of gods as well as burial rituals (Persephony: check and check); milkfish yellow, it's usually granulated into seed-sized bids. More so, frankincense has a strong Christian association with gift giving (the poem's "Take from my palm . . .") since it is mentioned among the treasures the mages presented to newborn Christ.

Two years later, in 1922, Marina Tsvetaeva would open a lyric poem in a voice of a lover "cast down from the chest of gods" with this quatrain: "In a deserted shrine / I tripled — as frankincense. / As seed and flame / I fell on the vertex." Here we have frankincense, seed (Persephone) and flame (sun-honey). Mandelstam's poem is a shrine, an altar, and the sacrificial gift altogether.

Poets in this anthology have denounced the clockwork mechanism of Russian verse. In a letter to a friend, Joseph Brodsky writes that metaphor, rhyme, and meter are all accidental, and the main concern of the poem is not *what* but rather *in what order*:

> You have to build composition. [...] Here's a compositional device: a break. Let's say you are singing verses about some damsel. You sing and sing, and suddenly— in the same meter—a few lines about something else. And do not explain anything. This has to be subtle, so that not to start a completely different tune. Thirty lines about your damsel and her dress and then five-six lines about an association you have with one of her ribbons. Composition, rather than plot. The real story here is not the damsel, but what's going on in your soul. Connect the stanzas not with logic, but with the motion of your soul—even if you are the only one who understands it.

Brodsky's poem "You have forgotten the village..." opens with an address to "you," the poet's lover, and a call, or perhaps a reproach, to her memory. Yet, having been summoned, this "you" immediately becomes forgotten by the poet. The dithyrambs to the addressee—something we'd expect from a love poem—never come. Instead, the speaker, having mentioned the not so memorable village "lost in the swampland," cannot stop remembering it. Each new turn of the line covers him under a wave of memory, jerks him forward from one detail to the next: *bolotah* (swamp)—*ogorodah* (gardens), *zlaki* (crops)—*bueraki* (ditches). The images are simplistic, bittersweet; the line breaks are painful—each forthcoming detail intensifies the bitterness.

Finally, a woman comes out onto the stage of the fifth line, but it's not our poet's "you." It's the dead "old Nastya," followed by her husband Pesterev, named here village-style, by his family name. Pesterev who, if not yet dead himself, must be sitting drunk in the cellar (a kind of a grave, no?), or making out of the headboard of "our bed" a certain something: possibly a gate. A place of intimacy, the final destination of every journey is being turned into a public place of neither here nor there, coming and going. But even this mutilation doesn't make the poet call out to the lover. Instead, he faithfully continues to describe the village: his "…And in winter they're chopping wood and turnips is all they live on," is an encyclopedic turn. He is resolute about describing the village in its entirety: *zimoj* (winter)—*drova* (fire wood) — *repe* (turnip) — *zvezda* (star) — *dyma* (smoke) — *nebe* (sky) — *okne* (window) — *pyli* (dust). This is the motion of his soul, or, if you wish, his junk river itinerary, or his refraction angle (the etymology of Nabokov's *refraction* is, in fact, Brodksy's *break*).

In the last line the "you" finally reaches some kind of a resolution: the "we" of "emptiness where once we loved." So what do we have here? An account of a heartbreak written without a single "I"! What a love poem: with every new line we witness the falling in love not with the female addressee, but with an unlovable, god and woman-forgotten village. Here's a lesson in composition: summon a lover and leave her waiting until the last line of a poem. Do not apply lessons in poetry composition to your normal life.

Acknowledgments

Gossip and Metaphysics includes new translations and co-translations of works by Anna Akhmatova, Daniil Kharms, Vladimir Mayakovsky, and Marina Tsvetaeva by the anthology's editors: Katie Farris, Ilya Kaminsky, and Valzhyna Mort. For permission to use previously published and copyrighted work, grateful acknowledgment is made to the following persons, organizations, and companies.

The footnotes and endnotes that accompanied some of these pieces in previous publications have been removed from the present collection in order to allow readers to experience the writings in ways closer to how their authors first presented them. We appreciate the critical and scholarly work of the editors and translators credited here, and we urge readers to consult the following books for additional information and explication.

Boris Pasternak

Epigraph from Czeslaw Milosz: from *Emperor of the Earth: Modes of Eccentric Vision* (University of California Press, 1977).

"Wild Vines" and "For Anna Akhmatova" are from *Collected Poems* by Robert Lowell. Copyright © 2003 by Harriet Lowell and Sheridan Lowell. Used with permission of Farrar, Straus and Giroux.

Part III from *Safe Conduct*, translated by Angela Livingston, is from *Pasternak on Art and Creativity* (Cambridge University Press, 1985). Copyright © 1985 Angela Livingstone. Used with permission of Cambridge University Press.

A letter from Boris Pasternak to Marina Tsvetaeva, translated by Margaret Wettlin and Walter Arndt, is from *Letters: Summer 1926*, edited by Yevgeny Pasternak, Yelena Pasternak, and Konstantin M. Azadovsky. English translation © 1985 Harcourt Brace Jovanovich. (First issued as an Oxford University Press paperback in 1988, then in paperback by New York Review Books in 2001.)

Marina Tsvetaeva

"Art in the Light of Conscience" and excerpts from "Poets With History and Poets Without History," translated by Angela Livingstone, are from *Art in Light of Conscience: Eight Essays on Poetry* (New York Review Books / Bloodaxe Books Ltd., 2010). Used with permission of Bloodaxe Books, on behalf of the translator and the estate (www.bloodaxebooks.com).

Excerpts of a letter from Marina Tsvetaeva to Boris Pasternak and a letter from Marina Tsvetaeva to Rainer Maria Rilke, translated by Margaret Wettlin and Walter Arndt, are from *Letters: Summer 1926*, edited by Yevgeny Pasternak, Yelena Pasternak, and Konstantin M. Azadovsky. English translation © 1985 Harcourt Brace Jovanovich. (First issued as an Oxford University Press paperback in 1988, then in paperback by New York Review Books in 2001.)

Osip Mandelstam

"The Necklace" and "Tristia" are from *Stolen Air: Selected Poems of Osip Mandelstam*, selected and translated by Christian Wiman, with an introduction by Ilya Kaminsky (Ecco Press, an imprint of HarperCollins Publishers, 2012). Used with permission of the translator.

"Leningrad" and "Your thin shoulders" are reprinted with the permission of Scribner Publishing Group, a division of Simon & Schuster, Inc., from *The Selected Poems of Osip Mandelstam* by Clarence Brown and W.S. Merwin. Copyright © 1973 by Clarence Brown and W. S. Merwin. Used with permission. All rights reserved.

Excerpts from "Conversation about Dante" are from *Osip Mandelstam: Critical Prose and Letters*, edited by Jane Gary Harris, translated by Jane Gary Harris and Constance Link. Copyright © 1979 by Ardis Publishers. Published in 2003 by The Overlook Press/ Ardis. Used with permission of The Overlook Press (www.overlookpress.com). All rights reserved.

The excerpts from "The Noise of Time" and "Alagez" are from *The Noise of Time*, translated by Clarence Brown (Northwestern University Press, 2002). Used with permission of Northwestern University Press.

Daniil Kharms

"Something about Pushkin" translated by Matvei Yankelevich with Eugene Ostashevsky, and "Gogol & Pushkin" and "Dear Nikandar Andreyevich" translated by Matvei Yankelevich, are from *Today I Wrote Nothing: The Selected Writings of Daniil Kharms* (Overlook Press, 2009). Copyright © 2007, 2009 by Matvei Yankelevich. Used with permission of The Overlook Press (www.overlookpress.com). All rights reserved.

Andrei Bely

"Pushkin and Gogol" and "Gogol and Mayakovsky," translated by Christopher Colbath, are from *Gogol's Artistry* (Northwestern University Press, 2009). Copyright © 2009 by Northwestern University Press. Used with permission of Northwestern University Press.

Excerpts from *The Dramatic Symphony*, translated by Roger and Angela Keys, are from *The Dramatic Symphony and the Forms of Art: A Novel with an Essay* (Grove Press, 1989).

Vladimir Mayakovsky

The excerpt from "The Cloud in Trousers" is from *The Bedbug and Selected Poetry* by Vladimir Mayakovsky, edited by Patricia Blake and translated by Max Hayward and George Reavey. Copyright © 1960 by Harper & Row, Publishers, Inc. Reprinted by permission of HarperCollins Publishers.

Excerpts from "I, Myself," translated by Katya Apekina: "Bad Habits," "The First Book," "1905," "1906," "11 Months of Butyrki," "The So-Called Dilemma," "Beginning of Mastery," "The Last School," "David Burliuk," "In the Smoking Room," "Memorable Night," "Next," "Burliuk's Strangeness," "Thus Daily," "Things Get Going," "The Yellow Blouse," "Naturally," "Called Up," and "October"; and "A Slap in the Face of Public Taste" from *Night Wraps the Sky: Writings by and about Mayakovsky*, edited

Anna Akhmatova

"On the Road," translated by Jane Kenyon with Vera Sandomirsk, is reprinted with the permission of The Permissions Company, Inc. on behalf of Graywolf Press, Minneapolis, Minnesota (www.graywolfpress.org).

"Pushkin's Stone Guest," translated by Janet Tucker, is from *My Half Century: Selected Prose*, edited by Ronald Meyer (Ardis Press, 1991; Northwestern University Press, 1997; The Overlook Press, 2013). Copyright © 1992 by The Overlook Press / Ardis. Used with permission of The Overlook Press (www.overlookpress.com). All rights reserved.

Excerpt from "Requiem," translated by Stanley Kunitz and Max Hayward. From *Poems of Akhmatova* (Mariner Books, 1997).

Joseph Brodsky

Epigraph from Seamus Heaney: from the essay "Joseph Brodsky, 1940–1996," from *Finders Keepers: Selected Prose 1971–2001* (Farrar, Straus and Giroux, 2003).

"On Love," Section X from "Nature Morte," "You've forgotten that village lost in the rows and rows" from "A Part of Speech," "Homage to Girolamo Marcello," and "To My Daughter" are from *Collected Poems in English* (Farrar, Straus and Giroux, 2000). Copyright © 2000 by the Estate of Joseph Brodsky. Used with permission of Farrar, Straus and Giroux.

"Letter to Horace" is from *On Grief and Reason: Essays* (Farrar, Straus and Giroux, 1996). Copyright © 1995 by Joseph Brodsky. Used with permission of Farrar, Straus and Giroux.

Other Books From Tupelo Press

Fasting for Ramadan: Notes from a Spiritual Practice (memoir),
Kazim Ali
Another English: Anglophone Poems from Around the World,
edited by Catherine Barnett and Tiphanie Yanique
Moonbook and Sunbook (poems), Willis Barnstone
Circle's Apprentice (poems), Dan Beachy-Quick
The Vital System (poems), CM Burroughs
The Posthumous Affair (novel), James Friel
Into Daylight (poems), Jeffrey Harrison
The Faulkes Chronicle (novel), David Huddle
Darktown Follies (poems), Amaud Jamaul Johnson
Dancing in Odessa (poems), Ilya Kaminsky
A God in the House: Poets Talk About Faith (interviews),
edited by Ilya Kaminsky and Katherine Towler
domina Un/blued (poems), Ruth Ellen Kocher
Phyla of Joy (poems), Karen An-hwei Lee
Engraved (poems), Anna George Meek
Boat (poems), Christopher Merrill
Mary & the Giant Mechanism (poems), Mary Molinary
Lucky Fish (poems), Aimee Nezhukumatathil
Long Division (poems), Alan Michael Parker
Intimate: An American Family Photo Album (memoir),
Paisley Rekdal
Thrill-Bent (novel), Jan Richman
Vivarium (poetry), Natasha Sajé
Calendars of Fire (poems), Lee Sharkey
Cream of Kohlrabi: Stories, Floyd Skloot
The Perfect Life (essays), Peter Stitt
Swallowing the Sea (essays), Lee Upton
Butch Geography (poems), Stacey Waite
Dogged Hearts (poems), Ellen Doré Watson

See our complete backlist at www.tupelopress.org